Critical Issues in Criminal Justice

Critical Issues in Criminal Justice

Historical Perspectives

Edited by:

Ernest Uwazie, Jennifer Noble, Ryan Getty, and Mercedes Valadez

California State University—Sacramento

Bassim Hamadeh, CEO and Publisher
Kristina Stolte, Acquisitions Editor
Alia Munoz, Project Editor
Alia Bales, Production Editor
Jess Estrella, Senior Graphic Designer
Danielle Gradisher, Licensing Associate
Natalie Piccotti, Director of Marketing
Kassie Graves, Vice President of Editorial
Jamie Giganti, Director of Academic Publishing

ISBN: 978-1-5165-3876-8 (pbk) / 978-1-5165-3877-5 (br)

Brief Contents

Section V: Additional Perspectives   307

Detailed Contents

Section II: Corrections 129

Section III: Law and Courts   175

CHAPTER 9
Justice Through Science: The Transformational
Impact of DNA Evidence in Criminal Justice   177
    Laurie Kubicek

CHAPTER 10
Child Pornography Offenses and Offenders: New
Challenges for the Criminal Justice System   195
    Alexa D. Sardina

CHAPTER 11
A Nation Talking to Itself About Justice: Fifty Years of Media Coverage of Criminal Justice   211

Jennifer Noble

Section IV: Special Topics

CHAPTER 12
Globalizing Criminal Justice Education: Building
Cultural Bridges for Career Enhancement 229

John P. J. Dussich

CHAPTER 13
From Past to Present: Understanding
the Influence of Immigration Status on
the Criminal Justice System   245

Mercedes Valadez

Section V: Additional Perspectives

HIGHLIGHT A

HIGHLIGHT B

HIGHLIGHT C

Preface

Ernest Uwazie

A s we approached the 50th anniversary of the Division of Criminal Justice at California State University, Sacramento, we took this opportunity to celebrate the evolution and progress of our program— from a small police science unit to the largest criminal justice program west of the Mississippi. Our faculty and staff had many ideas on how to mark this golden jubilee—looking back at our illustrious alumni and welcoming their return to campus and looking forward to creating new programs that will enrich our curriculum for the next generation of students. The division sought "big ideas" that would transform research and scholarly endeavors for faculty and students going into the next 50 years and continue our tradition of excellence in justice, education, and leadership.

The collection of chapters in this book embody the following goals: honoring the past and striving toward academic excellence in the future. This book will serve as a testament to what we do best as educators and scholars: pen our reflections of our passions about critical developments in the justice field and provide historical context and insight.

Often at the center of the criminal justice inquiry is the persistent question: Is criminal justice a science or an art? Perhaps, the evolution of the criminal justice program at California State University, Sacramento can attempt to answer the question. It started by offering four evening courses in Police Science and Administration in the Government Department in 1949, had its first full professor in 1952, and produced its first 17 graduates in 1957. In 1969, Police Science and Administration became its own department. Shortly after, it was renamed the Division of Criminal Justice. The division is currently housed in the College of Health and Human Services.

The vision of the Division of Criminal Justice is to be "a dynamic center for educating students to be future leaders with professional competencies and ethics, abilities and values that allow them to be productive and engaged members of a global society." Our interdisciplinary curriculum on the nature and causes of crime, as well as societal responses to the phenomena of offending, is taught by a balance of academic scholars, generalist faculty, and criminal justice practitioners in law enforcement, courts, and corrections. Furthermore, our criminal justice curriculum is enriched by a robust academic internship program for seniors, dedicated advising staff and faculty cohort advisors, crime scene lab, and various extra-curricular activities.

The Division of Criminal Justice's success in producing illustrious alumni in the various levels of leadership and service throughout the different local and state criminal justice agencies is a shining example of the value of criminal justice education. Arguably, criminal justice study is both about the science of trying to precisely measure or predict human nature or offending patterns and the art of understanding influential factors in moderating complex human behavior. Thus, a new type of college-educated criminal justice professional would have a profound impact on the system, from the desired goal of crime prevention to the constant attempt at reduction of recidivism rates and search for equal or equitable justice. For the criminal justice practitioner, real justice is about balancing the intersectionality of precision of criminogenic variables and routine judicial decisions, often indeterminate, at trials and sentencing. In retrospect, it was wise to envision, in the criminal justice reform era, that change in navigating the intersectionality of law and social policy, including justice rules and practice, should begin with solid, interdisciplinary criminal justice education.

In my contemplation of the future of the justice system in 50 years and beyond, the following themes emerged : (a) the increasing and changing role of technology and its impact in crime detection and evidence gathering; (b) managing the manifestations of poor human security conditions and recalcitrant vulnerable populations in court processing and resolutions of vexing non-violent criminal cases; (c) expansion of offender rehabilitation services and restriction of incarceration to the most dangerous in society; (d) new human traits and skill sets in conflict resolution for the criminal justice practitioners; and (e) increased collaboration among justice stakeholders, including the community, private sector, faith-based and nonprofit organizations.

In the pursuit of these emerging themes under the fulcrum of social justice, criminal justice personnel selection and training will become more urgent. Critical thinking and evidence-informed decision making will remain integral in the ever-increasing use of discretion in the justice system. Qualitative and quantitative measures of the effectiveness of the breadth and depth of justice processes, policies, and programs may fluctuate across political ideologies and generational divides, yet they remain present in the annals of justice. In all, criminal justice education will be shaped and led by a post-millennial, technology savvy, social media-driven generation. Perhaps this next generation will possess a new sense of patience, delayed gratification, heightened sensitivity to the environment, and greater value for human relationship building across and within local and global communities. In sum, as the 19th century French novelist Alphonse Karr would say, "The more things change, the more they stay the same." So, our justice system, both civil and criminal, is both a science and an art.

In conclusion, it has been a great pleasure to work with my esteemed colleagues, both junior and senior, in producing this volume. I am especially grateful to my coeditors, Dr. Ryan Getty, Jennifer Noble J.D., and Dr. Mercedes Valadez, whose able roles in the many reviews of the drafts and feedback to the respective contributors made the final product possible and completed for the 50th anniversary celebration. I acknowledge the clerical assistance of Danielle Chervin of the Division of Criminal Justice. I am also thankful to Chiefs Jones and Seale for their contributions from their professional experiences on policing and California's prison realignment, respectively, despite their busy schedules. Indeed, I may have initiated the project, but it's an idea that could have found rest in the cemetery of many great, unfulfilled dreams were it not for the contributors. Truly, this is the result of collaboration, mentorship, peer learning, patience, and passion. I hope that the energy and experience from this landmark project will lead to new ones and expand, as well as add value to the growth and imagination of the Division of Criminal Justice at California State University, Sacramento.

Finally, it is worth pointing out that each author is responsible for the contents of his or her contribution. My coeditors and I have taken good care not to distort or interfere with the content or meaning of each author's contribution or voice in the editing process. If otherwise, it is unintended, and we sincerely regret any errors or mistakes in this volume. The views expressed in this publication are solely those of the identified authors, and they do not necessarily represent the viewpoints or endorsement of the Division of Criminal Justice or California State University, Sacramento.

Please, direct comments or inquiries to

Ernest Uwazie
Lead Editor

Chapter 1

Introduction

Ernest Uwazie, Ryan Getty, Jennifer Noble and Mercedes Valadez

Background

Charles Dickens had a firm grasp on society to include past, present, and future behavior that he epitomized within his introductory paragraph in *A Tale of Two Cities*:

> It was the best of times, it was the worst of times, it was the age of wisdom, it was the age of foolishness, it was the epoch of belief, it was the epoch of incredulity, it was the season of Light, it was the season of Darkness, it was the spring of hope, it was the winter of despair, we had everything before us, we had nothing before us, we were all going direct to Heaven, we were all going direct the other way—in short, the period was so far like the present period, that some of its noisiest authorities insisted on its being received, for good or for evil, in the superlative degree of comparison only (Dickens & Schama, 1990).

The criminal justice system has gone through many eras since the turn of the 20th century. These eras, whether involving prisons, courts, or policing, have vacillated between increased professionalism of practitioners and focus on offender treatment to expanded punitive responses to, and repression of, crime. Within the various criminal justice milestones, the pendulum continues to swing between crime and due process models or vision of justice. Although this book is limited to some critical topics or survey of the more recent history, and arguably revolutionary phase, of the U.S. criminal justice system (1960s to present), the present owes much to the past's lessons and practices. The eclectic compilation of essays in this book attempts to highlight only some of the changes and continuities of the justice system, with some global or transnational intersections. As Dickens correctly states, we seem to relive and repeat history while at the same time strive for and experience better. This

1

seeming irreconcilable dichotomy still exists through policing philosophies, legislative mandates, prosecution strategies, sentencing guidelines, prison policies, and incarceration rates and tendencies. It is our sincere hope that we celebrate the successes over the past 50 years while learning from the mistakes or shortfalls as we chart new positive directions of criminological inquiry and societal response to offending. We believe through education and data-informed practices, our students, as future leaders, will envision and build on prior or ongoing successful strategies to meet and exceed Dickens's positive expectations of the future. Arguably, the status quo is not a future.

With this expectation of higher education and the criminal justice (CJ) system's "new" *raisons d'être*, the California State University, Sacramento's existence is storied and evolving. Like most criminal justice's degrees, CJ education evolved in the late 1960s with the creation of the Law Enforcement Assistant Administration's (LEAA) funds and initiatives as part of the Omnibus Crime Control and Safe Streets Act of 1968. The federal government created the LEAA as a response to systemic corruption and abuses, urban or race riots, and the lack of standardized education and training (U.S. Department of Justice, 1996) for law enforcement personnel . Prior to the LEAA, most CJ practitioners had, at most, a high school diploma. The few who actually received a bachelor's degree, majored in sociology, psychology, public administration, or business, as CJ degrees were not readily available due to demand and/or a university's profitability (Sherman, 1978). This dynamic changed with emphasis on a CJ degree due to the LEAA funding. Of critical note is the intellectual contributions and professional influences of August Vollmer, the "father of modern policing" in the United States, and a former president of the International Association of Chiefs of Police (Oliver, 2017). He was influential with the professional era of policing, especially with his leadership in establishing the first formal academic degree in criminal justice from the University of California, Berkeley. No one could have imagined the future impact on universities, students, and the criminal justice system and its practitioners over the next 50 years. Being educated on the long, complicated, and sometimes tortured history of the criminal justice field is a *sine qua non* to visioning and championing its future for a promising, better place.

Within this text, you will find chapter contributions primarily from the current faculty of the Division of Criminal Justice at California State University, Sacramento, plus a chapter by a guest keynote speaker at the division's first colloquium to internationalize the criminal justice curriculum. Each contributor was asked to author a chapter on a subject about which he or she felt passionate and provide some historical perspectives or relevance. Three shorter pieces on topical issues and contexts are included as an epilogue. It is the sincere wish of the editors and writers that the text help explain "how it was back then" and what has happened since. This "trip down memory lane" is meant to remind readers that the "good old days" weren't that good, and although much has been done to professionalize the criminal justice system in the last 50 years, much more can and should be done. Indeed, the height of the search for justice through the criminal justice system is yet to be achieved.

An Overview of the Chapters

Law Enforcement

Chapter 2 introduces the reader to a profound, newly formed, cooperative project between California State University, Sacramento and key local and state law enforcement agencies. Lately, strained relationships between the police and minorities have come to the forefront, highlighting need and offering a promising strategy for achieving the goal of diversity in law enforcement. Drs. Moffatt and Repa have pioneered a program called the "Law Enforcement Candidates Scholar" (LECS) in the Division of Criminal Justice in partnership with the Sacramento and surrounding community to promote diversity in law enforcement recruitment and hiring. This program is one of the few within the United States and owes its inception, implementation, and success to Moffatt and Repa. Years of planning and work culminated in the first graduates of LECS in 2016. These LECS graduates are not simply college graduates (they earned their degree while in the program) but rather a cohort of diverse volunteers chosen among many applicants who exemplified academic ability, leadership, cultural competence, and other skills necessary to succeed in law enforcement. Students within this program choose whether they want to be eventually hired by the

Sacramento Police Department or the California Highway Patrol, the two founding partners. The graduates are not only held to high academic standards, but also experience (and must pass) the hiring background specified by their chosen agency. The LECS program and its creators, Drs. Moffatt and Repa, believe the introduction of diversity at the college level enhances the partner agencies' vision and mission to serve a more diverse community. The LECS program is both innovative and promising.

Chapter 3's contribution is from another faculty member who has much policing experience. Dr. Huang's chapter addresses the economy, police staffing, and crime rates. With California's recession experience, he wanted to know if the major shift in economic downturn and the drastic practice of laying off police officers and rising unemployment had an effect in crime rates at local levels. Specifically, he looked at California state wide and local, Sacramento, violent and property crime rates in relation to the lack of "normal" police staffing and the state's unemployment rate. Examining the years 2000–2012, he found an inverse relationship between the variables of interest and violent/property crimes. Antithetically, he also found that violent crime spiked even when the (Sacramento) police force remained stable. He offers some interesting explanations and recommendations for these results.

Dr. Getty and Michaud's contribution in chapter 4 almost views "change" over the last 100 years in a rhetorical perspective; they argue that although many changes have occurred since the early 1900s, the criminal justice system seems to repeat similar mistakes throughout the decades. Starting with police (initiated) riots at the turn of the 20th century, the chapter highlights similar riots and calls for reform during the 1960s. As well, the federal government advocated police education in the "Reform Era" of the 1920s where police were afforded training and, hypothetically, a major shift away from the influence of politics in policing. Similar "reforms" were also repeated to some success in the 1960s. In all, they advocate criminal justice changes, specifically within policing, that have somewhat progressed, but much more is needed to be done.

Chapter 5 discusses law enforcement's use of force: a topic extensively talked and written about lately. When people think about law enforcement, the image that comes to mind is usually "traditional" uniformed local, county, or state patrol officers. Dr. Timothy Sowards expands this notion by including corrections officers and community corrections officers. In particular, he looks at legal and situational factors that influence use of force, use of force research and training, and the public perception of police use of force. Finally, he "projects" how law enforcement could manage the public's perception of use of force. This topic is of interest to potential and current law enforcement officers in addition to citizens who hope to better understand the factors influencing the police and media. In line with concepts from 21st-century policing recommendations, Dr. Sowards believes that stronger police–community relations may help quell the community's mistrust while decreasing anti-police sentiments, among other interesting recommendations.

Chapter 6 appeals to those wishing to get into the anti-terrorism field or study, as well as those who want to learn about the various aspects of terrorism. Dr. Davies Sasere's chapter includes the varying and troublesome definition of terrorism, why people may engage in terrorism, law enforcement's perceptions of it (pre- and post-9/11), and law enforcement's distinct roles in the mitigation, prevention, preparedness, and response to it. For those interested in the study and causes of terrorism, this is a must read. The "Homeland Security and Roles of Local Law Enforcement: A Paradigm Shift" chapter is very thorough and provides many citations and references for those who want to further their insights and knowledge of terrorism, homeland security, and law enforcement. Sasere's in-depth analysis and information will leave the academic and practitioner alike wanting for more.

Corrections

Chapter 7 explains some aspects of mass incarceration practices and how it affects minorities. There is ongoing controversy regarding the nation's direction toward mass incarceration. This trend is unfortunately marked by disproportionate incarceration of people of color. Dr. Gutierrez's rather extensive chapter examines the 1960s trend and lawmakers' policy of mass incarceration with direct negative impacts on minority populations. To put it bluntly, past changes in correctional policy (and court sentencing) have led to an overrepresentation of minorities in prison populations. The chapter analyzes the trends from four focal points. Drawing from the pre-civil right era up to the contemporary era, Dr. Gutierrez offers suggestions based on empirical evidence, how this happened, and how the CJ system could address this injustice. If one wondered how we have enabled Jim Crow–type laws, Dr. Gutierrez explains the historical significance and policy decisions affording these archaic practices to continue in correctional/sentencing decisions.

In chapter 8, Dr. Ernest Uwazie introduces the place and role of restorative justice in criminal justice, with both domestic and international experiences. Restorative justice theoretical framework may not be too familiar to most CJ students and some faculty, but its concepts and practices have been present for millennia, albeit informal in many contexts and cultures. To simplify the concept, the offender(s), victim(s), and community work in unison to heal each other (restore "wholeness") from the harm done by criminal acts. Dr. Uwazie's expertise and experience shine through in this chapter by helping the reader understand restorative justice in several contexts in prose that almost any person can understand. He has distilled rather abstract concepts and ideals (some might say foreign) into a cohesive and cogent framework, with thought-provoking questions. For those who seek a nontraditional yet promising system of justice, this chapter helps to show that other ways are feasible and possibly more effective in reducing recidivism and creating victim satisfaction.

Law and Courts

Chapter 9 may seem technical on its face, but truly it is very real in the operations of the court and is easy to understand. Professor Laurie Kubicek discusses the use of deoxyribonucleic acid (DNA) in a somewhat recent advent to the courts and criminal justice system. People (i.e., juries) expect DNA evidence on almost *every* case due to the "CSI effect" and the seriousness of penalties for convictions. Through her solid legal experience, Professor Kubicek educates the reader in the use of DNA while dispelling some of the fallacies. There is no doubt as to the impact of DNA evidence to help convict the guilty and exonerate the (convicted) innocent. Professor Kubicek uses several seminal court cases involving DNA evidence to illustrate its usefulness and misuse on the parts of the defense and prosecution. In all, DNA is only one piece of evidence in a criminal trial and has the ability to be (mis)used at trial in ways that the public never expected or, possibly, intended.

Chapter 10 delves into the certain aspects of crime child pornography. Dr. Alexa Sardina confronts the distasteful yet all too prevalent world of child pornography. Not many juveniles know they are committing a federal crime when they "sext" a picture of male/female (even simulated) sexual acts and/or depiction of genitalia. The "prank" of sending a picture of male/female sexual parts and/or sexual acts has become a very serious and prevalent crime. Through an historical review of child pornography, Dr. Sardina examines four categories of offenders: the curious, those who have a sexual interest in children, those who use the Internet to commit sexual offenses, and those who produce and distribute child porn. Within those categories, she relates current research and, further, adds the criminal justice response to child pornography. As well, she rounds out her chapter with the investigative process, prosecuting, and sentencing of child pornography offenders. Readers will also gain knowledge into the emerging world of "sexting" as it relates to legality and practice.

In another timely article, chapter 11 broaches the subject of the criminal justice system and the media's relationship. One can hardly turn on the TV or Internet without hearing about something involving the criminal justice system. Professor Jennifer Noble authored this chapter to educate the reader of the criminal justice system and the changes in the media's landscape. This topic touches on local and national stories/cases as they work their way through the criminal justice system, with an emphasis on different types of media. Professor Noble educates the reader on the history of criminal justice media coverage while explaining the key important contributions. Through her examples, the reader realizes the media's contributions to educating the public on topics such as wrongful convictions, prosecutorial misconduct, the effects of mass incarceration, inequities in bail, and other important leading reforms. Noble notes these system-wide criminal justice issues and examines trends that educate and influence readers, viewers, and lawmakers alike. Controversial new policies such as cameras in the courtroom are discussed as a way to illustrate that emerging technologies are here to stay, so will the criminal justice system's ability to adapt and ensure the rights of the accused are protected while conforming to the public's demand for transparency.

Special Topics

Chapter 12 draws from over six decades of practitioner and academic experience in international criminal justice education. Dr. John Dussich combines ideas and concepts from several different subjects and disciplines to explain the attractions and advantages of globalizing the criminal justice curriculum. Through a multi-methodological approach, he advocates global relationships and involvement to further knowledge and mitigate ethnocentrism. His multipronged approach involves faculty creating courses and employing texts that teach and/or accentuate internationalization, publishing in foreign language journals, finding sources and opportunities for students to learn abroad, and, generally, planning curricula with global inclusiveness. He believes one should not only learn about other cultures within the classroom, but also experience different cultures and CJ systems to have a more dynamic and enriching view of world-wide approaches to crime and punishment. In this way, students can broaden and enhance their future careers as well as develop a more positive attitude for social justice.

Chapter 13 involves aspects of immigration policy and various criminal justice practices as it pertains to immigration. Another hot topic in America today is immigration and its influence or place in the criminal justice system. Dr. Mercedes Valadez integrates 50 years of historical perspectives while discussing some misconceptions and realities of the relationships between crime and immigration. In a comparison, Dr. Valadez illustrates the disparities between immigrants and U.S. citizens in U.S. criminal courts while highlighting the role of the police in migration control and its concomitant effects. The recent U.S. policy of expanding immigrant detention centers and the role of the private, industrial prison complex, along with calls for reforms and even possible investigations into human rights violations, round out this compelling chapter. If one wants to be brought up to speed on the current state of affairs regarding immigration policy and practices in relationship to justice practices, this chapter will surely inspire a visceral response.

Chapter 14 provides an overview of the important topic of posttraumatic stress disorder (PTSD) and healing in criminal justice personnel management and training. It seems reasonable that first responders who deal with critical incidents are also victims of trauma and PTSD. The general public may assume the daily tasks of police, counselors, child abuse investigators and the like are "numb" to the horrors they see on a regular basis and confront these incidents with a routine-like attitude. Nothing could be further from the truth. First responders may hide their pain and trauma in an outward appearance of a "devil-may-care" attitude, but on the inside they feel pain and trauma similar to actual victims. Empathy is a basic response, and nothing can shield one from caring for another human being in crisis. In her chapter, Dr. Lynette Lee informs and educates those who deal with trauma realize its prevalence and toll on the individual, agency, and community, while giving counsel and informed advice to help ameliorate the damaging effects brought about by stress and trauma.

Finally, in chapter 15 Drs. Ernest Uwazie and Nicole Fox introduce the topic and concept of transitional justice, especially after state collapse or mass atrocity crimes, with two illustrative case studies from Rwanda and South Africa. Although this type of justice will not likely replace already established systems throughout the world, it provides a mechanism and alternative way of handling offenders while a (new) government is formed or attempts to re-establish a more traditional and legitimate form of criminal justice system. In essence, transitional justice establishes a pathway in the absence of a CJ system because of massive societal or governmental changes, especially in a failure or collapse of the nation-state or its social control system. The authors begin by illustrating two of the most flagrant and recent examples of genocide and human rights violations in Africa: Rwanda and South Africa. Anyone interested in how countries, specifically these African countries, handled justice in the wake of monumental change and a governmental vacuum ought to read this chapter. Other countries have known genocide in the 21st and late 20th centuries such as in Myanmar, the Sudan, Cambodia, Bosnia and Herzegovina, Somalia, and the list goes on. In the case of Rwanda, nearly 70% of ethnic Tutsis were systematically killed. Estimates range from half a million to one million casualties. To put this in perspective, that is more than the population of San Francisco, CA (856,095) and twice the size of Sacramento (486,189). Dead. As one could imagine, it would be difficult to reestablish any form of criminal justice under these circumstances. With help, Rwanda did it, and you can find out how in this chapter. In 1993 South Africa abolished the Apartheid regime. A somewhat awkward analogy for the United States would be sort of a combination the South, post-Civil War, and the civil rights era of the American 1960s and 70s. This analogy is only meant to impress the sudden societal change and the monumental task of restoring order among factions. It is impressive that South Africa established a Truth and Reconciliation Commission to "promote national unity and reconciliation in a spirit of understanding which transcends the conflicts and divisions of the past." You can read about how this worked within this chapter.

Three Highlights provide special perspectives about contemporary issues in the criminal justice field and practice. Highlight A by Police Chief Eric Jones focuses on the evolution of the vision of Principled policing, with reference to President Obama's Task Force on 21st Century Policing in late 2014. Principled policing relies upon leadership at all levels and embraces a cultural change. In part, this change involves less of the typical measurements of police effectiveness such as tickets, arrests, etc. and more on community relationship building through shared values and beliefs. Through this "building bridges" with the community, it is hoped that comprehensive community involvement in crime prevention and control can be achieved. Highlight B by Dr. Cecil Canton addresses the timely issue of implicit bias and law enforcement. He broaches the controversial subject of implicit bias and police use of deadly force and the need to recognize its adverse impact in police–community relations. Through some scenarios and examples of recent police shootings of minorities, he explains the phenomena of implicit bias in a scientific manner. He argues that overt bias is easily identifiable but implicit bias is much more insidious and operates subconsciously. In Highlight C, Probation Chief Lee Seale examines California's Juvenile Justice Realignment, after ten years of its implementation. After decades of harsh drug offenses, Three Strikes legislation, skyrocketing costs of incarceration, and constrained probation services, Senate Bill 81 passed in 2007 to reform and realign the juvenile justice system in California; it shifted from state to local or community control of the custody and services of offenders. Preliminary juvenile delinquency data are promising and encouraging, with lower rates of recidivism and reduced costs. He argues for increased efforts to maintain the achievements of the present juvenile justice reform, using evidence based practices and protective functions of local control and individualized treatment.

Some Concluding Thoughts

When this landmark 50th anniversary book project was proposed by Chair Uwazie in late spring semester 2017, it was done with knowing the California State University, Sacramento, Division of Criminal Justice had the opportunity to make a profound statement of legacy for prior graduates, some of whom helped write these chapters, and to provide an optimistic outlook for future graduates. The list of esteemed graduates from the division over time is too long to list, but it suffices that the division's faculty and staff have made a profound impact on local and state, if not national and international, CJ practitioners over the decades. The past and present faculty and staff are proud of this fact and will continue to earn students' trust through their commitment to a high standard of education. This book is only a small example of some of the works done by professors outside of their readily recognizable classroom contributions. Students often think that professors "only" work a few hours a day teaching classes. While this part of our main mission to excel at pedagogy is normally thought of first, it hardly answers what we do with the other "free time" afforded academics. Students do not typically see or hear about the countless hours spent researching and writing journal articles and books; working with various local, county, state, national, and international organizations to help with programs or evaluations of systems; working with the media to educate the public; cancelling/postponing vacations because of deadlines or committee commitments; and working on a multitude of division, college, and/or university committees for the betterment of students and faculty in addition to community service. This is only a smattering of what we do in our "free time" as our affirmed commitment to the division's goal of making the Division of Criminal Justice at California State University, Sacramento one of the best in the nation, and one of the largest. When you see us outside of class, please ask us what we're doing behind the scenes to help our students succeed, although you should prepare to be there a while—to hear the stories of the rigors of research and writing.

This book is dedicated to our past and present students, our past and present faculty and staff, and our future goals. May your learning be enriched as you enjoy reading the essays!

References

Dickens, C., & Schama, S. (1990). *A tale of two cities*. New York, NY: Vintage Books.

Oliver, Willard M. (2017). *August Vollmer: The father of American policing*. Durham, NC: Carolina Academic Press.

Sherman, L. W. (1978). The quality of police education: A critical review with recommendations for improving programs in higher education *The National Advisory Commission on Higher Education for Police Officers*. San Francisco, CA: Jossey-Bass.

U.S. Department of Justice. (1996). *LEAA/OJP retrospective: 30 years of federal support to state and local criminal justice*. Washington, DC: Author.

I

Law Enforcement

Chapter 2

Public Safety for All? A Modern History of Diversity and Inclusion in Law Enforcement

Shelby Moffatt and Melissa Repa

Introduction

On August 11, 2017, the Sacramento, California, community witnessed a rare sea-change (or more appropriately, "C change," in culture, communication and community) when Daniel Hahn took the city's oath of office in a swearing-in ceremony at California State University, Sacramento to become the 45th chief of police for the Sacramento Police Department. This day was obviously special and important to Chief Hahn and his family and friends, but to the many nameless, dispossessed, and voiceless citizens who previously encountered unwarranted harassment, discrimination, or bias from officers sworn to protect them, Chief Hahn's ascension to leadership represented more than a promotion. Chief Hahn, the city's first Black police chief, became a symbol of public trust and vindication for many who had lost hope in their law enforcement agency.

Chief Hahn appeared to be the change the Sacramento community had been long waiting for because he brought a sense of pride and excitement necessary to rebuild neighborhoods and a city, with a mindset needed to transform policing. At the same time, just feet away and positioned outside of the ceremony hall, protesters stood together in opposition of Chief Hahn not because he is a Black man, but because he is viewed as an extension of a corrupt system needing to be dismantled. Bretón (2017) reported that Hahn was "being thrown into the lion's den—a metaphorical one made up of police-union politics, civilian unrest over recent controversial shootings and a worked-up City Council placing many demands on the department" (para 16). The question that many of Chief Hahn's supporters and detractors would soon be asking was, "How would he respond to the city's first major critical incident involving use of force under his watch?"

Less than one year into office, Chief Hahn's leadership was directly tested in March 2018 when an unarmed Black man named Stephon Clark was shot by Sacramento police officers. The community waited and wondered what Chief Hahn's plan would be to address the shooting and repair police–community tensions rooted in historical injustices. Simply, how could he appeal to a community ready to protest any perceived acts of injustice while mollifying a police force who already felt victimized and forgotten? Moreover, would Chief Hahn be able to inspire culture change in both the community and his law enforcement agency while retooling his agency to be more reflective of communities served?

This chapter provides a modern, historical overview of diversity and inclusion in policing to contextualize how injustices and bias, over time, play a role in police–community mistrust. Also described are the benefits and importance of diversity and inclusion in law enforcement and multiple issues related to recruitment, hiring, and service training that can serve as barriers. The chapter concludes with a discussion of a 21st-century police recruitment model at California State University, Sacramento, entitled the Law Enforcement Candidate Scholars' (LECS) program. The LECS program is designed in partnership with local and state law enforcement agencies to prepare future law enforcement officers to be career-ready change agents. The LECS program draws from research on diversity and inclusion in law enforcement and infuses cultural diversity and leadership training into a pre-academy program to better prepare a diverse pool of candidates for the rigors of policing, to connect future police officers to positive mentors and a support network, and to enhance police–community relations.

Historical Context of Police-Community Relations

Humans have long subscribed to the belief that safety and security are necessary for civilizations to survive and prosper (Maslow, 1943), thus resulting in the creation of laws and systems of enforcement. Prosperous societies succeeded in part because they established and enforced rules and sought progress through intelligence, cultural/social success, economic/physical well-being and safety. Not always inclusive of all cultures or engendering trust, more successful societies quantified their triumphs on the sum of their achievements over their failures, but without regard for the dignity and respect of all people or the equality of opportunities (Mayer, Davis, & Schoorman, 1995). Nevertheless, true societal progress only occurs when purposeful and meaningful activities are conducted that serve all community members, leading to the central question of this chapter: Has the law enforcement system in the United States evolved to protect the safety of all members of the public?

The city of Sacramento, California, established in 1848 (gold was discovered), can be used as a compelling example of how relations between law enforcement and communities have evolved in America. Almost immediately, Sacramento needed to create stronger rules and a system of governance for its rapid increase in residents. Even though California was identified as a free state (non-slavery) before the start of the Civil War, the eventual capital of California (Sacramento) would not be inclusive to many of its residents of color under the rule of law until the passage of the 14th Amendment in 1868, which promised "due process and equal protection under the law." Yet, even 80 years after the passage of the 14th Amendment, African Americans and other persons of color were still being marginalized and denied basic human rights due to de jure and de facto laws informally identified as "Jim Crow" laws that institutionalized racial discrimination. Progress for racial and ethnic minorities (REMs) was limited not only because of written laws, but also because of a culture that promulgated distrust and segregation in a free society. By a well-defined standard of exclusion, African Americans and other REMs were prevented from acquiring economic wealth, legal protection, and social benefits that were afforded to their White counterparts.

For much of the 20th century, U.S. police departments were fashioned mostly out of White male officers who were traditional in nature and values, reflecting the status quo of the times. Even with the U.S. Constitution as established law, U.S. Supreme Court decisions directing officers to adhere to the rule of law and departmental rules and regulations that mandated officers serve and protect the public, officers often bypassed or refused to take an impartial spirit-of-the-law (Koh, 2002) approach when engaged with REMs, resulting in greater socially, culturally, and morally insensitive decisions. This generation of law enforcement officers was largely following and freely participating in practices of the dominant culture in America, which allowed for immoral and unlawful behavior under Jim Crow laws to be an accepted practice, with officers serving as enforcers of these laws (U.S. Department of Justice, 2018).

The de facto acceptance of indifference and injustice found in 20th-century American law enforcement was not a new occurrence in American history. The legacy of prejudice, discrimination, and racism by law enforcement officers against people of color was borne out of the onset of American slavery, which began during the antebellum Civil War period. The effect of slavery resulted in the creation of slave patrols, night watchmen, and paddy rollers (Haden, 2001), which were established mostly throughout the southern states to enforce hundreds of slave statutes enacted between the 1600s and 1865 that mandated the control, discipline, search, and capture of runaway slaves. Paddy rollers and other types of bounty hunters were so prevalent throughout the southern region of America that they eventually became a customary and routine part of law enforcement in the United States. These slave statutes were solidified as a part of the American landscape when President George Washington signed into law the Fugitive Slave Act of 1793. The Fugitive Slave Act not only strengthened protections of White wealthy land and slave owners, but also penalized anyone who felt morally compelled or refused to enforce the law (Paul, 2016).

The pulse of modern American law enforcement is inextricably linked to America's horrid past and mistreatment of REMs. For centuries, America's core group of citizens adhered to a mantra of "not my problem" regarding the outcome of REMs, which afforded law enforcement officers, who were members of the core group, similar excuses to be detached from their moral responsibility when engaged with REMs (Moffatt, 2015). In spite of these attitudes, a turning point in the behavior and culture of law enforcement occurred in the unlikely city of Sacramento, California, in 1948. By the end of World War II, people by the thousands migrated to the region in search of employment opportunities (Avella, 2003), resulting in another expansive population growth. Although the state of California, specifically the city of Sacramento, had diverse demographics, Sacramento still remained socially, culturally, and legally segregated like many of the cities in America. Nonetheless, unlike the Jim Crow laws that embraced segregation, Sacramento took an unusually progressive step forward in the law enforcement profession. In 1948, Robert Canson became the first African American police officer employed by Sacramento's Police Department. Officer Canson was one of nearly 300 sworn officers on Sacramento's police force. He trail-blazed the way for future REMs, women, and other underrepresented communities to enter law enforcement professions. Decades later, because of the Civil Rights Act of 1964, Equal Employment Opportunity Act of 1965, and other progressive laws, citizens of Sacramento witnessed increases of REM and other traditionally underrepresented groups reach the ranks of police officer, lieutenant, captain and, yes, chief of police. Yet, even after Officer Canson's extraordinary hire 70 years ago, thus far, he has never garnered historical acknowledgement by members of the Sacramento community nor been recognized as a major milestone in the Sacramento Police Department's nearly 170-year history.

Despite a few social advances, African Americans and others would continue to endure assaults and various types of harm from their police departments all across America. According to Fryer (2016), "Images of law enforcement clad in Ku Klux Klan regalia or those peaceful protesters being attacked by canines, high pressure water hoses, and tear gas are an indelible part of American history" (p. 1). Ultimately, persistent public discord and intolerance displayed by law enforcement officers were considered accepted practice in police departments across the country, manifesting in police distrust by REMs and in violent confrontations such as the Watts Riot in Los Angeles in 1965 and the Oak Park Riot in Sacramento in 1969 (City of Sacramento, 2018; Skelton, 2015). Alternatively, in the 1960s, victories in human rights saw the passage of the Civil Rights Act of 1964, the Voting Rights Act of 1965, along with the "Due Process Revolution" led by Chief Justice Earl Warren and landmark Supreme Court cases such as *Miranda v. Arizona* (1966), which gave greater rights to people detained by law enforcement officials. Despite these milestones, REMs and others continued to experience disparities and endure mistreatment and unjust actions by police forces paid to protect all citizens (Feld, 2003).

Improper practices and discriminatory behaviors enacted by traditional law enforcement agencies on REM communities became so prevalent that national commissions were created to investigate their wrongdoings. In 1968, the "Kerner Report" from the National Advisory

Commission on Civil Disorders concluded that institutional racism and poverty were influencing the level of violence in poor communities. The report also suggested that law enforcement agencies needed to defuse tensions with REM communities, create greater diversity within police ranks, and strengthen the image of law enforcement within REM neighborhoods (George, 2018; National Advisory Commission on Civil Disorders, 1968). Despite the forward-thinking recommendations for bettering police–community relations from the Kerner Report 50 years ago, law enforcement agencies are still in a quandary about REM communities and society in general. Moreover, many REM communities continued to struggle to obtain political, social, and economic equality. These inequities set the foundation for social disorganization (poverty) and a rise in criminal activity for African Americans and other REM communities (Walker, Spohn, & DeLone, 2012).

When the concept of social justice programs was initially presented to law enforcement agencies as a way to quell tensions and improve communities, many agencies balked or blatantly refused to attach social programs to law enforcement practices. Officers believed the concept of using social programs would not work due to insufficient manpower, expertise, or resources to manage or solve social problems (e.g., poverty, unemployment, alcoholism, etc.) that already existed in predominantly REM neighborhoods (Moffatt, 2015; U.S. Department of Justice, 2007). However, continuing economic disparities and major events in the United States involving police confrontations with unarmed citizens that have occurred in the last 20 years (e.g., Los Angeles (CA), Sacramento (CA), Ferguson (MO), New York City) are forcing agencies to review their current practices in police–community relations and recruitment and hiring. Hence, if tensions in communities are to be reduced and racial diversity in policing increased, law enforcement must take social and cultural risks with the communities they serve. Creating a strong public image and bridging divides should be their mantra rather than maintaining the status quo (Moffatt, 2015).

Cultural Diversity and Bias

One way to improve police–community relations is to recognize that past experiences of cultural groups can shape attitudes toward law enforcement. Research consistently shows that racial and ethnic minorities (REMs) are more likely than Whites to view law enforcement with suspicion and distrust (National Institute of Justice, 2018). The *Washington Post*'s (2001) and *Gallup*'s (2014) findings suggest a vast amount of discomfort, anger, and even anxiety still persists during investigative detentions (e.g., citations or arrests) or other general contacts (e.g., issued warnings, searches, or use of force) between REMs and law enforcement officers.

In 2001, the *Washington Post* surveyed nearly 2,000 adults and found 37% of African-Americans and 20% of Latinos/Latinas said they were unfairly stopped by police, compared to only 4% of Whites. In 2014, *Gallup* conducted related surveys measuring confidence in police and found comparable outcomes with only 59% of Whites and 37% of Blacks expressing a great deal of confidence in police. Moreover, only 45% of Blacks rated honesty and ethics of police officers as high, compared with 59% of Whites (Gallup, 2014).

Data on perceptions of law enforcement officers, along with protests of police in Sacramento and other communities, suggest many community members lack confidence in police officers and thus may be unwilling to trust and contact police when assistance is needed. Lack of trust and legitimacy is highlighted as a key issue in the report of the President's Task Force on 21st Century Policing (2015). The task force report discusses ways to rebuild trust by changing the culture of law enforcement from a purely "warrior" mind-set to a "guardian" mind-set in which law enforcement guards and protects the dignity of all people. The guardian mind-set would help law enforcement shift from an "us-versus-them" mentality to one that is more community oriented. Additionally, engaging REM communities with positive interactions with police is another strategy for improving relationships (President's Task Force on 21st Century Policing, 2015).

To further improve relationships within the community and enhance effectiveness of law enforcement encounters, police awareness and understanding of multicultural community influences is critical. Just as community members may have misconceptions and biases toward law enforcement officers that can lead to lack of trust, some officers may be predisposed to their own biases about REMs, people from low socioeconomic statuses, or other social groups, which can impact their effectiveness in protecting and serving their communities. The U.S. Department of Justice (DOJ) notes, "Bias and a lack of cultural competency are often cited interchangeably as challenges in police community relationships" (U.S. DOJ, 2018, para. 2). In addition, practices within an agency and in relationship with the public must be respectful, transparent, and trustworthy and give individuals a voice. To rebuild trust in policing after controversial police shootings, police departments like the Sacramento Police Department are implementing practices such as community forums, reforming use of force policies and enhancing training. These and other "procedural justice" practices can help build legitimacy with the public and enhance officer awareness of cultural influences in the community (President's Task Force on 21st Century Policing, 2015). Explicit biases and discriminatory enforcement of laws based on race are prohibited by the U.S. Constitution and other laws and policies, but even the most open-minded individuals and ardent defenders of social justice are prone to unconscious implicit-bias associations between REM groups and stereotypes, such as the negative association of REM communities with criminality (Carter, 2016). Thus, the goal for each of us is being aware that these biases exist and could lead to poor decisions and experiences by both law enforcement officers and the community.

Law enforcement officers need to be mindful of stereotypical expectations and generalizations that are inappropriate for a given situation. For example, if officers perceive peril from certain groups or in certain neighborhoods, they may react more aggressively and even escalate their use of force incorrectly. A majority of Americans do not believe that law enforcement officers are racist. However, "in the absence of proactive training and interventions, they are no more immune to unconscious bias than the rest of us" (Carter, 2016, p. 950). Clearly, bridging existing traumas felt by many living within REM communities means more awareness, understanding, and police training are needed to counteract biases.

Police Training

The California Commission on Peace Officer Standards and Training (2014) stated, "Peace officers need to recognize and respect the complexities of cultural diversity to develop skills necessary for identifying and responding to California's changing communities" (p. 45). Consequently, ethical leadership, cultural diversity, and discrimination are all learning domains taught in basic police academies in California and throughout the country. However, "tactical" police learning domains, such as de-escalation of force or mental illness response, crowd and riot control, and defensive tactics training also need to address unconscious biases that may lead officers to perceive a greater threat from REMs than others (Stoughton, 2014). By focusing more resources toward training, the hope for leaders in various law enforcement agencies is that unnecessary complaints of racial profiling, harassment, and tensions between officers and REM communities can be mitigated and tragedies can be averted.

Law enforcement agencies should continue to develop training on cultural diversity and inclusion in coordination with communities they serve and collaboratively identify ways to reduce crime and improve relationships and public trust in law enforcement. Women in Federal Law Enforcement (WIFLE), the National Organization of Black Law Enforcement Executives (NOBLE), and other leaders recommend that law enforcement agencies review their training procedures to ensure access and inclusion to diverse police candidates (WIFLE, 2016). For example, law enforcement agencies that require cadets to pay their own academy costs may discourage low income and REM candidates from participating. Likewise, residential academies, which require candidates to live away from home for 6 months or more, may not be accessible to candidates with families. In addition, opportunities for extra training, coaching, and mentoring support, particularly when candidates fail any learning domains (e.g., report writing, physical fitness, driving, etc.) is also encouraged to ensure all candidates are given the best opportunities to succeed.

To continue this model of inclusion, police academies need to be mindful of how the training practices may present possible cultural barriers to some cadets who are not familiar with the traditional culture of policing. Many academies use "paramilitary" boot camp models and emphasize the "warrior" mind-set. This type of culture develops leadership skills and builds character but also uses intimidation, humiliation, and fear tactics. When also incorporating a "guardian" mind-set, academies can ensure agency culture and performance measures are linked to the values of procedural justice with a focus on mutual respect, cultural awareness, and communication (President's Task Force on 21st Century Policing, 2015; WIFLE, 2016). By teaching and developing genuine community engagement beginning in academies, law enforcement's return on investment will greatly increase with community trust. This approach directly aligns with the President's Task Force on 21st Century Policing (2015), which suggests that "officers who feel respected by their organizations are more likely to bring this respect into their interactions with the people they serve" (p. 10).

Recruitment and Hiring in Law Enforcement

Research conducted by the U.S. DOJ and the Equal Employment Opportunity Commission (EEOC) suggests police diversity helps build trust and legitimacy on both sides of the law enforcement–citizen divide, reduces bias, and increases public safety (U.S. DOJ, 2016). The President's Task Force on 21st Century Policing (2015) recommended that law enforcement agencies strive "to create a workforce that encompasses a broad range of diversity including race, gender, language, life experience, and cultural background to improve understanding and effectiveness in dealing with all communities" (p. 16). Recruiting and retaining well-prepared and quality candidates for law enforcement careers for rapidly increasing numbers of REMs continues to be a challenge for police leadership across the country (Pearsall & Kohlhepp, 2010; WIFLE, 2016). This coincides with data that suggested representation of REMs and women in the law enforcement workforce does not mirror diverse communities (Bureau of Justice Statistics, 2015). Ironically, even though the city of Sacramento was proudly named by *Time* magazine as the most diverse city in America in 2002, the Sacramento Police Department, which promotes transparency, diversity, and inclusion as foundations of its administration, still has only 4.33% sworn Black officers, 10.61% sworn Latino/a officers and 9.12% sworn Asian officers in a department of nearly 700 sworn officers (City of Sacramento, 2016). This data does not reflect the diversity observed in the city of Sacramento, which includes a population of 13.4% Blacks, 28.3% Latino/a and 18.7% Asian individuals, respectively (City of Sacramento, 2016; U.S. Census, 2017).

The aforementioned data disparities may coincide with recruitment challenges cited by research on advancing diversity in law enforcement. A principal category impacting police recruitment in REM communities is the achievement gap in education. Candidates who struggle with basic scholastic concepts often do not meet agency requirements, thus negatively impacting agency goals for recruitment of students from REM populations (National Center for Educational Statistics, 2017). Additionally, candidates face several other barriers, such as lacking needed preparation and training to enter a sworn law enforcement academy; prior personal histories that delay or disqualify candidates from entering an academy; greater disinterest in law enforcement due to the multitude of negative images regularly displayed on media about police officers; and racial disparities in the criminal justice system (Moffatt, 2015; Kahn & Kirk, 2015). The U.S. DOJ (2016) also reported similar findings such as lack of trust; reputation of agency; lack of awareness of career opportunities; overreliance on tailored examinations for screening that may exclude members of underrepresented communities; residency restrictions; cost and complexity of application and training; and stringent and inflexible selection criteria. As of 2018, a new challenge for police recruitment in the state of California involves the strict selection criteria related to limits on recreational drug use, meaning law enforcement applicants who have used marijuana in their recent past may be automatically disqualified or delayed in the hiring process. Essentially, nearly every law enforcement agency across the country is impacted by a similar dilemma: Where will they find qualified candidates to fill numerous sworn officer vacancies?

Although a top priority for law enforcement agencies such as the Sacramento Police Department is to attract and retain a highly qualified workforce that represents the community (City of Sacramento, 2018), "changing the face" of policing by recruiting higher numbers of underrepresented individuals alone will not transform deeper issues challenging law enforcement (WIFLE, 2016). According to Walker and colleagues (2012), "Merely employing racial minority officers does not automatically eliminate police–community relations problems. The quality of policing is largely determined by the organizational culture of the department, which is the combined product of leadership by the chief, formal policies on critical issues such as the use of force, and rank-and-file officer peer culture" (p. 175). At the same time, current police culture, unconscious bias, and status quo recruitment practices affect the recruitment, hiring, and promotion processes within the organization. Twenty-first century law enforcement agencies can no longer be reactive and wait for potential candidates to seek them out.

One solution for agencies struggling to find qualified candidates may be as simple as being more proactive and creative in their recruitment strategies. Law enforcement agencies need to metaphorically "take the battle to the candidates" by connecting with them in their social environments. For instance, agencies can distribute recruitment materials at colleges and universities with high numbers of students who are racial and ethnic minorities; use various media platforms to attract wider and more diverse audiences; strengthen partnerships with REM organizations; encourage existing employees to be ambassadors of the organization; provide mentoring and establish a student or internship program; and even offer tuition reimbursements to appeal to candidates. These strategies and many more may help increase a law enforcement agency's recruitment and hiring numbers (WIFLE, 2016).

As the United States and California specifically continually increase in population, the importance of diversity and inclusion and targeted recruitment must be emphasized even more. Law enforcement must be committed to utilizing new tactics that recommit to the communities it serves. Growing populations of REMs will influence needed changes in a 21st-century workforce. One of the benefits of hiring a diverse workforce is that it can help ensure agencies cultivate diversity while employees are engaged and productive with different perspectives, ideas, and solutions that challenge the status quo and encourage new collaborations. Law enforcement agencies are in need of major cultural, compositional, and attitudinal restructuring, not only due to increased social pressures of diversity and inclusion, but also due to a moral obligation to redefine their legacies toward more inclusive organizations. A more improved paradigm that focuses on addressing barriers within law enforcement agencies (including recruitment, hiring, and retention processes) is needed. Fundamentally, if underrepresented communities are to believe inclusion, diversity, and improved relations with law enforcement are still possible in their neighborhoods, law enforcement must make a more concerted effort to bridge those gaps and to promote organizational change through innovation. Cities like Sacramento have the opportunity to become early adopters of innovations and plan changes in their police department that can spread beyond their communities (Repa, 2015). This includes engaging police officer candidates who reflect diversity of the broader population in the community using groundbreaking methods such as the Law Enforcement Candidate Scholars (LECS) program.

Law Enforcement Candidate Scholars Program

One innovative solution being implemented to address needs for greater public trust and transformative law enforcement recruitment, hiring, and training practices across California is the Law Enforcement Candidate Scholars (LECS) program. The LECS program, launched in fall 2016 at California State University, Sacramento, is an innovative "Scholars to Officers" program that provides students opportunities to participate in academic, cultural competence training and career and leadership development, which aids in obtaining skills necessary to succeed in a law enforcement career. The LECS program is contractually partnered with local and state law enforcement agencies that offer paid academies (California Highway Patrol and the Sacramento Police Department) to students to prepare and transform them to become sworn law enforcement officers in Sacramento and throughout California.

The LECS program consists of a two-phase process for students: training workshops in year one to help students meet the law enforcement agency entrance requirements, and an academic internship with the partnering agency in year two. Phase one training addresses skills identified as challenges for many police applicants and new recruits, including leadership in law enforcement, pre-employment application, written tests and reports, communication and cultural competence, academy culture, oral interviews, defensive driving, de-escalation force options, defensive tactics, and physical fitness training. The workshops are held both on campus and at police academies to create realistic scenarios to educate and enhance students' skills. The academic internship in phase two is an opportunity for LECS students to gain additional, practical hands-on experience with partnering agencies and the community while becoming more familiar with work culture. Pleasantly, upon graduation from the LECS program and the university, graduates will enter a sworn law enforcement academy as a paid cadet.

One of the cornerstones of the LECS program is its emphasis on transformational leadership and challenging the status quo to address societal disparities (Nevarez & Wood, 2010). Likewise, Chief Hahn's commitment to cultural diversity, inclusion, and challenging the status quo was demonstrated by his support at an unconscious bias training hosted by the LECS program in 2017. Training featured panelists who were local leaders, community organizers, and advocates for justice, frankly discussing unconscious bias, cultural competency, and how diversity and inclusion positively and negatively influence police–community relations. The unconscious bias training was a collaborative effort that allowed individuals' voices to be heard while restoring trust between law enforcement agencies and the community.

The LECS program is based on a cohort model (small learning community) that provides opportunities for students from many backgrounds (Kuh, 2008) to work, study, and train together in a high-impact educational practice. In addition, this learning format encourages students to become change agents in their communities and builds a network of support for future law enforcement officers throughout their careers, including both peer and professional mentors to motivate one another toward their future career goals. Strengthening social bonds is also an important part of the program, which is why LECS students from previous cohorts are expected to mentor new cohorts to help provide social networking, support, and leadership. Since many of the LECS students will join the ranks of law enforcement agencies as a cohort, they will be teammates ready to support others in their communities.

In the two years since the LECS program commenced, research and data collected on the perceived impact of the LECS program as it relates to community relations with law enforcement, academic success, and recruitment and hiring of students, including those underrepresented in law enforcement careers, suggests positive results. Research on the LECS program included quantitative data derived from an online survey provided to participants who volunteered to complete the survey. The vast majority of LECS students surveyed (92%) professed that the program positively impacted their academic success. Ninety-six percent of students surveyed felt the LECS program aided students (including those underrepresented in law enforcement) in recruitment and hiring and job placement in a law enforcement agency. Results from the survey also suggested that 91% of students think the LECS program positively impacts community relations with law enforcement. These data are critical considering past and current relationships with law enforcement.

One of the program's biggest points of pride is its 43 candidates originally selected in the inaugural cohort and 39 candidates selected for cohort 2. Collectively, LECS students are a diverse group of young women and men. Based on enrollment (39% Latino/a, 33% White, 9% Black, 7% Asian/Pacific Islander, 11% other), the program boasts a significant percentage of REMs (U.S. Department of Education, 2018), and nearly half (46%) of the students accepted into the program identified as female. Data on female candidates is significant because the majority of law enforcement agencies across the United States are deficient with female hires. The LECS program truly reflects broad multiculturalism found at California State University, Sacramento and in the general population of California.

Job placement data suggested that approximately 50% of continuing LECS students from the first two LECS cohorts (a total sample size of 82) passed the Peace Officers Standards and Training Entry Level Law Enforcement Test Battery (PELLETB) exam and initial background assessments required to be placed into academic internship positions or as conditional hires in their partnering law enforcement agencies. Proudly, over 50 students are expected to participate in cohort 3, demonstrating increasing popularity of the program by students who want to make a difference as agents of change in their communities. The LECS program emphasizes leadership and professional development in the field of law enforcement. Because of sensitive subject matters (e.g., cultural competence), applied lessons and strong mentorship, students in the LECS program have a greater appreciation for the institution of policing and the expectations and commitment required to be a highly qualified law enforcement cadet and future sworn officer.

The LECS program positively transforms young women and men into scholars ready for the challenges of being law enforcement cadets, while also preparing them for the rigors of their future careers as sworn officers. LECS students regularly experience real-life law enforcement scenarios with the assistance of sworn law enforcement instructors. This type of hands-on instruction requires students to critically think while performing difficult tasks. However, because the LECS program involves a great deal of academic, mental, emotional, and physical fitness training and activities, some participants come to the realization that they are not prepared for a career in law enforcement. The LECS pre-academy training program inevitably experiences a small degree of attrition for various reasons such as disqualifications for failing agency guidelines or agency background investigations; changes in lifestyles, resulting in changes in career choices; lack of commitment to the LECS values (leadership, education, diversity, commitment and innovation); and lack of readiness (socially, emotionally, or physically) for the rigors of the LECS program. Nonetheless, the LECS program is producing successful outcomes; compared with the overall acceptance and completion rates for individuals (not participating in the LECS program) applying to police academies, the LECS program job placement rates are very high (Oliver, 2015).

Qualitative data were also collected through surveys and analyzed for themes based on frequency and variety using phenomenological techniques. By analyzing survey participant responses, trends were noted regarding how students perceived the influence of the program on academic success, recruitment and hiring, and community relations with law enforcement. Themes that emerged from the surveys were as follows:

- **Leadership development:** Building skills and commitment through leadership.
  - "My leadership and communication skills [] improved immensely."
- **Career readiness:** Opportunities for career success and personal development.

- ○ "I plan on learning more as I progress with the career in law enforcement."
- ✦ **Overcoming challenges:** Addressing barriers to becoming a sworn law enforcement officer.
  - ○ "The physical fitness portion of the program and preparing for the Pellet B proved to be challenging at first."
- ✦ **Social exchange:** Improving social interactions and communications.
  - ○ "I continue to learn through each workshop and have made connections well with my peers and mentors."

The initial evaluation of the program revealed positive results of the LECS program on students' career outcomes with impactful results for academic success, recruitment and hiring, and community relations. Moreover, this unique "Scholars to Officers" leadership program is significantly helping college students to develop mentally, physically, socially, and culturally to succeed academically while helping them prepare for jobs in 21st-century policing. Future research can evaluate expectations of LECS students; examine specific influences of the LECS program on women and underrepresented minorities; and study efficacy of the program on long-term retention and promotion of local and state law enforcement officers. More importantly, the LECS program can be used as a model to develop law enforcement experiential learning opportunities for college students while addressing historical deficits in recruiting and championing the importance of inclusion and cultural competence. Positive outcomes already achieved by the program make it likely that the LECS program will not only be adopted by other agencies and on other campuses, but in other states as well.

Conclusion

Law enforcement is at a crossroads in our country's modern history of police–community relations and commitment to diversity in policing. Leadership within the Sacramento Police Department and other police agencies across the country has the opportunity to help restore trust in policing through new ways of approaching communities and recruitment and training of future law enforcement officers, such as with the LECS program model. Sacramento can be put in the national spotlight not as a disconnected community, but as an early adopter of innovations that move the needle toward cultural diversity and inclusion in policing.

Chief Hahn's swearing-in day brought with it positive change, growth, and feelings of optimism. His mere presence became a sense of reassurance to many of Sacramento's REMs and others across the country that the Sacramento Police Department could change the course of history. Nevertheless, critical to Chief Hahn's success are conscious decisions and changes he makes over the next few years in the midst of continued historically rooted community tensions. He has an unprecedented opportunity to transform public safety in Sacramento into a foundational model for other police departments also seeking greater diversity and inclusion using the LECS program, with lasting impacts for decades to come. It is time for law enforcement to apply lessons from the past to become a system that is truly for all members of the community and to recognize law enforcement candidates and officers who reflect, serve, and support positive change.

FIGURE 2.1   Chief Hahn and LECS students (Vernone, 2017).

Discussion Questions

1. After reading about historical injustices experienced by racial and ethnic minorities during encounters with law enforcement, what strategies would you use to enhance police–community relations in today's modern era?

2. What are the benefits and challenges associated with advancing a more diverse and culturally competent law enforcement workforce rather than the status quo?

3. How can culture change and professional development within law enforcement training academies help law enforcement become more inclusive and create a better public image?

4. How can student pre-academy career programs be used as a means to recruit and better prepare police candidates for a culture of diversity and inclusion in society?

References

Avella, S. M. (2003). *Sacramento: Indomitable city.* Mt. Pleasant, SC: Arcadia Publishing.

Bretón, M. (2017, August 11). How a White woman from Minnesota raised Sacramento's first Black police chief. *Sacramento Bee.* Retrieved from https://www.sacbee.com/news/local/news-columns-blogs/marcos-breton/article166659592.html

Bureau of Justice Statistics (BJS) (2015). *Local police departments, 2013: Personnel, policies, and practices.* Retrieved from https://www.bjs.gov/content/pub/pdf/lpd13ppp.pdf

California Commission on Peace Officer Standards and Training. (2014). *Expanded course outline.* Retrieved from https://post.ca.gov/Portals/0/post_docs/training/PC832Materials/ECO%20Exemplars/ECOs%20Comparison%20Example/ECO_COMP_A.docx

Carter, J. M. (2016). Whren's flawed assumptions regarding race, history, and unconscious bias. *Case Western Reserve Law Review, 66*(4), 947–956.

City of Sacramento. (2018). *Brief Sacramento police department history.* Retrieved from https://www.cityofsacramento.org/Police/About-SPD/Department-History

City of Sacramento. (2016). *Sacramento police department 2016 annual report.* Retrieved from https://www.cityofsacramento.org/-/media/Corporate/Files/Police/About-SPD/Annual-Reports/ar16.pdf?la=en

Civil Rights Act of 1964, Pub. L. 88-352, 78 Stat. 241 (1964)

Feld, B. C. (2003). The politics of race and juvenile justice: The "due process revolution" and the conservative reaction. *Justice Quarterly, 20*(4), 765–800.

Gallup (2014). *Gallup review: Black and white attitudes towards police.* Retrieved from http://www.gallup.com/poll/175088/gallup-review-black-white-attitudestoward-police.aspx

George, A. (2018). The 1968 Kerner commission got it right, but nobody listened. *Smithsonian.* Retrieved from https://www.smithsonianmag.com/smithsonian-institution/1968-kerner-commission-got-it-right-nobody-listened-180968318/

Haden, S. (2001). *Slave patrols: Law and violence in Virginia and the Carolinas.* Cambridge, MA: Harvard University Press.

Kahn, A. & Kirk, C. (2015, August 9). What it's like to be Black in the criminal justice system. *Slate.* Retrieved from http://www.slate.com/articles/news_and_politics/crime/2015/08/racial_disparities_in_the_criminal_justice_system_eight_charts_illustrating.html

Koh, H. H. (2002). The spirit of the laws. *Harvard International Law Journal, 43*(1), 23–40.

Kuh, G. D. (2008). Excerpt from high-impact educational practices: What they are, who has access to them, and why they matter. *Association of American Colleges and Universities.* Retrieved from https://keycenter.unca.edu/sites/default/files/aacu_high_impact_2008_final.pdf

Maslow, A. H. (1943). A theory of human motivation. *Psychological Review, 50*(4), 370.

Mayer, R. C., Davis, J. H., & Schoorman, F. D. (1995). An integrative model of organizational trust. *Academy of Management Review, 20*(3), 709–734.

Miranda v. Arizona, 384 U.S. 436 (1966). Retrieved from https://www.law.cornell.edu/supremecourt/text/384/436

Moffatt, S. (2015). *Criminal justice academy/career academy programs' influence on "at risk" youth success.* (Unpublished doctoral dissertation). California State University, Sacramento.

National Advisory Commission on Civil Disorders. (1968). *Report of the National Advisory Commission on Civil Disorders.* Retrieved from http://www.eisenhowerfoundation.org/docs/kerner.pdf

National Center for Educational Statistics. (2017). *Status and trends in the education of racial and ethnic groups 2017.* Retrieved from http://www.nces.ed.gov

National Institute of Justice (NIJ). (2018). *Race, trust, and police legitimacy.* Retrieved from https://www.nij.gov/topics/law-enforcement/legitimacy/Pages/welcome.aspx

Nevarez, C., & Wood, J. L. (2010). *Community college leadership and administration: Theory, practice, and change* (Vol. 3). New York, NY: Peter Lang.

Oliver, K. (2015). Investigation: Racial diversity lost in CHP hiring process. *KCRA.com.* Retrieved from https://www.kcra.com/article/investigation-racial-diversity-lost-in-chp-hiring-process/6422651

Paul, C. A. (2016). Fugitive Slave Act of 1850. *Social Welfare History Project.* Retrieved from http://socialwelfare.library.vcu.edu/federal/fugitive-slave-act-of-1850/

Pearsall, A. & Kohlhepp, K. (2010, April). Strategies to improve recruitment. *The Police Chief, 77,* 128–130.

Police Officer Standards and Training. (2014). *Expanded course outline.* Retrieved from https://post.ca.gov/Portals/0/post_docs/training/PC832Materials/ECO%20Exemplars/ECOs%20Comparison%20Example/ECO_COMP_A.docx

President's Task Force on 21st Century Policing. (2015). *Final report of the President's task force on 21st century policing.* Washington, DC: Office of Community Oriented Policing Services.

Repa, M. (2015). *Leadership to support e-quality for all: A study of a systemwide accessible technology policy implementation* (Unpublished doctoral dissertation). California State University, Sacramento.

Skelton, G. (2015, August 19). Amid an era rife with rebellion, the Watts riots were a wake-up call. *Los Angeles Times.* Retrieved from http://www.latimes.com/local/politics/la-me-cap-watts-20150820-column.html

Stoughton, S. (2014, December 12). How police training contributes to avoidable deaths. *The Atlantic.* Retrieved from https://www.theatlantic.com/national/archive/2014/12/police-gun-shooting-training-ferguson/383681/

The Washington Post. (2001). Discrimination in America. The Washington Post Online. Retrieved from The Washington Post. (2001). Discrimination in America.

The Washington Post Online. Retrieved from http://www.washingtonpost.com/wp-srv/nation/sidebars/polls/race071101.htm

U.S. Census. (2017). *Quickfacts: Sacramento city*. Retrieved from https://www.census.gov/quickfacts/fact/table/sacramentocitycalifornia,US/PST045217

U.S. Department of Education. (2018). *United States Department of Education lists of postsecondary institutions enrolling populations with significant percentages of undergraduate minority students*. Retrieved from https://www2.ed.gov/about/offices/list/ocr/edlite-minorityinst.html

U.S. Department of Justice. (2016). *Advancing diversity in law enforcement*. Retrieved from https://www.justice.gov/crt/case-document/file/900761/download

U.S. Department of Justice. (2018). *Community relations services toolkit for policing*. Retrieved https://www.justice.gov/crs/file/836486

Vernone, J. (Photographer). (2017, August 11). *Before his swearing-in ceremony, Hahn met with Sac State criminal justice students who have an interest in law enforcement careers*. [digital image]. Sacramento, CA: California State University, Sacramento. Retrieved from https://www2.calstate.edu/impact-of-the-csu/student-success/Profiles/Pages/Daniel-Hahn.aspx. Copyright © 2017 by Jessica Verone. Reprinted with permission.

Voting Rights Act of 1965, Pub. L. 89-110, 79 Stat. 437. Retrieved from http://library.clerk.house.gov/reference-files/PPL_VotingRightsAct_1965.pdf

Walker, S., Spohn, C. & Delone, M. (2012). *The color of justice: Race, ethnicity, and crime in America* (5th ed.). Belmont, CA: Wadsworth.

Women in Federal Law Enforcement. (2016). *Transforming law enforcement by changing the face of policing*. Retrieved from http://www.wifle.org/publications.htm

Chapter 3

Economy, Police Staffing, and Crime Rates
The 12-Year Experience in California

Shihlung Huang

Introduction

Like most states in the United States, California experienced a recession-like distressed economy after the 2008 financial crisis. Followed by a housing bust in 2006, many businesses went bankrupt and the unemployment rate spiked from 4% in 2002 to 12% in 2010. In turn, the collapse of the housing market and distressed economy abated the resources of both state and local governments. Major sources of revenue were redirected for programs that were not related to solving problems of public safety. In response to the severe shortage of revenue, California introduced a myriad of measures to balance the budget, including the cutbacks of law enforcement police forces. At the onset of the revenue shortfalls, common budget balancing tactics were manifested in furloughs and pay cuts for government employees and public safety officers (Zvonicek, 2012). During the initial phase of the budget crisis, people seemed to pull together and endure. Presently, people are beginning to feel more concerned, especially in the face of a reduction in the number of sworn officers that resulted in layoffs and stifled local law enforcement efforts to respond to calls for service. People become increasingly frightened when local politicians, especially police leaders, continue to stress impending crime waves, which they tout as being the result of officer shortages. Most public administrators and elected officials continue to advocate for the hiring of more, not less, police officers to deter the expected crime wave prompted by the economic recession (Kuruvila, 2010).

If gun purchase can serve a proxy indicator of fear of crime, it looks like Californians are fearful of the surge of crime due to the compound effect of bad economy and reductions in full-time law enforcement officers. Gun sales have been escalating for the past few years and reached a record high in 2012 in California (Zimmerman, 2012). More people appear to be purchasing guns for self-protection and as deterrence for burglary and other crimes rather than for hunting game. So, the question becomes, "Will high unemployment rates lead to increases in violent and property crime?" Additionally, will a shortage of officers contribute to a rise in these types of crimes? And finally, does *crime* really increase in periods of *recession*, or is this simply a myth? It is fair to assume that in times of dire need more people will turn to crime for food and other essential items when the economy is bad and when fewer officers are on the street to deter perspective perpetrators. But are these fair assumptions? This chapter will use California and its capital city, Sacramento, to gauge the impact of unemployment and change of police presence on crime. The results here will shed light on this theoretical implied relationship.

Economy and Crime

While the general public assumes the predictable relationship between a poor economy and high levels of crime, criminologists are less certain of the direct correlation. Proponents maintain that when more legitimate job opportunities are available, illegitimate means become relatively less desirable (Becker, 1968). Additionally, some economists have estimated that a 1% increase in the unemployment rate would lead to a 1% to 2% increase in property crime (Donohue & Levitt, 2001; Wilson, 2011). However, more opponents contend that it is empirically challenging when trying to associate unemployment with crime from a historical perspective. A typical example is crime rates during the Great Depression. When the unemployment rate was 25%, instead of the expected chaos and social disorder, the crime rate actually fell in many cities (Wilson, 2011). This low crime rate may point to the fact that under duress people who were experiencing widespread poverty and unemployment actually united, rendering mutual support and collective action, while closely supervising and caring for youth (Wilson, 2011).

In addition, the unemployment rate may not be an accurate barometer of economic stability and is an insufficient measure when attempting to connect unemployment and crime as it estimates only the percentage of the labor force that is looking for work and hasn't found it. In fact, those who are neither working nor looking for work are the ones who are most vulnerable to criminal activity if one subscribes to the belief that a faltering economy leads to increases in crime. The University of Michigan's Consumer Sentiment Index is another indicator that can be used to assess the economy/crime puzzle. This index conducts interviews with thousands of people asking them about their overall financial situation, their confidence in the government to solve economic problems, and their plans for purchasing durable goods. However, this tool is used to gauge self-assessments of people's financial well-being rather than their *true income*. Levitt (2004) believes this measure is a good indicator for the direction of stock prices and less frequently the crime rate.

Police Staffing and Crime Rates

It is logical to assume that increased police presence inhibits the commission of crimes. Prominent criminologist James Alan Fox painted a grim picture when he indicated that "the next crime wave will get so bad, that it will make 1995 look like the good old days" (as cited in Levitt & Dubner, 2006, p. 2). As a direct result of the enactment of the Violent Crime Control and Law Enforcement Act (or Crime Bill) of 1994, substantial funds (over $7.5 billion) were funneled to law enforcement agencies, resulting in the addition of more than 100,000 officers (Gutierrez, 2003). As noted by Gutierrez (2003), the implementation of community policing strategies seems to have had an impact on the implementation of strategies that attempt to attack the root causes of crime (namely social disorder, citizen mobilization, and proactive efforts to thwart crime) during the later portion of the 1990s. Another widely cited example is the reduction of crime in New York City for its doubling of the police force and its aggressive tactics of CompStat (Eterno & Silverman, 2005). Deterrence theory by Stafford and Warr (1993) suggests that the enhanced likelihood of being caught endorsed the concept of police presence as general deterrence. Routine activity theorists also implied that crime occurs when there is a motivated offender, an attractive target, and a lack of capable guardianship (Cohen & Felson, 1979). Given this, to prevent crime from happening, police officers and their presence (as well as community mobilization) would serve as capable guardians to deter a motivated offender from committing criminal acts.

Impact of 2008 Economic Downturn on Police Staffing

The economic crisis that began in 2008 has reversed the steady increase in police officers in this country. With the collapse of housing market in 2006, businesses were forced to shut their doors, all levels of government revenue dwindled, and unemployment rates experienced a steady increase (Zvonicek, 2012). A report from Community Oriented Policing Services (COPS) (2011) revealed the severe impact of the declining economy on county law enforcement budgets and documented ways these counties have responded. Their findings indicated that these counties were making comprehensive cuts in every area including but not limited to critical services and police personnel in an attempt to balance the budget. These measures, including furloughs and layoffs of sworn officers, are more drastic than the previous survey in which cuts were only limited to spending and hiring freezes (Community Oriented Policing Services, 2011).

A recent survey indicated that the current recession has led to the largest loss in revenues and spending cutbacks in the history of the survey, and the revenues have continued to decline for 4 years in a row (Hoene & Pagano 2010). In every corner of the United States, municipal, county, state, and tribal law enforcement agencies are being forced to lay off officers and civilian staff or modify their operations as a result of budget cuts. Over the last two years, many agencies have experienced considerable effects from budget constrictions, including mandatory furloughs and hiring freezes, resulting in significant reductions in staffing levels never experienced before. For example, in Paterson, New Jersey, the police department laid off 125 officers, a quarter of their entire force, in April, 2011. More than 30 lieutenants and sergeants were also relegated back to patrol. Violent crime jumped 15% in 2010 over the previous year's level (Henry, 2011). In January 2011, Camden also made headlines when its police department let go 163 officers, leaving it with only 204 sworn officers. This number was the lowest since 1949 (Goldstein, 2011). With a population of 102,000, the police department in Flint, Michigan, also cut two-thirds of their officers over a 3-year period and, on a typical day, only six officers were on patrol at any given time. The city was (and still is) suffering from an unusually high rate of violent crime and is perennially one of America's murder capitals per capita (LeDuff, 2011).

In Sacramento, California, municipal police and the sheriff's department were faced with the same dilemma: which officers should be laid off and what strategies can be employed to cope with severe budget cuts. The shrinking of Sacramento's police force has been extreme; the department has lost more than 300 sworn officers and civilian staff members and more than 30% of its budget since 2008. The police department is forced to do more with less to balance the budget and keep the department afloat:

> He (the police chief) was forced to lay off sworn officers and civilian employees; eliminated the vice, narcotics, financial crimes and undercover gang squads, sending many detectives back to patrol; and thinned the auto theft, forensics and canine units. Police officers no longer respond to burglaries, misdemeanors or minor traffic accidents. Earlier this year, the traffic enforcement unit was disbanded. The department now conducts follow-up investigations for only the most serious crimes, like homicide and sexual assault. Chief Braziel noted that "You reach the point where there is nothing left to cut." (Goode, 2012)

The sheriff's department was also faced with a $10 million cut and was forced to lay off 118 deputies in 2013. This cut has forced a realignment that moved officers working in the county jail to work on patrol. This move further put public safety in jeopardy when fewer officers at the jails were handling an increasing number of inmates (including more violent ones) as a result of prison realignment (Branan, 2013).

California's Economy and Crime Rates

The unemployment rate in California jumped from 5% in 2000 to 12% in 2010, causing severe concerns that an impending crime wave was afoot. As posited prior, it is only reasonable to assume that crime will increase during difficult economic times. With the largest state population and an economy the size of a country's (fifth largest in the world), it stands as a great indicator of the impact these budgetary reallocations will have on citizens in California. How does California's crime rate fare in light of its dotcom and housing busts? Does it follow the national trend? Or does it tell a different story? Some figures are presented next that might help sort out these questions.

As indicated in Figure 3.1, both violent and property crime maintained an overall downward trend despite the two periods of low unemployment during 2000–2012. A closer looks reveals that as violent crime went up at the peak of the housing bust (2006), it then tapered off until 2010, picking up again in 2012. Property crime shows a slightly different pattern: It went in tandem with unemployment rates at the onset of the housing boom (2001–2004) and slightly increased as unemployment improved after 2010.

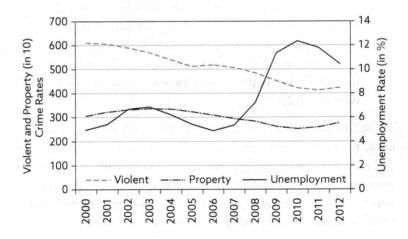

FIGURE 3.1   Unemployment rate, violent, and property crime rate in California, 2000–2012.
Sources: Bureau of Labor Statistics, 2013 and California Department of Justice, 2014.

The implication in Figure 3.1 did not support what conventional wisdom tells us about the relationship between a bad economy and an increase in crime. On the contrary, it painted a completely different picture, suggesting that a good economy brings with it more crimes, in particular, property crimes. The reason behind this may be that affluence brings with it more vice, as when the economy is good, consumers are purchasing more luxurious goods, and criminals take advantage of this windfall and engage in more property crimes. The raw numbers may also suggest that unemployed workers will not necessarily will resort to crime during hard times. For some reason, they have managed to maintain a crime-free lifestyle under severe economic pressure.

California Police Staffing and Crime Rates

Figure 3.2 provides an indication of the relationship between police staffing and crime rates during 2000–2012.

Given the figure, what can be said about the fiscal crisis effects on law enforcement staffing in California? Examining these raw numbers might lead to an explanation of the relationship (if any) of how the reduction of the police forces has affected crime rates. To answer this question,

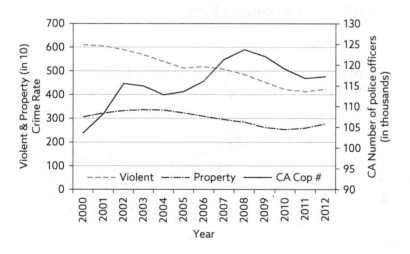

FIGURE 3.2   California police staffing and crime rate, 2000–2012.
Source: California Department of Justice, 2013.

the number of law enforcement officers and crimes rates is displayed to reveal specific trends. As Figure 3.2 shows, California suffered from officer cut-backs for two periods after 2008. However, an examination of crime rates showed a different pattern with a slight rise in 2001–2002 but a tapering off after that. It is interesting to note that crime rate did not pick up, but instead showed a continuing downward trend during the 4-year continuous layoff of officers. When the number of officers slightly increased, so did the crimes after 2011. It is difficult to make meaningful conclusions, here, in whether the number of officers matters.

Economy, Police Staffing, and Crime at the Local Level: Sacramento

Since using the state of California presents some degree of difficulty in discerning the impact of either the economy or police staffing, it is posited that a close examination of local police departments will shed light on their relationships, if any, between the economy and police staffing. Sacramento is the capital city of California, with a population of one half million people. The major employer is state government, and the economy and unemployment rates follow the same pattern of that found at the state level (Bureau of Labor Statistics, 2013). Figure 3.3 provides some indication of the dynamics found in the state capital.

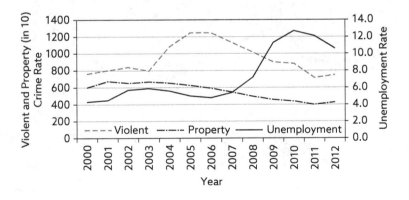

FIGURE 3.3 Sacramento unemployment and violent and property crime rate.
Sources: Bureau of Labor Statistics, 2013 and California Department of Justice, 2014.

The situation in Sacramento mirrors that of California as a whole. Sacramento unemployment follows an exact pattern, and the property crime rate maintained a steady downward trend (Bureau of Labor Statistics, 2013). It is logical to assume that property crime would rise during the period when the economy flourished, as there were more valuables available for perpetrators. On the contrary, the violent crime rate showed an uptick from 800 to more than 1,200, a 50% rise, during the housing boom from 2002 to 2006. The two emerging patterns associated with the violent crime rate were increases in aggravated assault and rape, much more than robbery and homicide. There is no mentioning from either media or law enforcement agencies regarding this puzzling trend. One might assume it may have been the higher alcohol consumption and enhanced interactions during the good times leading to more incidents of altercation and violence. Again, what remains an interesting and important significance when examining this figure is the inverse relationship between the economy and crime rates. That is, crime does not go up when the economy goes into a tailspin. On the contrary, crime goes down.

Were there more crimes when the number of patrol officers in the Sacramento Police Department decreased from 800 to 650, a reduction of 18% during 2008–2012? The answer is mixed. Both violent and property crime continued to drop when the police force was cut during the first 2 years (2009–2010). But both crime categories started to pick up at the

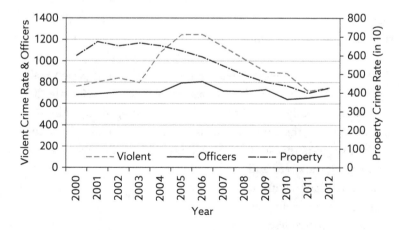

FIGURE 3.4   Police officer, violent and property crime in Sacramento, CA.
Sources: Sacramento Police Department, 2014 and California Department of Justice, 2014

third year, 2012, when the police force faced further cuts. Sacramento police officers remain steady in 2000s, but both violent crime—except 2003–2006—and property crime continued on a downward trend. There doesn't appear to be a significant relationship between a visible police presence and the crime rate. It also seems that the unemployment rate shows more impact on crime than the number of officers. The number of police officers as a deterrent effect of crime should have more impact on property crimes than violent crime because, theoretically, property crime is normally the result of calculated reasoning, whereas violent crimes are more impulsive. However, in Sacramento, violent crime spiked even when the police force remained stable.

What Lies Ahead?

As indicated, the ebb and flow of unemployment rates and police staffing levels in recent years suggested their impact on crime rates were not as significant as most people might have believed. The results of this preliminary assessment indicate that their relationship is inconclusive at best. Crimes in all categories continued to drop during this major economic recession despite the unprecedented cutbacks in law enforcement officers at state and local levels. However, the tables presented in this analysis also show that both violent and property crimes started to rise in 2011 at both the state and local levels—at a time when unemployment showed some signs of improvement and more laid-off officers were reinstated. While some might consider this uptick merely an accidental blip, more stakeholders were concerned that a reversal of this downward trend would soon emerge when the implementation of prison realignment (AB 109) in California counties reached its zenith (Goode, 2012).

It should be duly noted that this fear and warning of impending crime and disorder in the communities is not without merit. Conventional wisdom suggests that longer prison sentences work to keep dangerous criminals off the street, and the declining crime rate in the past decades is a direct correlation with the reduction in crime reported. Incapacitation appears to be the new goal of those who would agree that policy makers should stay the course and continue with the crime control model of criminal justice processing (Levitt, 2006; Wilson, 2011). Assembly Bill

109 in California (or prison realignment) may change all that. Under the Federal Court decree to reduce overcrowded prisons, the state of California has been releasing 30,000 state inmates to its 58 counties for supervision and management. These inmates are considered nonserious, nonviolent, nonsexual felony offenders who will continue to serve their time either in county jails or some other alternative criminal sanction. Although the state provides some funding to cover the cost of supervising these felons, county leaders are gravely concerned that these additional burdens on top of their overwhelming, underfunded, and understaffed county jails and law enforcement sectors might push them to brink of financial insolvency (Branan, 2013; Goode, 2012).

It is a relief to see the declining crime rate in light of the recession-like economy and the severe cutbacks on law enforcement officers in the past decade. In this new decade, California is faced with different challenges when a significant number of state felons begin serving their time in the community rather than behind bars. California has been the leader in innovative and progressive policies and programs in this country and the world. This state also has the largest criminal justice system and prison population in the nation. Experts are closely watching how the state of California weathers this daunting task as well as its impact and implications.

Discussion Questions

1. Identify and discuss the theories and commonsensical reasoning on the relationship between economy and crime rate.

2. Discuss the possible impacts of economic downturn to law enforcement and other components of the criminal justice system.

3. What could be the plausible reasons to explain why a severe economic recession was not leading to higher crime rates during the housing crisis in California and the United States?

4. Discuss the different impacts of economic downturn to violent crimes, property crimes, and other type of offenses.

5. What are the strategies for law enforcement leaders to maintain public safety and enhance funding during an economic recession?

References

Becker, G. (1968). Crime and punishment: An economic approach. *Journal of Political Economy, 76*(2), 169–217.

Branan, B. (2013, June 11). Sacramento County sheriff warns of big patrol cuts at budget hearing, *Sacramento Bee,* p. 1B.

Bureau of Labor Statistics (2013, June). *OES employment and wages by occupation 2003–2012.* U.S. Department of Labor, Washington D. C.

California Department of Justice (2014). *Crime in California–2014.* Office of the Attorney General, Department of Justice. Sacramento, CA: Criminal Justice Statistics Center

Cohen, L. & Felson, M. (1979). Social change and crime rate trends: A routine activity approach. *American Sociological Review, 44*(4), 588–608.

Community Oriented Policing Services (2011). The impact of economic downturn on American police agencies. A Report of the U.S. Department of Justice, Office of Community Oriented Policing Services. Washington, DC: Author.

Donohue, J. & Levitt, S. (2001). Legalized abortion and crime. *Quarterly Journal of Economics, 116*(2), 379–420.

Eterno, J. & Silverman, E. (2005). The New York City Police Department's Compstat: Dream or nightmare? *International Journal of Police Science and Management, 8*(3), 218–231.

Goldstein, J. (2011, March 6). Police force nearly halved, Camden feels impact. *New York Times.* Retrieved from https://www.nytimes.com/2011/03/07/nyregion/07camden.html.

Goode, E. (2012, November 3). Crime increases in Sacramento state workers after deep cuts to police forces. *New York Times.* Retrieved from https://www.nytimes.com/2012/11/04/us/after-deep-police-cuts-sacramento-sees-rise-in-crime.html

Gutierrez, R. S. (2003). *Social equity and the funding of community oriented policing.* New York, NY: LFB.

Henry, S. (2011, April 18). Cops protest as Paterson lays off 125 police officers; mayor hopes to hire some back. *Associated Press.* Retrieved from https://www.deseretnews.com/article/700128192/Paterson-lays-off-125-police-officers.html

Hoene, C. and Pagano, M. (2010). *City fiscal conditions in 2010.* Washington DC: National League of Cities, Research Brief.

Kuruvila, M. (2010, July 14). Oakland talks break down; layoffs for 80 cops. *San Francisco Chronicle*. Retrieved from https://www.sfgate.com/bayarea/article/ Oakland-talks-break-down-layoffs for-80-cops.php

LeDuff, C. (2011, April 15). Riding along with the cops in murder town, U.S.A. *New York Times*. Retrieved from https://www.nytimes.com/2011/04/17/magazine/ mag-17YouRhere-t.html.

Petersilia, J. (2014). California prison downsizing and its impact on local criminal justice systems. *Harvard Law & Policy Review, 5*, 327–345.

Levitt, S. (2004). Understanding why crime fell in the 1990s: Four factors that explain the decline and six that do not. *Journal of Economic Perspectives, 18*(1),163–190.

Levitt, S. & Dubner, S. (2006). *Freakonomics: A rogue economist explores the hidden side of everything.* New York, NY: William Morrow and Company.

Sacramento Police Department (2014). *Internal Report.* Sacramento, CA: Public Affairs Office.

Stafford, M. & Warr, M. (1993). A reconceptualization of general and specific deterrence. *Journal of Research in Crime and Delinquency, 30*, 123–135.

Wilson, J. (2009, January 8). Crime and economy don't tell whole story. *Los Angeles Times*. Retrieved from https://www.latimes.com/opinion/editorials/la-oe-wilson8-2009jan08-story.html.

Wilson, J. (2011, March 28). Hard times, fewer crimes. *Wall Street Journal*. Retrieved from https://www.wsj.com/articles/SB100014240527023040665045763455 53135009870

Zvonicek, R. (2012) *A study of the California furloughs and their effects on state workers.* Master thesis in California State University, Sacramento.

Zimmerman, J. (2012, December 18). Gun sales hit all time high in wake of tragedy. *The Press-Enterprise*. Retrieved from https://www.pe.com/2012/12/18/ gun-sales-hit-all-time-high-in wake-of-tragedy

Chapter 4

Has Policing Changed? Lessons Through the Looking Glass

Ryan Getty and Andrew C. Michaud

Introduction

Regardless of recent, progressive reforms to policing, not much has changed. Though this notion may seem somewhat pessimistic and discouraging, it is actually meant as a lesson to ensure future generations of students and practitioners recognize the past experiences and lessons while building on new, forward-looking policing philosophies.

This chapter will discuss reforms dating back more than a century, with parallels drawn to modern-day tactics and philosophies. Controversial subjects, such as police use of force, police deviance, and community relations, will be examined in a historical and present-day context and suggestions will be made for modifications and improvements.

Through the recognition of what has historically worked and what has not worked, students should be able to reason through various scenarios to satisfy public expectations of modern police practices. It is only then that communities across the country and the police may come to an understanding of what are just and proper police policies and practices.

Historical Police Reform

Regardless of the origins and reasons for the creation of law enforcers, police across the United States had similar duties and responsibilities. The most important of these were duties associated with keeping the peace and apprehending offenders. Although there was a plethora of news accounts of mob lynching, arrestees absconding, and officers extorting others, people were likely less concerned with what police were

51

doing because their daily struggle for survival took precedence. Even news of abuses were likely short-lived because of the overriding need to survive. This dynamic of lack of police accountability continued until the early 20th century when police reforms were first established.

The first police reform action was the 1919 Chicago Crime Commission (Chamberlin, 1920). By 1931, seven local, 16 state, and two national commissions had been established to investigate policing methods and processes. Even President Herbert Hoover established the Wickersham Commission in 1929 to review the criminal justice system (National Commission on Law Observance and Enforcement, 1931). The Commission's 1931 "Report on Lawlessness in Law Enforcement" clearly highlights the critical need for reform (Lester, 1997). It was not long after the conclusion of the Wickersham Commission in 1931 that police were once again at the forefront of public discourse.

In 1932, after the ending of World War I, veterans, their families, and sympathetic groups marched on Washington, DC (Oritz, 2006). The Bonus Army, as it was known, wanted veteran compensation for their service to the country. President Hoover ordered the full might of the military to descend on the group. However, it was the police who shot protesters and ultimately killed two veterans. This and other non-democratic actions, such as strike breaking, perpetuate the historical notion that police are a means of social control in a financial oligarchical government (Mitrani, 2013). This conception did not subside with the emergence of the turbulent 1960s and 1970s.

The American 1960s and 1970s experienced many political and cultural movements. Numerous government and police abuses led to landmark Warren Court decisions that are routinely accepted today. Due to police abuses, basic constitutional concerns such as due process, civil rights, search and seizure, and use of force were at the forefront of discourse yet again.

Though many of these subjects had been decided in the preceding cases and years leading up to the Warren Court decisions, it seemed to be a time for revolutionary criminal justice system reform in America. The Court tackled questions of Fourth Amendment rights against unreasonable or limited search and seizures in *Mapp v. Ohio* (1961), *Terry v. Ohio* (1968), and *Chimel v. California* (1969); Fifth Amendment rights against self-incrimination (*Miranda v. Arizona*, 1966); Sixth Amendment rights requiring council during interrogations (*Escobedo v. Illinois*, 1964); and availability of publicly funded council (*Gideon v. Wainwright*, 1963). The criminal justice system in general, and the police specifically, were in an uproar based on these liberal interpretations of the Constitution. But police began to adapt, if not eventually conform (Pye, 1968). Somewhat more important to citizens' redress was the practical application of an 1871 statutory provision within 42 United States Code, Section 1983 based on the Court case *Monroe v. Pape* (1961). The statute allowed for plaintiffs to sue police officers who violated the plaintiff's rights, but this was rarely used prior to the Court's decision. While suing police is almost commonplace today, historically it was difficult to surmount the power of qualified immunity (certain immunities for government officials), which resulted in lawyers focusing on these types of civil rights violations (Baud, 2018).

Today's media coverage and criticism of the police may seem subdued compared to some of the 1960s and 1970s daily media accounts of police beating and tear-gassing protesters at the 1968 Democratic National Convention in Chicago and the 1970 shooting on Kent State University grounds by the national guard, for which police were also blamed (Klatch, 2002). In addition to well-publicized abuses, the police were embroiled in a scandal that would have national ramifications.

Based on allegations of corruption against the New York Police Department in the 1960s and early 1970s, the Knapp Commission was formed (United States Accounting Office, 1998). Some of the dynamics of corruption and police subcultural behavior uncovered in the Knapp Commission were made famous in media by the film *Serpico* (Lumet, 1973). This negative publicity further made illicit practices by police more apparent.

These examples further the chapter's argument that history is repeating itself and police are making the same mistakes today that were made over their 100 years of formal existence. One can argue these mistakes were made while professionalization of policing was still evolving and there were many lessons learned. This argument is somewhat satisfactory except for the fact that many more commissions and Department of Justice investigations regarding police misbehavior took place after this term of professionalization. However, as new educational and procedural reforms were proposed, the police were still making the same, century-old mistakes.

Contemporary Police Reform

Standards for police education and training had not systematically existed before the 1970s (Oliver, 2016). Many officers who were employed prior to established requirements did not have to conform to the new, basic mandated training and educational minimum standards. For those newly hired, training beyond the minimum police academy requirements typically consisted of rookie officers being "tested" by veterans in a street fight with a suspect (today, probably outlawed as hazing). This holdover practice is continued in various forms although is reinforced informally through rumors within departments as to whether a rookie can hold his or her own in a fight or pressure situation (according author's experiences and personal interviews).

The pessimistic appraisal of professionalization, beginning in the 1970s and progressing throughout the 1980s, is partially unfair. Many innovative and progressive events happened during this time of unprecedented 1980s high crime levels. At the forefront were important items such as hiring standards, mandatory police academy attendance and requirements, field training basics, as well as legislated in-service training. These reforms were initiated on the recommendations of the President's Commission on Law Enforcement and Administration of Justice (1967), which was groundbreaking in that it reviewed all aspects of the criminal justice system with a full chapter devoted entirely to "the police."

Within the commission's report, the police were systemically critiqued on their function in society, operational problems, police hiring practices, education, and standards. The commission charged policing to make improvements in these and many other areas. Several of the commission's non-binding recommendations were partially and slowly realized, but policing did not change. What reforms did occur, and their significance, will be discussed in the next section.

The 1980s criminal justice system was known for police policy and procedural shifts on a national scale, partially due to the unprecedented rise in crime (continuing from the 1970s) and the fear of crime becoming pervasive for communities who were not accustomed to crime (Boggess, Bound, 1997). With the national increase in crime rates, police shootings, use of force, and corruption also seemed to also increase (Dombrink, 1988). The federal government felt the need to intercede in some cases where police departments seemed to have a pattern of corruption and/or abuse. One possible intervention is a consent decree: an agreement between a police department and the U.S. Department of Justice, as certified by a court, that states the department will address a series of agreed-on concerns within a specified period of time (Dabney, 1963). As will be argued later, federal U.S. Department of Justice (USDOJ) investigations and subsequent consent decrees tend to have only short-term effects on the behavior of departments.

The quintessential example of the 1980s federal government's good intentions gone awry is the Miami Police Department's approach under affirmative action hiring while "complying" with a USDOJ consent decree. This consent decree was part of a larger goal mandated by the USDOJ and courts to make departments across the U.S. more racially diverse and representative of their respective jurisdictional populations (U.S. Department of Justice, 2017). The city of Miami felt it had to act quickly to comply with the consent decree but also seemed to blatantly and negligently disregard acceptable police hiring practices. In less than a decade after implementing the new hiring standards to meet the consent decree guidelines, nearly 10% of the entire Miami Police Department was either suspended or fired due to corruption allegations or criminal charges ranging from drug trafficking to murder (Lersch, 2001). This pattern of federal government intervention and local law enforcement minimum compliance continued for decades.

Partially due to the rise in crime rates, there were requests for more professionally trained police to efficiently and effectively prevent crime and deter criminals and arrest offenders. These were fueled by three meaningful events that happened in and around the 1990s to progress police reforms. They were the Rodney King beating and its aftermath; the passing of the Violent Crime Control and Law Enforcement Act of 1994; and police adopting empirically sound techniques.

It cannot be overstated how much the Rodney King beating in 1992 impacted police at the time. Officers and supervisors of the Los Angeles

Police Department (LAPD) were taped beating motorist Rodney King in an apparent "contempt of cop" or for "pissing off the police," as it is known in police circles. "Contempt of cop" refers to person(s) not doing or saying what an officer expects, which results in informal sanctions. Van Maanen (1978) identified citizens who encountered police and did not act in an acceptable manner as "assholes" by police definition. Recent research found "assholes" tend to get the contempt-of-cop treatment under certain circumstances, such as no witnesses, neighborhood context, etc. (Skogan & Frydll, 2004). However, the decades-old, seminal observations of Bittner (1975) and Van Maanen (1978) are still cogent today. As witnessed in the Baltimore Police Department's alleged treatment of giving Freddie Gray a "rough ride" (Fernandez, 2015), contempt of cop still exists, to a certain extent.

Police are supposed to be above petty grievances such as disrespect and reacting to verbal abuse (see *City of Houston v. Hill*, 1987). Despite this, the riots that followed the beating suggested underlying tensions between police abuse of force and the public, particularly the minority populations. The fallout from the King incident resulted in property damage that amounted to greater than $1 billion dollars' damage and led to the resignation of the LAPD Chief of Police. In addition, 60 people were killed in the looting and fires, 10 were shot by police, and 44 deaths were attributed to "other homicides or incidents tied to rioting" (*Los Angeles Times Staff*, 2016). This was only the beginning of riots, deaths, and property damage precipitated by police actions in the late 20th century and early 21st century.

The next major event in the 1990s progression of professionalization of police was the passing of the Violent Crime Control and Law Enforcement Act of 1994. This law included provisions for a ban on certain assault weapons, federal three-strikes punishments, monies to help prevent and investigate violence against women, sex offender registration and tracking, monies for boot camps for juveniles, a greater budget, more support, and additional police to help with America's transition to community-oriented policing.

By signing this bill into effect, the Clinton administration allotted for the hiring of 100,000 new police officers to enact community policing, with $1.3 billion in funds in 1995 and another $7.5 billion authorized from 1995–2000. As a comparison, there were 873,356 law enforcement officers nationwide in 1995 as reported by the Uniform Crime reports (Banks, Hendrix, Hickman, & Kyckelhahn, 2016). This unprecedented addition of officers nationwide would have represented a nearly 10% overall increase in officers and a substantial influx of rookie officers to handle complex criminal justice and policing issues.

This addition of more police had some unintended detrimental effects to underserved, inner-city inhabitants (Reiman & Leighton, 2017). It is certain that not all the ills of police can be traced to the increase in new officers, but there is a correlation between the number of officers and the amount of arrests. It is also deducible that the number of arrests have an inverse relationship with cooperation and trust in the police. In an effort to address this and fear of crime, other programs such as problem-oriented policing (POP), broken windows policing (BW), zero-tolerance policing (ZTP), and weed and seed (W&S) were practiced.

Tillyer (2018) recently found that "agencies engaged in greater *and* specific COP activities experience an increased likelihood of arrest in violent crime incidents" (p. 526, emphasis in original). COP is community-oriented policing whereupon the police are more engaged in problem solving through community input and involvement (Community Oriented Policing Services & U.S. Department of Justice, 2018). Tillyer (2018) also correctly felt that support for the effectiveness of COP was mixed with respect to COP's expectations of citizen involvement, organizational transformation, and problem solving. To date, very few peer-reviewed, academic journal articles are overly positive about COP's effectiveness at the organizational level and none at the national level. Beyond "Solomon" Zhao's COPS office–funded studies in the late 1990s and early 2000s, not many rigorous or positive-finding studies were published. Researchers have identified that COP is expensive and time consuming, the benefits (if any) are not realized quickly, and the officers have difficulty transitioning to "social workers" not doing "real police work." The fad of COP may have passed with the massive COP budget cuts and allotments, but other programs, such as California's Strengthening Law Enforcement and Community Relations Grant, have gained popularity and expect to include community involvement, problem solving, and working on the legitimacy of the departments involved (Board of State & Community

Corrections, 2015). The blending of fair and just law enforcement with positive community relations is elusive, but this goal seems to be the same for citizens and the police.

A component of community-oriented policing (COP) is problem-oriented policing (POP). As first envisioned by Goldstein (1979, 1990), POP involves the police working through a SARA (scanning, analysis, response, and evaluation) process to determine what the community needs and to allot resources. Optimally, the community is involved but not necessarily required. Essentially, POP is a best-practice crime analysis policy for crime prevention and deterrence (Center for Problem-Oriented Policing, 2018). Despite promising results, the caveat is that POP is generally focused on one or two major problems while significant time and resources are committed to focused outcomes. Comparatively, COP is more general and holistic while POP is more strategically focused with (in these authors' opinion) more precise outcomes.

Broken windows (BW) and zero-tolerance policing (ZTP) are almost inextricably intertwined. From the time of Kelling and Wilson's (1984) strategic release within *Atlantic Monthly*, the influential, theoretical policy has taken root in almost every law enforcement agency in the United States, to some degree. At the time, the New York police commissioner (and later LAPD chief of police) applied BW in 1990 to the New York Transit Police with "aggressive order-maintenance" policing in an attempt to decrease historically high crime rates. With his success, he was hired as the New York City police commissioner and immediately began a crackdown on quality-of-life issues. Broken windows theory assumes that if minor blights and neighborhood disorders are repaired, criminals will not see the area as hospitable to criminogenic incursion (Wilson & Kelling, 1982). Aside from the arguments of criminals being able to recognize and take advantage of any broken window opportunities, the crackdown of minor infractions was not a boon to police–community relations then nor now. Such tactics as ZTP were included in BW and remain to this day. A recent example is Eric Garner's police choke-hold death due to the New York City Police Department's continued practice of BW and ZTP (Baker, Goodman, & Mueller, 2015). The bottom line was that a minor infraction for selling untaxed cigarettes was seen as disorder and allowed to be handled customarily. Broken windows quickly devolved into zero-tolerance policing by way of correcting minor infractions so that more serious crimes would not occur. The major problems with ZTP are that it is often unforgiving, takes the common sense out of police discretion, and disproportionately affects the poor and inner-city minorities (Burke, 1998). Any progress gained though community relations and COP could easily be undone by BW/ZTP practices. What Bratton and his contemporaries did not understand was that BW in its purist form advocated for Wilson's (1968) service-style policing, helping communities to police themselves through increased collective efficacy and informal social control. Simply, the police should have helped the community help themselves. Instead, the police inaccurately implemented ZTP and claimed victory while alienating communities. It is true that crime rates dropped after implementing ZTP, but crime rates were inexplicably dropping across the United States by the time Bratton implemented his practices in New York and Los Angeles. This did not stop Bratton from becoming a self-proclaiming crime czar and publicizing his successes as the way to fight crime (W. Bratton & Kelling, 2006; W. Bratton & Knobler, 1998; W. J. Bratton, 1999; Ritter, 2007). Unfortunately, many police chiefs modeled their BW/ZTP tactics after his very high-profile and non-empirically tested methods. Today, law enforcement can still see the results in lawsuits and community distrust by applying the well-intended broken windows theory in a discriminatory manner.

Weed and seed was another politically expedient way for the police to fight the war on drugs. Weed and seed was started in 1991 with the strategy of "'weeding out' criminals" and "'seeding' [for] prevention, intervention, treatment, and neighborhood revitalization services" (U.S. Department of Justice, 2004, p. 1). Yet, this strategy for the war on drugs soon devolved mainly into "weeding" with no or little "seeding." Further, citizens perceived an increase in gangs and drugs (Bridenball & Jesilow, 2005). There is no doubt that these citizens blamed the police for the lack of seeding. Although weed-and-seed funds were reallocated after 9/11, some local jurisdictions still informally practice weed and seed.

Many drug houses were raided because of local ordinances aimed at eliminating crack houses that later would evolve into "problem houses" in predominately minority and inner-city areas (Cohen,

2015). The result was disorganization in stable neighborhoods and crime diffusion and displacement, thereby developing new, adjacent criminogenic areas and neighborhoods that lacked the collective efficacy to fight off crime. It is no surprise that citizens blamed the police for negative outcomes.

These negative outcomes and subsequent loss in faith of police are further exacerbated by scandals. One such notable scandal known as the "Rampart Division Scandal" involved the Los Angeles Police Department in 1997 and 1998. This case of corruption involved 24 officers and consisted of a bank robbery, "false imprisonment and beating of an arrestee," and theft of cocaine, to name a few offenses committed (Los Angeles Police Department, 2000, pp. 2–3). This further facilitated distrust, animosity, and contempt for the police, in addition to the loss of institutional legitimacy and respect.

Hardly any modern decade has been unaffected by police scandal and reform. The constant has been the police having problems and the government's and people's reactions to police abuses or misconduct. It is unlikely there will be a time in the future where police will not misbehave or abuse power, but that will not keep police from trying to change or the people from pushing for reforms.

Lack of Police Progress

While officer-involved shootings of unarmed citizens are generally the exception, the media firestorm regarding the Michael Brown shooting in Ferguson, Missouri, catalyzed demonstrations and riots in several cities where police–community relations were strained. Jurisdictions that had demonstrations/riots appeared to be the departments that traditionally had issues with police-citizen relations and use of force. While media's possible manipulation of facts may explain some of the citizen furor, the police are also culpable. The reasons police keep repeating the same 100-year-old mistakes are complicated at best.

Hiring

As mentioned earlier regarding the Miami incident, police hiring practices have had controversies. Arguably, police have not changed their hiring practices since the early 1900s. There has been a longstanding argument of whether police should have a four-year degree. In fact, it started with August Vollmer (1917) and was reiterated in the government findings, resulting in major criminal justice reforms (President's Commission on Law Enforcement and Administration of Justice, 1967). No national commission or governmental agency—except Minnesota with a minimum two- or four-year degree as a licensing requirement—has pressed higher educational requirements for local police in the last half-century. Early opposition (e.g., Fuld, 1917) was present and is still present today.

With many studies purporting the drawbacks of a higher education requirement, such as no benefits regarding perceived job satisfaction, views of top management, or role orientations (Paoline, Terrill, & Rossler, 2015), "officers are less supportive of abuse of authority but [the result is] fairly small in magnitude" (Telep, 2011, p. 392). Only 30% of Minnesota officers believe a four-year degree (increasing from a minimum two-year degree) should be required (Hilal, Densley, & Zhao, 2013). It is no wonder with the mix in literature that police educational reforms have not taken place since the early 1900s. This educational requirement vastly affects recruitment, particularly minority recruitment.

Police have been actively recruiting minorities for decades. Minorities were rarely considered for police service in the United States until the Civil Rights Act of 1964. Inroads in the LAPD started as early as 1886 for African Americans and 1845 for one woman (Los Angeles Police Department, 2018) and (National Center for Women and Policing, 2013), but overall acceptance lagged behind lawful inclusion (Sklansky, 2006). The active recruiting of minorities is commonplace, although minorities are difficult to hire and retain. The Bureau of Justice Statistics (2012) found "4 out of 5 agencies with 100 or more officers targeted women and minorities with special recruitment efforts, [and] women only represented 12.1% of the officers in agencies that targeted female applicants in 2008" while minorities were 24.3% represented by targeted agencies in contrast to those agencies that did not target minorities

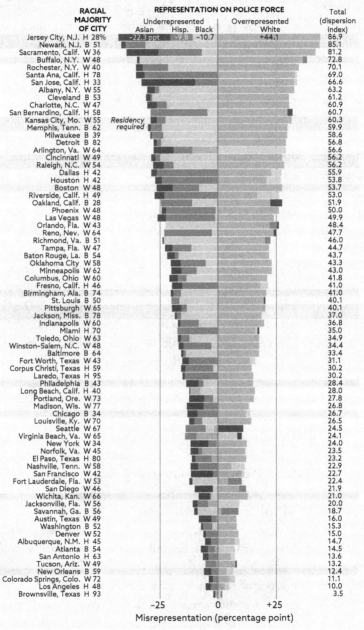

Which U.S. City Has The Least Representative Police Force?

The race gap between officers and residents in cities with the 75 largest police forces, 2010

FIGURE 4.1   Minority representation by the largest 75 police departments in the U.S.

Source: American Community Survey, Equal Employment Opportunity Commission, 2010.

(8.9%) (Reaves, 2012, pp. 12–13). Throughout history, those agencies that actively recruit minorities tend to be better represented. However, a recent story found minorities were woefully underrepresented in departments that had residency requirements (Ungar-Sargon & Flowers, 2014). More telling was how many of the nation's 75 largest cities are overrepresented by White officers. Figure 4.1 denotes these cities and how overrepresented the cities are from extremes such as Jersey City, New Jersey, at 44.1% to Brownsville, Texas, at 3.5%.

Some of the more counterintuitive findings represented in the figure include the LAPD (only 10%) and the Atlanta Police Department (14.5%) while seemingly forward-thinking and innovative police departments such as Sacramento (81.2%) and San Jose, California (66.6%), do not seem to be representative of the community at all. In fact, many of the large departments in liberal and progressive California are not representative.

Training

Before the 1967 President's Commission on Law Enforcement and Administration of Justice, little thought was given to state licensing and certification of police officers. Even after the formation of police officer standards and training (POST) in all states, requirements were substandard. For example, the Texas legislature established a legislative body to oversee peace officer training and education in 1965, but it was not funded until 1967. The basic peace officer course in the early '70s consisted of 140 hours of instruction (Texas Commission on Law Enforcement Standards and Education, 2008). Today, peace officer academies typically last an average of 840 hours (Reaves, 2016). The increase in hours over the decades has centered on liability issues such as use of force, weapons use, legal education, and tactical driving (Reaves, 2016; Texas Commission on Law Enforcement Standards and Education, 2008). The increase in hours seems to be focused on reducing department liability rather than teaching new recruits how to police. The practical side of policing is left to the various departments through the field training program.

The Field Training and Evaluation Program (FTEP) started around 1972 in San Jose, California (Michigan National Association of Field Training Officers, n.d.). This post-academy training was borne out of civil liability and the need for realistic training beyond the controlled atmosphere of the basic academy. What was once seen as superfluous to "needed training" has now become required in most states (McCampbell, 1987). This transitional phase from book learning in the academy to practical applications is paramount for rookies.

While some research had criticized the basic academy as outdated or ineffective in certain areas (Bradford & Pynes, 1999; Bykov, 2014; Chappell, 2008; Marion, 1998; McDermott & Hulse, 2012; Talley, 1985; White, 2008), other research has identified the FTEP as the lynchpin for incorporating academics with socialization skills and practicing realistic procedures (Campa, 1993; Hundersmarck, 2009; Pitts, Glensor, & Peak, 2009; Hoover Group of Reno, 2002). In fact, field training officers and practical training are so important that researchers predict future deviance based on the trainees' field trainer (Getty, Worrall, & Morris, 2014). It stands to reason that if field training programs', their trainers', and trainees' expectations are held to a high standard, the end result should be a higher level of practicing ethical officers. Unfortunately, no national standard for a field training program or training officers has been adopted (National Association of Field Training Officers, 2017). Trainers often relay practical lessons so the trainee reacts in accordance with what the trainer has learned from their street experience, not necessarily what policy dictates. Detrimental mantras include, "It's better to be tried by 12 than be carried by six" (i.e., shoot first and ask questions later) and "When in doubt, use more force." Sayings like these reinforce the "us-versus-them" paradigm, and as long as there is a division by those serving and served, doubt and accusations of racism and favoritism will continue.

Weapons Availability

The use of intermediate weapons such as chemical weapons (mace), conductive electrical devices (tasers), and PR-24s (police batons) have become center stage in the use of nonlethal ways to de-escalate historically deadly force situations. It is no wonder that typical citizens believe that police use too much force when they see many popular television programs demonstrating sophisticated, nonlethal weapons and tactics to subdue people with deadly weapons. To make matters worse, dash cams and officers' body cameras are expected to relay all the relevant facts to every concerned citizen. This is not reasonable, but people expect to "be there" with all the facts involved while not accounting for the legalistic threshold of *Graham v. Conner* (1989). There have been many cases since *Graham v. Conner*, but none have had the profound impact of "reasonableness" in shooting a person.

It is reasonable in the face of mounting negative media coverage to question an officer's decision to shoot. One could also ask why the federal government has not prioritized invention and use of nonlethal use-of-force methods. It is unrealistic to believe police want to shoot people. It is much more likely that police are as afraid as "normal people" and often do not have the training, experience, nor equipment to deal with deadly-force situations. After all, according to the latest police-citizen contact survey, 85% of persons who requested police were satisfied with the police response and 9 in 10 persons who requested police assistance reported they would contact police again (Durose & Langton, 2013). So, one must wonder why this level of satisfaction would not be shared by the broader population.

Police are hampered with a lack of both training and technological advancements. No other government agencies are so encumbered by bureaucratic and legal constraints, nor as scrutinized, as law enforcement agencies. As mentioned before, local law enforcement is the only visual representatives of the federal, state, and local arm of the executive branch. A citizen cannot usually address local procedures he or she feels are unfair but rather, must hear his or her case before the state appellate or Supreme Court. There is no quick or definitive resolution at the street level because that is not the legalistic or bureaucratic way.

Law enforcement efficiency and effectiveness are hampered through selection, training, and hiring. It is irresponsible to blame the typical officer in the absence of global circumstances involving unnecessary use of force when decades of evidence and studies have shown that macro forces such as the hiring and substandard training/education of unqualified people make a difference. This, in conjunction with the lack of acceptable less-than-lethal weapons available to street officers has significantly eroded faith and legitimacy in the police.

Conclusion: Where Do We Go From Here?

Police should be representative of the people with whom they serve. That aphorism is as applicable today as when Getty's father said it in the 1970s. As well, national committee recommendations and hearings since the early 1900s have recommended reform due to corruption and use of force. The main assumption of this chapter has been that nothing has changed with regards to pertinent police reforms except technological advancements in information gathering and dissemination. Essentially, this means many of the recent controversial officer-involved shootings and media-reported police deviances are due to three issues: hiring, training, and lack of technological advancements. Many inroads have taken place in these areas, but they do not solve the reality of police situations. One can easily criticize front-line police in a controversial shooting, but it is unlikely people will blame historically systemic causes.

Discussion Questions

1. What are the major differences between early policing practices and philosophies and modern policing practices and philosophies?
2. What commissions shaped the progressive nature of policing and how did it change practices?
3. What obstacles do the police have in the early 1900s versus the "modern" police? Are there any advantages to policing in any time period?

Application Exercise

1. You are the chief of police of a medium-sized police department. One of your more decorated officers has become involved in a questionable shooting. What would you do given various levels of citizen trust? In other words, you have little, some, and great trust between citizens and your department. Describe how you would handle a publicized and contentious officer-involved shooting accompanied with various levels of community trust.
2. You have the ability to form policy. What would you do to immediately stop questionable shootings? Be sure to involve as many

"caretakers" (such as faith-based resources, the unions representing police, the local and state governments, the media, and so forth) as you can.

3. How do you change the historical trend of lack of minority and female hiring in police departments? Research the issues involved and summarize what you would do differently than what is recommended.

4. Would you train officers differently? Why do you take this position?

5. What resources would you give officers that may create different outcomes with regards to officer-involved shootings?

References

Baker, A., Goodman, J. D., & Mueller, B. (2015, June 13). *Beyond the chokehold: The path to Eric Garner's death*. Retrieved from https://www.nytimes.com/2015/06/14/nyregion/ericgarner-police-chokehold-staten-island.html

Banks, D., Hendrix, J., Hickman, M., & Kyckelhahn, T. (2016). *National sources of law enforcement data*. Washington, DC: U.S. Department of Justice.

Baude, W. (2018). Is qualified immunity unlawful? Retrieved from https://ssrn.com/abstract=2896508 or http://dx.doi.org/10.2139/ssrn.2896508

Bittner, E. (1975). *The functions of police in modern society: A review of background factors, current practices, and possible role models*. New York, NY: J. Aronson.

Board of State & Community Corrections. (2015). *Strengthening law enforcement and community relations grant*. Retrieved from http://www.bscc.ca.gov/downloads/AgendaIteme H - Attachment H - 4 Strengthening Grant RFP -FINAL 1-29-16.pdf

Boggess, S., & Bound, J. (1997). Did criminal activity increase during the 1980s? Comparisons across data sources. *Social Science Quarterly* (University of Texas Press), 78(3), 725-739.

Bradford, D., & Pynes, J. E. (1999). Police academy training: Why hasn't it kept up with practice? *Police Quarterly*, 2(3), 283–301.

Bratton, W., & Kelling, G. (2006). There are no cracks in the broken windows. National Review. Retrieved from http://www.nationalreview.com/blogs/print/216913

Bratton, W., & Knobler, P. (1998). *Turnaround: How America's top cop reversed the crime epidemic*. New York, NY: Random House.

Bratton, W. J. (1999). Great expectations: How higher expectations for police departments can lead to a decrease in crime. In R. H. Langworthy (Ed.), *Measuring what matters: Proceedings from the Policing Research Institute meetings*. Washington, DC: National Institute of Justice.

Bridenball, B., & Jesilow, P. (2005). Weeding criminals or planting fear: An evaluation of a weed and seed project. *Criminal Justice Review, 30*(1), 64–89. doi:10.1177/0734016805275682

Burke, R. H. (1998). The socio-political context of zero tolerance policing strategies. *The socio-political context of zero tolerance policing strategies, 21*(4), 666-682.

Bykov, O. (2014). Police academy training: An evaluation of the strengths and weaknesses of police academies. *Research Journal of Justice Studies and Forensic Science, 2*(1), 140–159.

Campa, E. E. (1993). *The relationship of reading comprehension and educational achievement levels to academy and field training performance of police cadets* (Unpublished doctoral dissertation). Texas A&M University, College Station, Texas.

Center for Problem-Oriented Policing. (2018). What is POP? Arizona State University. Retrieved from http://www.popcenter.org/about/?p=whatiscpop

Chamberlin, H. B. (1920). The Chicago crime commission: How the business men of Chicago are fighting crime. *Journal of the American Institute of Criminal Law and Criminology, 11*(3), 386–397.

Chappell, A. T. (2008). Police academy training: Comparing across curricula. *Policing: An International Journal of Police Strategies & Management, 31*(1), 36–56.

Chimel v. California, 395 U.S. 752 (1969)

City of Houston v. Hill, 482 U.S. 451 (1987)

Cohen, A. (2015, August 12). How White users made heroin a public problem. *The Atlantic*. Retrieved from https://www.theatlantic.com/politics/archive/2015/08/crack-heroinand-race/401015/

Community Oriented Policing Services, & U.S. Department of Justice. (2018). *About*. Retrieved from https://cops.usdoj.gov

Dabney, S. M. (1963). Consent decrees without consent. *Columbia Law Review, 63*(6), 1053-1064.

Dombrink, J. (1988). The touchables: Vice and police corruption in the 1980's. *Law and Contemporary Problems, 51*(1), 201-232.

Durose, M., & Langton, L. (2013). *Requests for police assistance*. Washington, DC: U.S. Department of Justice Retrieved from https://www.bjs.gov/content/pub/pdf/rpa11.pdf.

Escobedo v. Illinois, 378 U.S. 478 (1964).

Fernandez, M. (2015, April 30). Freddy Gray's injury and the police "rough ride." *New York Times*. Retrieved from https://archive.is/qMNGK

Felix, L. F. (1917). University lectures for police. *Journal of the American Institute of Criminal Law and Criminology, 8*(3), 464-464.

Getty, R. M., Worrall, J. L., & Morris, R. G. (2014). How far from the tree does the apple fall? Field training officers, their trainees, and allegations of misconduct. *Crime & Delinquency, 62*(6), 1–19. doi:10.1177/0011128714545829

Gideon v. Wainwright, 372 U.S. 335 (1963)

Goldstein, H. (1979). Improving policing: A problem-oriented approach. *Crime & Delinquency, 25*(2), 236–258.

Goldstein, H. (1990). *Problem-oriented policing*. New York, NY: McGraw-Hill.

Hilal, S., Densley, J., & Zhao, R. (2013). Cops in college: Police officers' perceptions on formal education. *Journal of Criminal Justice Education, 24*(4), 461–477. doi :10.1080/10511253.2013.791332

Hoover Group of Reno. (2002). *The Reno model PTO program: An executive summary of the art of post-academy police training*. Reno, NV: Author.

Hundersmarck, S. (2009, August). Police recruit training: Facilitating learning between the academy and field training. *FBI Law Enforcement Bulletin, 78*, 26–31.

Kelling, G. L., & Wilson, J. Q. (1984). Broken windows: The police and neighbor-hood safety. *Atlantic Monthly, 249*(3), 29–38.

Klatch, R. E. (2002). The development of individual identy and consciousness among movements of the left and right. In D. S. Meyer, N. Whittier, & B. Robnett (Eds.), *Social movements: Identity, culture, and the state*. New York, NY: Oxford University Press.

Lersch, K. M. (2001). Drug related police corruption: The Miami experience. In M. J. Palmiotto (Ed.), *Police misconduct: A reader for the 21st century*. Upper Saddle River, NJ: Pearson.

Lester, R. E. (1997). *Records of the Wickersham Commission on law observance and enforcement*. Bethesda, MD: University Publications of America.

Los Angeles Police Department. (2000). *Rampart area corruption incident*. Los Angeles, CA: Author. Retrieved from http://assets.lapdonline.org/assets/pdf/boi_pub.pdf.

Los Angeles Police Department. (2018). *125 years of African-Americans in the LAPD*. Retrieved from http://www.lapdonline.org/home/content_basic_view/47101

Los Angeles Times Staff. (2016, April 26). The L.A. riots: 25 years later. *Los Angeles Times*. Retrieved from http://timelines.latimes.com/los-angeles-riots/

Mapp v. Ohio, 367 U.S. 643 (1961)

Marion, N. (1998). Police academy training: Are we teaching recruits what they need to know? *Policing: An International Journal of Police Strategies & Management, 21*(1), 54–79.

McCampbell, M. S. (1987). *Field training for police officers: The state of the art.* Washington, DC: National Institute of Justice.

McDermott, P. J., & Hulse, D. (2012). Focus on training: Interpersonal skills training in police academy curriculum. *FBI Law Enforcement Bulletin, 81*(2).

Michigan National Association of Field Training Officers. (2018). A history of the San Jose police department field training program. (April 22, 2018). *Miranda v. Arizona*, 384 U.S. 436 (1966)

Mitrani, S. (2013). *The rise of the Chicago police department: Class and conflict, 1850–1894.* Champaign, IL: University of Illinois Press.

Monroe v. Pape, 365 U.S. 167 (1961)

National Association of Field Training Officers. (n.d.). Home page. Retrieved from http://nafto.org

National Center for Women and Policing. (2013). *A history of women and policing.* Retrieved from http://womenandpolicing.com/history/historytext.htm

National Commission on Law Observance and Enforcement. (1931). *Report on the enforcement of the prohibition laws of the United States.* Department of Justice.

Oliver, W. M. (2016). Celebrating 100 years of criminal justice education, 1916–2016. *Journal of Criminal Justice Education, 27*(4), 455–472. doi:10.1080/1051 1253.2016.1186992

Ortiz, S. R. (2006). Rethinking the bonus march: Federal bonus policy, the veterans of foreign wars, and the origins of a protest movement. *Journal of Policy History,* 18(3), 275-303.

Paoline, E. A., Terrill, W., & Rossler, M. T. (2015). Higher education, college degree major, and police occupational attitudes. *Journal of Criminal Justice Education,* 26(1), 49–73. doi:10.1080/10511253.2014.923010

Pitts, S., Glensor, R. W., & Peak, K. J. (August 2007). The police training officer (PTO) program: A contemporary approach to postacademy recruit training. *The Police Chief,* 74, 114-118.

President's Commission on Law Enforcement and Administration of Justice. (1967). *The challenge of crime in a free society.* Washington, DC: United States Government Printing Office

Pye, A. K. (1968). The Warren Court and criminal procedure. *Michigan Law Review,* 67(2), 249-268.

Reaves, B. A. (2012). *Hiring and retention of state and local law enforcement officers, 2008–Statistical tables.* Washington, DC: Bureau of Justice Statistics Retrieved from https://www.bjs.gov/content/pub/pdf/hrslleo08st.pdf.

Reaves, B. A. (2016). *State and local law enforcement training academies, 2013.* Washington, DC: U.S. Department of Justice Retrieved from https://www.bjs.gov/content/pub/pdf/slleta13.pdf

Reiman, J., & Leighton, P. (2017). *The rich get richer and the poor get prison* (11th ed.). New York, NY: Routledge.

Ritter, N. (2007). *LAPD Chief Bratton speaks out: What's wrong with criminal justice research—and how to make it right.* Washington, DC: National Institute of Justice.

Sklansky, D. A. (2006). Not your father's police department: Making sense of the new demographics of law enforcement. *Journal of Criminal Law & Criminology, 96*(3), 1209–1243.

Skogan, W., & Frydll, K. (Eds.). (2004). *Fairness and effectiveness in policing: The evidence.* Washington, DC: National Academies Press.

Talley, R. A. (1985). A task inventory follow-up evaluation of the Oakland basic police academy curriculum: A survey study (training, law enforcement, entry-level) (Doctoral dissertation). Retrieved from http://proquest.umi.com/pqdweb?did=753276751&sid=1&Fmt=2&clientId=10361&RQT=309&VName=PQD

Telep, C. W. (2011). The impact of higher education on police officer attitudes toward abuse of authority. *Journal of Criminal Justice Education, 22*(3), 392–419. doi:10.1080/10511253.2010.519893

Terry v. Ohio, 392 U.S. 1 (1968)

Texas Commission on Law Enforcement Standards and Education. (2008). *History of the BPOC course.* Austin, TX: Texas Commission on Law Enforcement Standards and Education.

Tillyer, R. (2018). Assessing the impact of community-oriented policing on arrest. *Justice Quarterly, 35*(3), 526–555. doi:10.1080/07418825.2017.1327609

U.S. Department of Justice. (2004). *The weed and seed strategy.* Washington, DC Retrieved from https://www.ncjrs.gov/pdffiles1/207498.pdf.

U.S. Department of Justice. (2017). *The civil rights division's pattern and practice police reform work: 1994–present.* Washington, DC: Author.

United States General Accounting Office. (1998). *Law enforcement information on drug-related police corruption.* Washington, DC: United States General Accounting Office.

Ungar-Sargon, B., & Flowers, A. (2014, October 1). Reexamining residency requirements for police officers. *FiveThirtyEight*. Retrieved from https://fivethirtyeight.
com/features/reexamining-residency-requirements-for-policeofficers/

Van Maanen, J. (1978). Observations on the making of a policeman. In P. K. Man-
ning & J. V. Maanen (Eds.), *Policing: A view from the street* (pp. 292–308). Santa
Monica, CA: Goodyear.

Violent Crime Control and Law Enforcement Act of 1994,, H.R. 3355 (1994).

Vollmer, A. (1917). Police schools. *Journal of the American Institute of Criminal Law
and Criminology, 8*(3), 463–464.

White, M. D. (2008). Identifying good cops early: Predicting recruit performance
in the academy. *Police Quarterly, 11*(1), 27–49.

Wilson, J. Q. (1968). *Varieties of police behavior.* Cambridge, MA: Harvard University Press.

Wilson, J. Q., & Kelling, G. C. (1982). Broken windows: The police and neighborhood safety. *The Atlantic Monthly, 249*(3), 29-38.

Chapter 5

Law Enforcement Use of Force and Public Perceptions

Timothy Sowards

Introduction

There are numerous aspects of law enforcement in America society. From the federal, state, county, and local municipalities, law enforcement actions remain relatively standardized. Regardless of the jurisdiction, law enforcement officers are required to follow the United States Constitution and their state constitution as well as legislative laws. There are three main roles for law enforcement agencies. The traditional police and sheriff role, which involves investigation and enforcement, the corrections officer's role of supervision of incarcerated individuals, and then, finally, the community corrections aspect, which overlaps all aspects of law enforcement but mainly focuses on supervision of convicted or adjudicated offenders in the community. Law enforcement is governed by the Constitution of the United States. The Constitution outlines how law enforcement officers are to interact with the public and convicted offenders. Over the last 10 years, law enforcement officers have dominated the media relative to their actions and use of force decisions. Much of this can be attributed to the improvement in cell phone and body camera technology, as well as social media. Media attention, along with an individual's social experiences, influences how individuals perceive law enforcement. Law enforcement today is facing a negative public perception that rivals that of police during the 1960s and 1970s civil rights movement in our country. There are changes occurring in the day-to-day operations of law enforcement, some of which revolve around the discussion of reasonable use of force. Therefore, both law enforcement agencies and elected officials are reexamining the future expectations of law enforcement in America.

21st-Century Issues in Law Enforcement

This chapter takes an in-depth look at the pressing issues facing law enforcement in the 21st century, focusing on law enforcement officer use of force and public perceptions. Public opinion is critical to government agencies. However, this opinion tends to fluctuate dramatically and may critically impact organizations (Ohiagu, 2009). In today's democratic society of law, it is important that public sentiment be considered when public policy decisions are being made. When departments fail to consider the opinions of the public, departments may encounter public outrage and consequences such as the riots and public protest in Ferguson, Missouri, in 2014 (Basu, Yan, & Ford, 2014) and Rodney King in Los Angeles, in 1991 (Harris, 1999).

Public sentiment against law enforcement is on the rise in many communities (Norman, 2017; Schuck & Rosenbaum, 2005). This negative perception is apparent in many media venues, new scholarly articles, and surveys conducted by law enforcement agencies (Tooley, 2009). People develop opinions in multiple facets, with numerous influences and experiences throughout their lives. This development and interaction is the process of socialization (Berger and Luckman, 1966). Law enforcement agencies are accountable to citizens in the communities they serve. Public opinion and support are vital to the success of any civil service agency (Ohiagu, 2009). Law enforcement agencies should attempt to gauge and measure citizens' perceptions, especially around controversial issues such as law enforcement officers' use of force. A citizen's interaction, experience, and perception of law enforcement officers use of reasonable force is critical in creating a positive social environment in the community.

Fifty Years of Use of Force

The principles of proper use of force are derived from constitutional mandates, case law, legislative mandates, and governmental policy (Hicks, 2003). Regardless of your rank in law enforcement, every sworn officer is required to follow the hierarchy of law. The broadest aspect of this law is the United States Constitution and Unites States Supreme

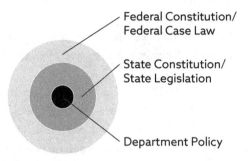

Federal Constitution/
Federal Case Law

State Constitution/
State Legislation

Department Policy

FIGURE 5.1   Hierarchy of law.

Court rulings (federal), followed by each individual state constitution and state laws (state). Finally, the most restrictive aspect of use of force comes down to departmental policies (local). Figure 5.1 demonstrates how the local-level policies must conform to state law and the state must remain within the laws and Supreme Court (federal) decisions.

History of Use of Force in America, 1950s to 1970s

The 1940s through the 1960s saw a dramatic change in civil rights and political agendas. This was a unique time in United States history; the tensions between the public and law enforcement were extremely high. The high tensions were regarding the citizens who continued to challenge issues related to civil rights such as employment, housing, political representation, and other social concerns. The treatment of Black citizens and minorities by law enforcement officers varied dramatically based on jurisdiction and department. However, the majority of interactions between minorities and law enforcement officers during this time of protest and civil unrest led to confrontation and inflammatory interactions in the community (Brickley, 2014).

Historically, from the early 1950s to the mid 1980s, the Supreme Court of the United States (SCOTUS) scrutinized law enforcement officers' use of force through the due process model of the 14th Amendment (*Rochin v. California*, 1952) and the Eighth Amendment standard of cruel and unusual punishment. The SCOTUS decision in *Rochin v. California* (1952) created the term "shock the conscience."

According to the SCOTUS decision, this term is legally defined as an action that is perceived to be so unjust that it "shocks the conscience" of the magistrate. *Rochin v. California* (1952) now provided a subjective guideline for judges in determining excessive force claims against law enforcement officers.

Rochin v. California (1952) was the guide for determining law enforcement actions until 1972 when the Second District Court of Appeal ruled on *Johnson v. Glick*. Johnson was a pretrial detainee. This meant he was arrested, booked into jail, and appeared before the magistrate but was not a convicted criminal. As *Johnson* returned from court, he was beaten and held in a cell for numerous hours by correctional officers without medical treatment. The excessive use of force and failure to provide medical treatment in *Johnson* did not fall under the Eighth Amendment's cruel and unusual punishment standard as Johnson was not a convicted criminal. Therefore, the Second District Court of Appeal created a four-part test in determining whether the constitutional line has been crossed and a 14th Amendment violation had occurred.

The four-part test is as follows: "A court must look to such factors as the need for the application of force, the relationship between the need and the amount of force that was used, the extent of injury inflicted, and whether force was applied in a good faith effort to maintain or restore discipline or maliciously and sadistically for the very purpose of causing harm" (*Johnson v. Glick*, 1972). Before *Johnson v. Glick* (1972), a magistrate's decision was extremely subjective. In effect, the four-part test provided more objective factors that helped define the "shocks-the-conscience" standard. The 14th Amendment was the "law of the land" for pretrial detainees until 2015 when the SCOTUS ruled in *Kingsley v. Hendricks* (2015). In that case, the SCOTUS decided the Fourth Amendment's "objective reasonableness" standard must be applied to pretrial detainees instead of the 14th Amendment's "due process and shock-the-conscience" standard (*Kingsley v. Hendricks*, 2015).

Use of Force Standard, 1980s to Current

Given the public sentiment from the previous decades, during the 1960s to 1980s, enormous pressures were placed on federal, state, and local governments to reform law enforcement encounters with citizens, and many of these pressures came in the face of litigation and court decisions (Brickley, 2014). The civil rights movement and its leaders pressured the Supreme Court of the United States (SCOTUS) to make amendments to policies to protect individual's rights and force Congress to draft legislation for criminal justice reform (Nunnelley, 1991).

During this time of reform, the SCOTUS decided two monumental use of force cases in the early 1980s. Prior to 1983, common law in the United States permitted law enforcement officers the ability to utilize deadly force on fleeing felons. Modern American law has dramatically changed, and with it the punishments for felony and misdemeanors have changed as well. Before the 1980s, law enforcement officers could use deadly force on fleeing felons. Examples of felonies in which officers could use deadly force prior to *Tennessee v. Garner* (1985) were if an offender just committed a felony crime such as a burglary, rape, murder, assault with deadly weapon, vehicle theft, possession of drugs for sale, etc. Under these circumstances, law enforcement officers were authorized to use deadly force to apprehend (i.e., seize) the offender. The facts of *Tennessee v. Garner* are this: On October 3, 1974, at about 10:45 p.m., in Memphis, Tennessee, a 15-year-old teenager named Edward Garner was suspected of burglarizing a residence. Officers responded and observed Garner running across the yard approaching a 6-foot chain-link fence. Officers believed the suspect at the time to be 17 or 18 years old. Officers believed Garner to be unarmed, but Garner had started to flee by climbing a fence. The officers believed that Garner would escape, based on the fact that Garner had just committed a burglary (felony) and was attempting to flee the scene, and one of the officers open fired and killed Garner.

Today, this type of use of deadly force is illegal. However, in 1974 this was a legal and justified shooting under established law. The father of Garner brought suit against the city of Memphis and alleged a violation of the Civil Rights Act of 1871 (*Tennessee v. Garner*, 1985). In 1985, the SCOTUS issued a decision that deemed the apprehension of a suspect with the use of deadly force was a seizure, and, more importantly, the "totality of the circumstance" must be reviewed under the Fourth Amendment's "objective reasonableness" standard. The SCOTUS also determined that the mere fact that a felon is fleeing does not justify deadly force. In addition, the suspect must present a serious threat to officers or the community (*Tennessee v. Garner*, 1985). *Tennessee v. Garner* (1985) was one of the first cases where the SCOTUS moved away from the 14th Amendment's "shock-the-conscience" standard and started to view the use of force by officers as a "seizure," which is governed by the Fourth Amendment.

In 1989, the SCOTUS issued its landmark decision that outlined specific, objective factors that could be used to determine if the force used by officers was reasonable. The Fourth Amendment has an "objective reasonableness" component to search and siezure. The decision, *Graham v. Connor* (1989), finally provided law enforcement officers, courts, and litigants nationwide with guidelines for determining "reasonableness" in use of force situations (*Graham v. Connor*, 1989). *Graham v. Connor* (1989) defined reasonableness as a central issue in physical force cases and examined the reasonableness of the officers' actions in light of circumstances at the time of the incident. The Court stated that all claims that law enforcement officers have used excessive force—deadly or not—in the course of an arrest, investigatory stop, or other "seizure" of a free citizen, should be analyzed under the Fourth Amendment and its "reasonableness" approach (*Graham v. Connor*, 1989).

The reasonableness of a particular use of force must be judged from the perspective of a reasonable officer on the scene rather than with the "20/20 vision of hindsight" according to *Graham v. Connor* (1989). The evaluation of reasonableness must consider that officers are often forced to make split-second judgments in circumstances that are tense, uncertain, and rapidly evolving about the amount of force that is reasonable given a particular situation (*Graham v. Connor*, 1989). The Court, determining whether a particular application of force was reasonable, requires a careful, case-specific review of the following *Graham* factors:

1. Requirement to perform official duties
2. Degree of intrusion (level of force used)
3. The severity of the crime in question
4. The apparent threat posed by the suspect
5. Whether the suspect was trying to resist or flee (*Graham v. Connor*, 1989)

The Court also noted in *Graham v. Connor* (1989) that a use of force situation must be judged from the perspective of a reasonable officer on the scene coping with a tense, quickly evolving situation and not from a perspective of 20/20 hindsight.

In the *Graham v. Connor* (1989) decision, the Supreme Court of the United States also laid out something called officer subject factors. These are factors that officers must consider before determining the amount and level of force they will utilize (*Graham v. Connor*, 1989).

Graham v. Connor officer subject factors include the following:

1. Number of officers versus suspects
2. Prior contacts with law enforcement
3. Special knowledge or skill of the officer(s)
4. Apparent age, size, and relative strength of the suspect
5. Officer injury or exhaustion
6. Mental illness or subject under the influence
7. Environmental factors
8. Proximity to potential weapons (*Graham v. Connor*, 1989)

If force is applied in a "good faith effort" to maintain and restore order, and is not implemented either maliciously or sadistically, then no criminal or civil liability is implied or could exist. *Graham v. Connor* (1989) established a legal standard dictating that police use of force at any level can be justified so long as the officer is acting as other reasonable officers would under the same circumstances.

Issues About Current Use of Force Standards

In 2016, the Police Executive Research Forum (PERF) authored a report called "The Guiding Principles on Use of Force." PERF is an independent research organization. PERF authors numerous law enforcement articles and is a resource for law enforcement managers. The 2016 report has 30 recommendations for agencies to implement. PERF understands that *Graham v. Connor* (1989) is the governing law. However, PERF appeals to law enforcement managers to further restrict an officer's ability to use force. These restrictions focus mainly on how officers interact with offenders who are armed with a weapon other than a firearm, shooting from or at vehicles, and interacting with suicidal individuals (PERF, 2016). The PERF report was the first attack on the *Graham v. Connor's* (1989) objective reasonableness standard.

The second "attack" came during the 2018 California legislation session when Assembly Bill 931 was authored and proposed to abolish *Graham v. Connor* (1989) and the Fourth Amendment standard of "objective reasonableness" and move California to a "necessary" use of force standard. This necessary use of force standard would require officers in California to never make a mistake. If an officer shot an unarmed suspect regardless of the facts leading to the confrontation, they could be criminally prosecuted. The criminality revolves around the fact the unarmed suspect was unnecessarily shot as the suspect did not present an imminent threat of death or great bodily injury to the officer or the public since the suspect was unarmed. The necessary force doctrine would move California law enforcement officers away from making decisions to only utilizing deadly force once they have been fired on.

California's Assembly Bill (AB) 931 was placed on suspense in the Senate Appropriations Committee and will not be voted on in 2018 (California Legislation Information, 2018). However, the attack on *Graham v. Connor's* (1989) objective reasonableness standard is not over. Law enforcement use of force is violent and ugly. As media coverage of law enforcement use of force interactions increases, law enforcement agencies must intervene, train, and educate the community. If departments fail to educate the community, then anti-law enforcement advocates will continue to pressure legislators to pass legislation like AB 931.

Current Use of Force Continuums and Resistance

It is vital that a law enforcement officer understands how the United States Constitution's Fourth, Eighth, and 14th Amendments, along with the SCOTUS decisions such as *Tennessee v. Garner* and *Graham v. Connor*, can affect officers' use of force decisions. The following sections should provide context as to the officers' authority for force, levels of force, and an officer's response table.

Law enforcement officers are authorized to use force in five situations:

1.   Defense of self

2. Defense of another
3. To effect an arrest
4. To overcome resistance of an offender
5. To prevent escape

There are three levels of use of force an officer can choose from:

1. The highest level is deadly force, which includes the use of a firearm and/or any force likely to result in death.
2. Next is the moderate or intermediate level of nondeadly use of force, which includes the use of a K-9, chemical agents (including oleoresin capsicum or tear gas (CN or CS)), police impact weapons (batons), electronic control devices (ECD), personal body weapons (punches and kicks), and vascular neck restraint.
3. Finally, the lowest level or nondeadly use of force includes officer presence, verbal commands, pushing or pulling, open-handed restraints, joint manipulation, balance displacement, takedowns, pressure points, and other body mass maneuvers (e.g., bar arm takedowns, twist-lock control holds, wrist locks, body mechanic takedowns, and grabbing and pushing) (Sowards, 2018).

Table 5.1 is an action and response chart that is taught in California Peace Officers Standards and Training (POST) Academies (California Peace Officer Standards and Training, 2015). This chart provides an example of a suspect's actions and what would be considered a reasonable reaction.

Hypothetical

To begin to appreciate the complexity of the situations officers encounter where force might be necessary, one must conceptualize force not as a static concept, but rather as a continuum of responses ranging from verbal commands to deadly force. To evaluate any use of force situation, one must first review the reason an officer is using force (defense of self, defense of another, effect an arrest, overcome resistance, prevent escape), then review the officer's standing relative to the *Graham* factors (why he or she was there, the severity of crime, the threat posed by the suspect, fleeing or evading, the degree of intrusiveness), then one must review the level of force used (deadly, intermediate, and low level). Finally, one reviews the officer's level of force based on the eight officer/subject factors (as outlined in *Graham v. Connor*) to determine if the officer's use of force was objectively reasonable relative to the totality of the circumstances.

TABLE 5.1

Action	Description of Action	Reasonable Response to Action
Cooperative	Subject offers no resistance	• Mere professional appearance • Nonverbal actions • Verbal request and commands
Passive non-compliance	Does not respond to verbal commands but also offers no physical form of resistance	• Officer's strength to take physical control including lifting/carrying • Control holds and techniques to direct movement or immobilize a subject
Active resistance	Physically evasive movements to defeat an officer's attempt at control, including bracing, tensing, running away, or verbally signaling an intention to avoid or prevent being taken into or retained in custody	• Control holds and techniques to control the subject and situation. • Use of personal weapons in self-defense and to gain advantage over the subject. • Use of devices to secure compliance and ultimately gain control over the situation
Assaultive	Aggressive or combative, attempting or threatening to assault the officers or another person	• Use of devices and/or techniques to secure compliance and ultimately gain control of the situation. • Use of personal body weapons in self-defense and to gain advantage over the subject
Life-threatening	Any action likely to result in serious injury or possibly the death of the officer or another person	• Utilizing firearms or any other available weapon or action in the defense of self of others.

One example scenario is as follows: Probation Officer Smith, who is 6' tall and 200 pounds, and his partner, Officer Jones, who is 5'4" tall and weighs 150 pounds, are conducting a probation supervision check at the home of a juvenile probationer who is 6'3" tall, weighs 220 pounds, and is a high school wrestler. Upon entering the home, the officers observe the probationer, who appears to be under the influence of a narcotic, and on the kitchen table is a white crystal-like substance later identified to be methamphetamine, which is probable cause for an arrest. The officers ask the probationer to turn around and place his hands behind his back so that officers can place him in handcuffs and proceed to search him incident to arrest. The probationer refuses. The officers request again for the probationer to comply with the lawful order and again he verbally refuses and says, "Get out of my house, or I will throw you out!" Officers are in full uniform and equipped with firearms, taser, chemical agent, and a baton and now must decide on what force option they are going to deploy to take the probationer into legal custody. The officers decided they have a good rapport with the probationer and attempt to utilize "open-handed restraint tactics" (see Table 5.1). Officer Smith grabs the probationer, who immediately pulls away from Smith and starts to wrestle Smith to the ground. Officer Jones grabs his baton and starts to strike the probationer. These baton strikes are ineffective in subduing the probationer. The probationer is now starting to go after Officer Smith's head region. Officer Jones draws and deploys his taser but the probes miss, thereby making the taser ineffective as well. At this time, the probationer grabs Smith around the neck and starts to choke him. Officer Jones grabs his firearm and places the barrel of the gun to the probationer's head and shoots the probationer. Once shot, the probationer releases his hold of Smith. Officer Jones calls for medical assistance while Smith starts first aid. Is the force used in this scenario reasonable? To evaluate the scenario under the totality of the circumstances, the following *Graham* factors must be considered:

1. Why the officers are there (to perform a probation supervision compliance check)
2. The severity of the crime at issue (possession of illegal substance, violation of probation, and assault on a peace officer)
3. The degree of intrusion (officers start with hands-on tactics, deployed baton and attempted taser, and utilized their firearm, deploying deadly force)

4. The apparent threat posed by the suspect (probationer was attempting to choke and kill Officer Smith)

5. Whether the suspect was trying to resist or flee (probationer refused to abide by the verbal commands of the officer, and when an officer attempted to place him in custody, the active resistance and fight began)

This situation was rapidly evolving, requiring officers to adapt and react to the suspect's actions in mere seconds. Most officers would conclude the scenario with a deadly force option. Some officers may have chosen a different intermediate force option or started with a higher level of force on first contacting the suspect. Regardless of how any one specific officer reacts, one might argue the facts support a deadly force result.

Officer subject factors:

1. Number of officers versus suspects (two officers 6'0", 200 pounds and 5'4", 150 pounds versus a suspect who is 6'3", 220 pounds)

2. Prior contact with law enforcement (subject is on probation)

3. Special knowledge or skill (subject is a "good-size" high school wrestler)

4. Apparent age, size, and the relative strength of the suspect (even though the probationer is a juvenile, the size of the probationer is 6'3", 220 pounds, and the fact he is in high school sports and works out on a regular basis as a wrestler, puts him in better shape than the two officers)

5. Officer injury or exhaustion (Officer Smith was being choked)

6. Mental illness or subject under the influence (probationer appeared to be on methamphetamines and acting aggressively/irrationally)

7. Environmental factors (in probationer's house, limited ability to deploy intermediate force options like a chemical agent or baton)

8. Proximity to potential weapons (probationer himself is a weapon at this point when he is choking the officer)

Under the totality of the circumstance, one might argue this was an entirely reasonable use of force. The officers were in the home legally performing their duties. The probationer was actively resisting, started to attack the officer and, in fact, attempted to kill the officer. The officers attempt to start at a minimal level of use of force with hands-on tactics but given the probationer's actions, the officers ended with the most severe amount of force, deadly force. This entire force encounter possibly lasted less than 60 to 90 seconds. Even though the probationer is a juvenile, the courts would determine his age to be irrelevant because his size alone negates his juvenile status.

Use of Force Research

Use of force in law enforcement is the same regardless of actual job title or rank. Law enforcement's use of force is judged on facts and circumstances despite whether the person is a probation officer, police officer, sheriff deputy, or correctional officer. Each of these positions are considered law enforcement and any law enforcement officer must be able to justify their use of force based on the suspect's actions.

An encounter between a resistive citizen and law enforcement could result in a use of force confrontation. Most encounters however, do not involve the use of force. The Bureau of Justice Statistics reports that between 2001 and 2011 there were more than 43 million contacts between police and law enforcement and approximately 1% resulted in a use of force or threat of force situation (Bureau of Justice Statistics, 2011). In 2012 alone, the Uniform Crime Report reported there were over 12 million arrests in the United States and only 410 uses of deadly force, which is equal to .00003% (Uniform Crime Report, 2012).

In 2016 the *Washington Post* created an interactive database that tracks officer-involved shootings. The database collects a wealth of information from ethnicity, age, gender, state, body camera information, fleeing the scene, armament, and mental health status. The data for the database is derived from local news reports, law enforcement websites, social media, and by monitoring independent databases that track officer-involved shootings such as Killed by Police (2017) and Fatal Encounters (2017). Finally, the data placed into the database is investigated by *Washington Post* journalists. Table 5.2 is a compiled list of officer-involved shootings from January 1, 2015, to August 12, 2018. Included in Table 5.2 is the California deadly use of force statistics. The armed/unknown statistic

TABLE 5.2   Officer-Involved Shootings January 1, 2015, to August 12, 2018

Nationwide	Total	White	Black	Hispanic	Other	Unknown	Armed/ Unknown
Total 1/1/15–8/12/18	3,570	1662	829	595	144	340	3,324
Unarmed	228	97	96	49	9	4	
California							
Total 1/1/15–8/12/18	556	154	87	221	31	63	491
Unarmed	75	23	23	26	0	1	

includes suspects who had a gun, knife, vehicle, replica weapon, or another object.

Contrary to the public perception and the media portrayal of law enforcement officers, the data does not support the notion that law enforcement officers are using excessive use of force on a "regular" basis. Furthermore, the statistics do not support the notion that officers are using force *daily* on members of the public. Table 5.2 does demonstrate that officers are having deadly force encounters; there are numerous reasons why those encounters are occurring, and each interaction must be judged on its own merits. One might argue that law enforcement deadly force encounters closely mimic the populations in which officers serve. In California, Hispanics are the majority of the population, followed by Whites, then Blacks, and the "minority" is Asian and others. When researchers look at the officer's shootings in California, they are a close representation of the population census as a whole (Census Bureau, 2010). Regardless of the statistics, law enforcement officers should continually strive to have positive interactions in the community and minimize use of force when safe to do so. Law enforcement training is vital to assisting officers in reducing and reacting reasonably to use of force situations.

Training

Law enforcement officers undergo multiple hours of training at state-regulated academies. California has a minimum standard of 664 hours, Florida 770 hours, and New York 636 hours (International Association of Directors of Law Enforcement Standards (IADLES),

2018). Each state sets its training hours and curriculum. Even though there is a lack of a national training standard, there are associations such as the International Association of Directors of Law Enforcement Standards (IADLES), which reviews and collaborates with other states police officer and standards training (POST) programs to help ensure similar curriculum. Most academies will cover topics such as ethics, professional conduct, use of force, firearms, patrol tactics, intermediate force options, physical skills training, physical conditioning, report writing, scenarios, legal education, searching, diversity training, community policing, scenario training, and numerous other topics of training at the entry level (IADLES, 2018).

Each state sets the minimum amount of in-service training hours. For example, California POST regulates a mandatory requirement of training of 12 hours in "perishable skills" training every 2 years. Perishable skills training includes emergency vehicle operations training, defensive tactics, firearms, crowd control, and intermediate force options training. The 12 hours of perishable skills training every 2 years is the *minimum* training requirement. Most agencies only complete the minimum because training is expensive and has a large impact on a department's ability to deploy resources in the community (California Peace Officer Standards and Training, 2018).

Research has demonstrated that utilizing scenario-based training is an effective way to ensure academy cadets are prepaired to graduate and enter real-life situations (Andersen, 2017; Lynch, 2005). Law enforcement officers have a multitude of use of force options, ranging from the lowest level of force to deadly force. Most law enforcement agencies will use scenario and practical hands-on training exercises to help the officer learn and demonstrate how to properly handle a call for service. This training includes officer handling tense and uncertain situations that could result in a use of force encounter. Good scenario training will make an officer escalate and deescalate in force options during the scenario.

When law enforcement officers respond to a call for service, officers have three primary concerns. First, the crime. Second, any information about weapons, and finally, the threat to the community, victim, or officer (California Peace Officer Standards and Training, 2015). When officers enter a basic academy in California, they are instructed in a process designed to improve their reaction time to a critical threat. This process is called the OODA loop. OODA stands for officers observe, orient, decide, and act (California POST, 2015). When officers arrive on the scene, they start the OODA loop. Officers are constantly evaluating and responding to a suspect's action, regardless of the suspect's age. Law enforcement officers are trained to evaluate a suspect's actions and react to those actions regardless of age or race (California POST, 2015).

Controversial Use of Force Example

The presentation of controversial interactions between civilians and law enforcement on the 24-hour news cycle can affect public opinion and can shape a person's socialization decisions. This section highlights three significant incidents that elicit strong public reaction and outcry and led to riots in the community. The three incidents are the Rodney King riots of 1991, the BART shooting of Oscar Grant 2009, and the Ferguson, Missouri, riots of 2014. In the Rodney King incident, a citizen-produced video was released to the media almost immediately. In the other incidents, the footage was streamed live, uploaded to the Internet, and blogged about in real time.

The 1991 Rodney King situation in Los Angeles, California, resulted in multiple days of riots in the community. The riots were in response to White police officers using excessive force on an African-American individual named Rodney King. Officers struck King multiple times, and it was believed by officers that King was under the influence of narcotics, which limited his ability to feel pain (*New York Times*, 1992). The exoneration of the White officers ignited outrage in a community that felt repressed by law enforcement. One area that has not been deeply researched was the influence of media on the Rodney King riots. The use of force on Rodney King was one of the first where modern media broadcasted a law enforcement officer use of force to the public's front room.

The accidental shooting of Oscar Grant by BART Police Officer Johannes Mehserle on January 1, 2009, is the incident that lead to the movie *Fruitvale Station*. Oscar Grant was on the Bay Area Rapid Transit train returning from a New Year's Eve event in San Francisco. BART officers responded to a call of a fight on the train. Upon responding, the officers noticed several loud and unruly person(s) on the train. While attempting to investigate the situation, Officer Mehserle attempted to handcuff Oscar Grant. However, given the dynamic conditions of the encounter, Officer Mehserle mistook his firearm for his taser and shot and killed Oscar Grant. The use of social media sent the video viral. The community of Oakland, California, was already seething about the treatment of its citizens at the hands of law enforcement, and they rioted.

On August 9, 2014, Officer Darren Wilson attempted to communicate with suspect Michael Brown who was walking down the middle of the street. The interaction between Officer Wilson and Brown has been disputed; however, the evidence demonstrates that Michael Brown attacked Officer Wilson who responded by shooting and killing Michael Brown. The video, physical evidence, and eyewitness testimony further enraged a community that felt oppressed by law enforcement. The result of the shooting and eventually the grand jury's decision not to indict Officer Wilson sparked multiple days of riots. These riots were a demonstration of the public's opinion about the stressed relationship between the law enforcement agencies and the community.

The Future

This chapter discussed officer use of force and the authority that governs officer use of force. However, one of the principal issues facing law enforcement is the citizen's perceptions of the excessive use of force. Lieutenant Colonel Dave Grossman (1996) outlined the theory that there are three types of people in the world: the sheep, the wolf, and the sheepdog. The wolves are the criminal element in society, and they prey on the sheep. The sheep are the common law-abiding citizens who go about their day and rarely think of the wolves. The sheepdogs are the law enforcement officers whose primary duty is to protect the sheep from the wolves. Most of society does not fully comprehend the role of the sheepdogs. An example of when the sheepdogs stop protecting the sheep can be seen in Chicago where police lost the confidence and support of the citizens in the community which they serve (Police Accountability Task Force, 2016). The 2016 Chicago Task Force Report found distrust for law enforcement. Citizens believed officers were racist and used excessive force. The report noted that in response to the citizens' distrust, law enforcement officers reduced their proactive approach to policing. The sheepdogs were no longer actively protecting the sheep; they were waiting for the wolves to attack and then they responded. With the lack of proactive policing in 2016, Chicago earned the number-one slot for the highest murder rate in the nation (Police Accountability Task Force, 2016).

There is a 50-year high of anti-law enforcement sentiment in society today (Krayewski, 2017). The 24-hour news cycle and the use of cell phones and social media have brought attention to the daily activities of law enforcement that has never in our nation's history been seen before. There is a common public perception that law enforcement use of force is out of control. Regardless of the statistical evidence that proves otherwise, citizens perceive there is a problem with law enforcement officer use of force. There are numerous variables that correlate to a citizen's opinion on law enforcement. Many of these variables are age, race, socioeconomic status, education, contact with law enforcement, and the media. These variables have been tested over time and have demonstrated some level of predictability of citizens' perceptions of law enforcement (Brown & Benedict, 2002; Callanan & Rosenberger, 2011; Cheurprakobkit & Bartsch, 1999; Maxson, Hennigan, & Sloane, 2003; National Institute of Justice, 2003). Anti-law enforcement movements like Black Lives Matter, along with the media's selective coverage on officer-involved shootings, is perpetuating discourse between the community and the law enforcement officers serving in the community (Brown & Benedict, 2002; Dowler, Fleming, & Muzzatti, 2006). The Pew Research Center conducted a survey about law enforcements perception of the media and 81% of officers felt they were unfairly treated by the media (Pew Research Center, 2017). Regardless of the support or opposition, there is a need to facilitate communication, training, and education between the law enforcement agencies and all community members.

Law enforcement departments must continually reach out and work to improve their relationship within the community. Improved community relationships may be accomplished if the departments start to create community forums where community members can be heard. These forums can be an opportunity to train and educate the community about the role and duties of law enforcement. Hollywood has done an excellent job of educating the public with unrealistic expectations of real law enforcement work. Each law enforcement officer needs to take the time to interact with the individuals in the community positively and provide realistic expectations. Departments and officers must learn to communicate more effectively with the community, hear the community concerns, and be proactive to the perception of community members. However, community members need to be open to these conversations as well.

Law enforcement agencies need to ensure they are proactive in responding to community needs, are proactive in conducting use of force training to both officers and community members, and are proactive in developing community relationships. Otherwise, law enforcement agencies will be reacting to litigation, public demonstrations, and bad legislation.

The criminal justice system is at a crossroads with numerous issues, such as decriminalizing drugs, overcrowding in prison, changes in sentencing standards, the role of community corrections and, of course, the philosophy and legal justifications for the use of force. The media and some members of the public are advocating for significant law changes relative to some of these issues. If legislation like Assembly Bill 931 is chaptered into law, citizens could see a mass exit of law enforcement officers and the inability to replace them. Chicago has demonstrated what happens to a community when the sheepdogs stop protecting the sheep. It is difficult to see if the next 50 years will be better or worse than the last 50 years for the career of law enforcement.

Discussion Questions

1. Discuss the four major aspects of the criminal justice system.

2. How do the Fourth, Eighth, and Fourteenth Amendments to the Constitution impact law enforcement officers' use of force?

3. What was the impact of *Tennessee v. Garner* and *Graham v. Conner* relative to use of force?

4. How does the media (news, social, other) influence public perception of law enforcement as a whole?

5. How does the media (news, social, other) influence public perception of law enforcement use of force situations?

6. Whats is your opinion of law enforcement in your community and what should happen to improve that relationship?

References

Andersen, J. (2017). Highly realistic scenario-based training simulates the psychophysiology of real world use of force encounters: Implications for improved police officer performance. *Journal of Law Enforcement*. Retrieved from http://www.jghcs.info/index.php/l/article/view/461

Basu, M., Yan, H., & Ford, D. (2014, November 25). Fires, chaos erupt in Ferguson after grand jury doesn't indict in Michael Brown case. *CNN*. Retrieved from http://www.cnn.com/2014/11/24/justice/ferguson-grand-jury/index.html

Berger, P. L., & Luckman, T. (1966). *The social construction of reality: A treatise in the sociology of knowledge.* Garden City, NY: Doubleday.

Brickley, T. (2014). *Perception of police in public housing communities* (Doctoral dissertation). Retrieved from: https://scholarcommons.sc.edu

Brown, B., & Benedict, W. R. (2002). Perceptions of the police: Past findings, methodological issues, conceptual issues and policy implications. *Policing: An International Journal of Police Strategies and Management, 25*(3), 543–580. Retrieved from http://www.emeraldinsight.com/1363-951X.htm

Bureau of Justice Statistics. (2011). *Data collection: Police-public contact survey.* Retrieved from https://www.bjs.gov/index.cfm?ty=dcdetail&iid=251

Bureau of Justice Statistics. (2013). *Estimated number of persons supervised by adult correctional systems, by correctional status.* Retrieved from https://www.bjs.gov/content/pub/pdf/cpus14.pdf

Callanan, V. J., & Rosenberger, J. S. (2011). Media and public perceptions of the police: Examining the impact of race and personal experience. *Policing & Society, 21*(2), 167–189. doi:10.1177/0734016811428779

California Legislative Information (2018). Criminal procedure: Use of force by peace officers. *Assembly Bill 931(2017–2018)*. Retrieved from http://leginfo.legislature.ca.gov/faces/billNavClient.xhtml?bill_id=201720180AB931

California Peace Officer Standards and Training Commission. (2015). *POST learning domain 20 and 33*. Retrieved from www.post.ca.gov

California Peace Officer Standards and Training Commission. (2018). *Perishable skills/communications requirement for CPT*. Retrieved from www.post.ca.gov

Census Bureau. (2010). *Population by race and Hispanic or Latino origin, for all ages and for 18 years and over, for California: 2010.* Retrieved from https://www.census.gov/content/dam/Census/library/publications/2011/dec/c2010br-02.pdf

Cheurprakobkit, S., & Bartsch, R. A. (1999). Police work and the police profession: Assessing attitudes of city officials, Spanish-speaking Hispanics, and their English-speaking counterparts. *Journal of Criminal Justice, 27*(2), 87–100.

Davis, R. L. (2015, December 18). *Law enforcement leads the change* (Blog). Retrieved from https://obamawhitehouse.archives.gov/blog/2015/12/18/law-enforcement-leads-change

Dowler, K., Fleming, T., & Muzzatti, S. L. (2006). Constructing crime: Media, crime, and popular culture. *Canadian Journal of Criminology and Criminal Justice, 48*(6), 837–850.

Fatal Encounters. (2017). *Fatal encounters with law enforcement database.* Retrieved from www.fatalencounters.org

Johnson v. Glick, 481 F.2d 1028 (1973)

Graham v. Connor, 490 U.S. (1989)

Grossman, D. (1995). *On killing: The psychological cost of learning to kill in war and society.* Boston, MA: Little Brown.

Hanser, R. (2014). *Community corrections.* Thousand Oaks, CA: SAGE.

Harris, P. (1999). *Black rage confronts the law.* New York, NY: New York University Press.

International Association of Directors of Law Enforcement Standards. (2018). *Post portal.* Retrieved from https://www.iadlest.org/post-portal

Kappeler, V. (2013). *The history of policing in the United States, part 6.* Retrieved from http://plsonline.eku.edu/insidelook/history-policing-united-statespart6#ga=1.56739946.1341012897.1458944691

Killed by Police. (2017). *Database of officer involved shootings with citizens.* Retrieved from www.killedbypolice.net

Kingsley v. Hendricks, No. 14-6368. (2015)

Krayewski, E. (2017). Survey of police finds most cops believe protesters motivated by anti-police sentiment, incidents of police violence are isolated. *Pew Research Center.* Retrieved from http://reason.com/blog/2017/01/11/survey-of-police-finds-most-cops-believe

Lynch, M. D. (2005). Developing a scenario-based training program: Giving officers a tactical advantage. *FBI Law Enforcement Bulletin, 74,* 1.

Maxson, C. L., Hennigan, K., & Sloane, D. C. (2003). Factors that influence public opinion of the police. *U.S. Department of Justice, Office of Justice Programs, National Institute of Justice.* Retrieved from https://www.ncjrs.gov/App/Publications/abstract.aspx?ID=197925

National Institute of Justice. (2003). *Factors that influence of public opinion of the police.* Retrieved from https://www.ncjrs.gov/pdffiles1/nij/197925.pdf

New York Times. (1992, March 20). *Sergeant says King appeared to be on drugs.* Retrieved from https://www.nytimes.com/1992/03/20/us/sergeant-says-king-appeared-to-be-on-drugs.html

Norman, J. (2017, July 10). Confidence in police back at historical average. *GALLUP*. Retrieved from https://news.gallup.com/poll/213869/confidence-police-back-historical-average.aspx

Nunnelley, W. A. (1991). *Bull Connor.* Tuscaloosa, AL: University of Alabama Press.

Ohiagu, O. P. (2009). Modern public relations is founded on a fresh realization of the supremacy of public opinion. *African Journal of Communication & Development, 3*(1), 77–93.

Pew Research Center. (2017). *Most officers say the media treat police unfairly,* January 25, 2017. Retrieved from http://www.pewresearch.org/fact-tank/2017/01/25/most-officers-say-the-media-treat-police-unfairly/

Police Accountability Task Force. (2016). *Recommendations for reform: Restoring trust between the Chicago police and the communities they serve.* Chicago, IL: Author. Retrieved from https://chicagopatf.org

Police Executive Research Forum. (2016). *Guiding principles on use of force.* Retrieved from https://www.policeforum.org/assets/30%20guiding%20principles.pdf

Rochin v. California, 342 U.S. 165, 172 (1952)

Rogovin, C. H., & Velde, R. W. (1969, August 31). Law enforcement assistance administration. *National Institute of Justice.* Retrieved from https://www.ncjrs.gov/pdffiles1/nij/2157.pdf

Sowards, T. (2018). *Perceptions of reasonable use of force by probation officers and civilians* (Unpublished doctoral dissertation). Walden University, Minneapolis, MN.

Schuck, A. & Rosenbaum, D. (2005). Global neighborhood attitudes toward the police: Differentiation by race, ethnicity and type of contact. *Journal of Quantitative Criminology, 21*(4), 391–418. doi:10.1007/s10940-005-7356-5

Tennessee v. Garner, 471 U.S. 1, 7 (1985)

Tooley, M. (2009). The media, the public, and the law enforcement community: Correcting misperceptions. *Police Chief, 77*(6). Retrieved from http://www.ncjrs.gov/App/publications/abstract.aspx?ID=249912

Uniform Crime Reporting. (2012). *Justifiable Homicide by Law Enforcement.* Retrieved from https://ucr.fbi.gov/crime-in-the-u.s/2012/crime-in-the-u.s.-2012/offenses-known-to-law-enforcement/expanded-homicide/expanded_homicide_data_table_14_justifiable_homicide_by_weapon_law_enforcement_2008-2012.xls

Washington Post. (2018). *Fatal force database.* Retrieved from https://www.washingtonpost.com/graphics/2018/national/police-shootings-2018/?noredirect=on&utm_term=.be0048a0ad7b

Chapter 6

Homeland Security and the Future of Criminal Justice

Davies Sasere

Introduction

Terror and acts of terrorism are not a new phenomenon in the United States or global justice systems; they have remained constant in the history of humanity, unpredictable and the most dangerous phenomena of modern times (Nemeth, 2017). Whereas the phenomenon is relatively new in the US, emerging during the 1960s, due to major social changes such as the Civil Rights Movement, most of America's experience with terrorism is with domestic (American-born) terrorists and extremists, most notably the Ku Klux Klan. The terrorist events of September 11, 2001, has spurred major global attention particularly due to the scale of damage that accompanied the attacks and the loss of human lives (Ogundiya & Amzat, 2008). The discussion in this chapter maps key historical changes and trends in terrorism in the United States since the 1960s and underlines the vital importance of history in understanding critical contemporary issues. The chapter further explores the responses and challenges, as well as an analysis, of future trends in terrorism prevention and legal prohibitions.

Defining Homeland Security and Terrorism

However, there are varying definitions and designations of terrorism and groups across the sociopolitical spectrum and culture. Historically, the concept of homeland security in the United States has taken many dimensions, especially in classification of terrorist acts in defense of the homeland. As Reese (2013) espoused, the U.S. government does not have a consensus definition of the homeland security with local, national, and international considerations. The ambiguity and overlapping definitions of the term reflects and reinforces the confusion in the mission of homeland security, with possible unintended consequences for national homeland security operations.

Most of the definitions of homeland security include terrorism prevention and disaster response, but many do not include border security, immigration, general resilience, or maritime security (Reese, 2013). However, the Department of Defense (DOD) offers the most exhaustive definition of the term as "the protection of US sovereignty, territory, domestic population, and critical defense infrastructure against external threats and aggression, or other threats as directed by the President" (Scaparroti, 2007, p. vii).

In the same vein, defining terrorism is a complex and controversial phenomenon with varied degrees and is implemented for different reasons. Not surprisingly, as the meaning and usage of the term have changed over time to describe the politics and discourse of each successive era, terrorism has remained ambiguous in attempts to construct one consistent definition (Barghothi, 2005; Cooper, 2008; Mahan & Griset, 2008; Spindlove & Simonsen, 2010). Much of the discussion about terrorism has involved attempts to find a consensus and universally acceptable definition of the concept. There are currently various definitions of the phenomenon (Gibbs, 1989; Mahan & Griset, 2008; Spindlove & Simeonsen, 2010; United Nations, 2005). In November 2004, the United Nations reaffirmed the definition of terrorism as any act "[i]ntended to cause death or serious bodily harm to civilians or noncombatants with the purpose of intimidating a population or compelling a government or an international organization to do or abstain from doing any act" (United Nations, 2005, p. 23).

The U.S. DOD conceptualized terrorism as the unlawful use of or threatened use of force or violence against individuals or property to coerce or intimidate governments or societies, often to achieve political, religious, or ideological objectives (Banks, de Nevers, & Wallerstein, 2008; Hoffman, 2006). The definition espoused by the DOD is arguably the most comprehensive, highlighting terrorist threat as much as the actual act of violence and targeting societies and governments. Ideally, what actually defines terrorism is not the motive, but the means utilized in driving the motives.

Trends and Developments in Terrorism

Acts of terror have permeated the U.S. homeland from the 19th century, and they continue to date. Terror and extreme violence were embedded into the social and political fabric of organizations such as the Black Panther Party, Ku Klux Klan (KKK), the Workers Party, Communist agitators, Students for a Democratic Society (SDS), and the Weathermen of the Vietnam era to undermine governing authority (Brister, 2010). While much could be espoused about the nature of the threats and trends of terrorism as well as violence throughout U.S. history, this chapter focuses on key events or developments from the 1960s to modern era. The internal urban violent activities of the 1960s was in response to experiences of injustice and inequality that resulted in public protests and movements led by Dr. Martin Luther King, Jr., and others operating from a higher moral plane, and challenged the status quo of police abuse of power and injustice, and are hence not included as part of the analysis, here.

Most of the early U.S. experiences with terrorism involved domestic (American-born) terrorists and extremists, most notably the Ku Klux Klan and Timothy McVeigh in the 1995 Oklahoma City bombing. International terrorism was not a serious threat until the Cold War era and the worldwide attacks on U.S. interests by Al-Qaeda based in the Middle East. Over the last 50 years, America has experienced a significant number of terrorist acts, as highlighted with the tragic 9/11 attacks on the World Trade Center in New York and the U.S. Pentagon building. Hewitt (2003) estimated that well over 3,000 incidents of terrorism occurred between 1954 and September 10, 2001, in the United States and Puerto Rico. Although foreign actors have initiated a handful of the incidents, Americans have carried out most of the attacks on the U.S. homeland (McVey, 2003; Oliver, 2006; Rehm, 2000).

During the 1950s and 1960s, some leftist-oriented extremist groups employed a "vanguard" strategy with a belief that revolutionary conditions rarely occur from within an exploited group or class (Federal Bureau of Investigation (FBI), 2006). The right-wing movements began in the 1960s, with an ideology that permeates an uncompromising belief in ethno-national or religious superiority by extremist groups such as the Klu Klux Klan (Martin, 2003). During this era, counterterrorism efforts were focused on the KKK, the Weathermen, the Black Panthers, the Students for a Democratic Society (SDS), and other developing and evolving terrorist groups (Nemeth, 2017).

Terrorist activities during the 1970s were mainly perpetrated by the leftist groups such as the Jewish Defense League (JDL) (Kushner,

1998). The primary goal of the group was to protect the Jewish residents, particularly the poor and the elderly. Other terrorist groups of the 1970s included the anti-Castro Cuban group, the Weather Underground Organization (or Weathermen), Omega 7, and the Croatian nationalists. These groups detonated several bombs, including the U.S. Senate bombing on March 1, 1971, and the U.S. State Department building on January 29, 1975 (FBI, 2006).

Between 1970 and 1980, a number of right-wing radical supremacist groups, otherwise known as White supremacist groups, such as the American Neo Nazi Movement, the Aryan Nations, the Skinheads, the Order, etc., emerged as an elaborate paramilitary organization (Barkum, 1989). The era also marked the growth of anti-abortion groups, such as the American Life League and National Right to Life Committee, after the U.S. Supreme Court Decision in *Roe v. Wade* in 1973. During the 1980s, there were increased incidents of terrorism against U.S. interests abroad, which led to the FBI's characterization of "state-sponsored" and "autonomous" terrorist organizations as the centerpiece of international terrorism. State-sponsored terrorism refers to those countries mostly in the Middle East and South Asia that violate international law by using terrorism as a tool of foreign policy (FBI, 2006).

In the mid-1980s, after the terrorist attacks at airports in Athens and Rome, the U.S. Director of Central Intelligence created a Counterterrorist Center to unify activities across the Directorate of Operations and the Directorate of Intelligence, with representation from the FBI and other agencies. Another U.S. counterterrorism response during this era includes the adoption of Biological Weapons Anti-Terrorism Act of 1989 (Maggs, 2010; Nemeth, 2017).

By the 1990s, terrorism in the United States escalated to a malicious and vitriolic form of antigovernment appeal characterized by actors such as Ted Kaczynski, the Unabomber, and Timothy McVeigh, who sought to destroy what they perceived to be corrupt culture and government. Militia groups such as the Michigan Militia and the Patriot Movement were the most prominent right-wing groups of the decade; these groups perpetuated the tragedies of Ruby Ridge (1992) and Waco (1993), (Freilich et al., 2001). The April 19, 1995, bombing of the Alfred P. Murrah Federal Building in Oklahoma City by Timothy McVeigh was the most notable terrorist act of the 1990s (FBI, 2006).

In addition, the pre-9/11 era witnessed the rise of Islamic jihadists who perpetuated a series of international attacks, mostly coordinated by Osama bin Laden and others against U.S. interests around the globe. Some of the tactics adopted by the terrorists included hijackings, terror in the skies, embassy bombing, attacks on naval targets, and the kidnapping of American personnel (Nemeth, 2017). In response to the new trend of terrorism, the U.S. government adopted new tactics and methodologies to combat domestic and international terrorism, including the promulgation of the Omnibus Counterterrorism Act of 1995; Executive Order 12947, signed by President Bill Clinton on January 23, 1995, which prohibited transactions with terrorists who threaten to disrupt the Middle East peace process and later expanded to include freezing the assets of Osama bin Laden and others; and the U.S. Antiterrorism and Effective Death Penalty Act of 1996, in response to the Oklahoma City bombing, which prohibits persons from providing material support to foreign terrorist organizations (Maggs, 2010; Nemeth, 2017).

The nature of modern violence experienced in the 21st century makes it clear that law enforcement has entered a unique stage of public safety. The terrorist attacks of September 11, 2001, altered law enforcement perceptions and responses to terrorism in the United States, as well as prevention strategies overseas. In 2013, there were 12,000 terrorist attacks worldwide (University of Maryland, 2014) (see also the appendix of the chronicle of terror acts). With a surge in terrorist activities around the world in the post-9/11 era, there is a great pressure for law enforcement to be more prepared in detection, prevention, and prosecution tactics and techniques.

The function of law enforcement in the post-9/11 era under homeland security is more focused on crime control, to identify potential threats and intelligence gathering. The events of 9/11 have changed the roles and responsibilities of policing in America and around the world. Many academic literatures, government publications, and public statements from government officials and politicians emphasize the impact of 9/11 on local law enforcement (DeLone, 2007; Henry, 2002; Oliver, 2006). For instance, Oliver (2006) contended that the events of 9/11 have thrust American policing into a new era, wherein homeland security is the dominant strategy.

The main legislative response to the terrorist attacks of 9/11 in the United States was the 2001 Uniting and Strengthening of America to

Provide Appropriate Tools Required to Intercept and Obstruct Terrorism or USA PATRIOT Act (Thomas, 2002). The USA PATRIOT Act led to the creation of the Department of Homeland Security, with the initial legislation encompassing 40 federal agencies. Among other provisions, the act granted sweeping powers to the executive branch and its law enforcement agencies, including the power of detention and surveillance, designation of any group as terrorist organization, and designation of domestic terrorism as a new crime. Arguably, the new powers at times undermine due process procedures and other adverse actions of law enforcement that may not be congruent with the First and Fourth Amendment rights (Thomas, 2002). Notably, the most sweeping legislative and direct response to 9/11 attacks was the creation of the Department of Homeland Security (DHS) on November 19, 2002. The DHS combined 22 different federal departments and agencies into a unified, integrated Cabinet agency. The DHS was charged with the primary purpose for homeland security missions and to ensure accountability in the execution of those missions. The legislative mandate for the creation of DHS was based on the recognition of massive intelligence and information-sharing failures that occurred prior to 9/11.

The future of DHS depends on the demand due to circumstance, incident, and event, and whether the functions of response remain local or national responsibilities. In as much as terrorism continues to exist, the importance of DHS cannot be overemphasized.

In addition to the Homeland Security Act of 2002 (Pub. L. 107-296), the Border Protection, Anti-Terrorism, and Illegal Immigration Control Act of 2005 was also enacted in further response to terrorism. There is no doubt that social development has influenced the transformation of terrorist attacks and the emergence of new strategies. However, the United States has responded forcefully to the threats of terrorism both within the U.S. homeland and outside, with constant policy strategies and financial as well as intelligence support for international peace and global security (Vavrenyuk, 2018).

Why Do Individuals Engage in Terrorist Acts?

A common belief is that terrorism stems from a "deprivation theory." The theory attributed participation in terrorist acts to living conditions of poverty, economics, and lack of education (Dekmejian, 1995; Faksh,

1997). Hafez (2003) and Martin (2006), argued that terrorism is based on extremism and antisystem ideologies with radical or reactionary outcome. Furthermore, Plous and Zimbardo (2004) contended that violent extremism is motivated by revenge and retribution. The increasing tension against the United States from nations and groups around the world, coupled with an estimated 655,000 Iraqis killed in Iraq from 2002 to July 2006, directly and indirectly related to the United States–led Iraq War (Cable News Network, 2006), are often cited as contributing factors for terrorism against the United States and her allies.

Factors that lead individuals to commit violent crimes or engage in terrorism are complex and ambiguous (Gartenstein-Ross & Grossman, 2009; Silber & Bhatt, 2007). Most academic literature examines radicalism in general (Gartenstein-Ross & Grossman, 2009; Precht, 2007; Silber & Bhatt, 2007), but only a limited number of studies have examined radicalism in relation to crime and terrorism (Mouras, 2013), which indicates a substantial gap in literature. Wilner and Dubouloz (2010) noted that an individual's decision to engage in terrorism or criminal behavior involves both emotional and mental processes. Existing research has focused on the phases of criminal behavior and characteristics of an individual terrorist's activities and the goals of terrorists (Gartenstein-Ross & Grossman, 2009; Precht, 2007; Silber & Bhatt, 2007). Precht (2007) for instance, contended that there is no common characteristic of a domestic terrorist. To buttress Precht's (2007) assertion, Silber and Bhatt (2007) argued that there are limited features available for law enforcement or intelligence agencies to predict the trajectory of individual's profile and engagement in terrorist activities.

Domestic terrorism can be driven by diverse motivations, including racial hatred, White supremacy, grievances against government policy, and an inordinate desire to subvert and undermine democratic state (Nemeth, 2017). During the 1990s, the likes of Ted Kaczynski and Timothy McVeigh adopted a virulent form of anti-government sentiment and tried to destroy what they perceived as a corrupt society and government (Nemeth, 2017).

Criminal Justice: The Future of Terrorism

Terror and threats of terrorism are very serious and petrifying aspects of modern society. So, what can be done to prevent terrorism in United States? Many of the strategies employed by various governments have proven to be ineffective or inadequate, as can be seen in the series of domestic terrorism in recent years in the United States. The U.S. government has enacted multiple legislations, taken a hard line against negotiating with terrorists, undertaken military interventions, taken action against nations providing safe haven to terrorists, applied economic sanctions, conducted covert and undercover operations, and prosecuted terrorists as criminals (Mullins, 1997). Some actions have proved to be effective and others have not worked as expected. Only by fully understanding the terrorist threats and their modus operandi can terrorists be defeated or significantly weakened.

The tragic events at the World Trade Center and the 2005 Oklahoma City bombing clearly dispel any notion that the United States is immune to terrorist acts. Understanding this sinister kind of threat is the best way to prepare for it. The concept of terrorism is a dynamic phenomenon and is ever changing with new actors and tactics. If terrorists fail to alter their tactics or structure, they can become isolated, dissected, and destroyed by security forces. It is no coincidence that basic tactics of terrorism through violence or threats remain relatively constant; terrorists will continue to improvise in future tactical trends and develop innovative strategies. However, it is imperative for law enforcement, security institutions, and the military to update a practical text on terrorism.

National defense and criminal intelligence operations are based in part on building information to explore the possibility of future pathways and future trends. Predicting the direction of future terrorist activities is very difficult, but it is a necessary component for the U.S. government and law enforcement agencies. It is wise to take a step back, assess, and determine what we are doing and what needs to be done to protect the homeland. Current initiatives and practices have left us with many unknowns. For example, why do we do what we do? How real is the threat described? If the threats are so real, why have they not occurred with greater frequency? Is there any evidence that if the frisk and search on people at the airport is randomly applied or eliminated that it would lead to an increase in terrorism incidents? There has yet to be one event of terrorism involving aircraft since 9/11. Most recent threats to homeland security have been limited to homegrown domestic terrorism. These questions and concerns need to be fully explored if we have to innovate and respond to future terrorism threats.

Although they may not form a common front, terror and criminal networks will continue to intersect. Whereas terrorists desire to destabilize society and inflict harm on citizens, criminals need government stability to operate. Cyberterrorism has yet to reach its full potential, and the United States remains vulnerable to attack. The future path of radicalization will change, but its direction remains questionable. Finally, terrorist networks and their operations may bifurcate, as we have seen in Al Qaeda and the evolution of the Islamic State in Iraq (ISIS). However, small attacks, especially homegrown terrorists, will continue, while sophisticated and larger attacks will evolve from large organizations with better network and logistical support. DHS must thrive into the next century, developing and adopting other strategies other than law enforcement techniques; in some cases, technology can be used as alternative. In most cases, homeland security professionals should be innovative and do things differently from the status quo. This thinking was espoused by Nemeth (2017), and includes the following practices:

+ Targeting terrorists through behavioral profiling
+ Conducting random rather than mandatory checkpoints at air and transport facilities
+ Allowing air frequent fliers to skip security systems
+ Disbursing budgetary allotments at the local level
+ Decentralizing more DHS operations to the states and local agencies
+ Allowing local agencies to assume some of the DHS functions

Changes in how war is fought affect the structure of civil society. For instance, Qutb (1965) opined that the existence of the jihadists' communities is threatened by Muslims who do not accept the jihadists' philosophy and by the non-Muslim West. In this case, the jihadists' can use terrorism as a social order to disrupt their enemies' societies and their way of lives. This philosophy continues to drive the course of most terrorist organizations such as Al Qaeda and ISIS. Thus, combating terrorism is more than a matter of taking the battle to an enemy, or using military force. All levels of society must become involved in homeland security.

Criminal Justice Model

Understanding the historical antecedents and modern view of terrorism within the framework of counter-terrorism provides both opportunities and challenges for criminal justice system. The imperative to prevent and respond to terrorism has led to consolidated efforts by criminal justice practitioners to anticipate risks or threats in pursuing homeland security (McCulloch & Pickering, 2009). Combating the terrorist threat is uniquely suited to a shift to prevention because the term "terrorism" itself is preemptive, existing prior to and beyond any formal verdict. Terrorism is a concept that arises primarily in the arena of politics rather than the courts.

Counter-terrorism measures, particularly those implemented in the wake of the 9/11 attacks, have seen homeland security and criminal justice integrated to an unprecedented extent. The integration of homeland security and criminal justice involves the blurring of the intercept between the state's domestic and international coercive capacities. Thus, preventive measures within homeland security embraces not only a temporal shift that predicts potential attacks, but also a geographic shift that merges or distorts domestic and international dimensions of criminal justice and homeland security. The integration or intersection between criminal justice and homeland security has resulted in a number of tensions (McCulloch & Pickering, 2009), for example, the tensions between the ideal of an impartial criminal justice system and the politically charged practice of homeland security. Another key issue relates to transparency required within the criminal justice framework through the presentation of evidence at trial and covert action designed to disrupt and counter terrorist acts. Counter-terrorism is simultaneously a highly visible public spectacle and a highly secretive and broadly unaccountable function of the state (Leuprecht 2007; Manson 2007; Tham 2007).

Often, the government argues that the rationale for integrating homeland security into criminal justice and preventing terrorism through prevention measures is that the human costs of terrorist incidents are so high that the due process protection afforded to terrorists during prosecution is unreasonable or unaffordable. On this basis, governments adopt a series of new laws intended to preempt harmful acts and manage the risk of terrorism through disruption, restriction, and incapacitation. However, when the criminal justice process adheres to the principles of the rule of law and human rights, in counter-terrorism activities, they can offer a peaceful, accountable, and legitimate response to terrorism. This kind of criminal justice response to terrorism can help avoid or mitigate the risk of unreasonable and/or unlawful use of force outside the protections and procedural guarantees offered by the due process of law (Lafree & Hendrickson, 2007). It also reinforces a society's commitment to the rule of law and human rights, even when living under terrorist threats.

In addition to the appropriate laws, policies, and practices, criminal justice practitioners must develop continuous capacity-building and specialized training to effectively respond to the increasing and complex nature of terrorism. This will require an integrated approach that is coherent, sector-wide, and human rights–based and sustainable and will include all components of the criminal justice system such as law enforcement, the prosecution, and the judiciary and the correctional system. The approach will also require a comprehensive capacity-building approach, which may involve law reform initiatives, judicial reforms, and an enhanced public integrity. There is no doubt that effective coordination across the criminal justice system remains one of the essential preconditions to the successful strategy for the prevention, mitigation, and response to terrorism.

The role of the criminal justice system in countering terrorism is a challenging one, but the main objective of counter-terrorism strategies must be to prevent terrorist activities. Future terrorism prevention will require a well-funded criminal justice strategy and a comprehensive system of substantive offenses, investigative powers and techniques, evidentiary rules, and international cooperation (Cassese, 2006). The goal is to proactively integrate substantive and procedural mechanisms to reduce the incidence and severity of terrorist acts within the constraints and protections of the criminal justice system under the rule of law.

The adoption of the criminal justice model can be challenging, especially for less well-resourced states, to implement all the recommended measures for law enforcement and criminal justice systems in addition to the requisite training. Criminal justice systems will have to approach these challenges differently, relative to their level of development, legal tradition, cultural circumstances, and institutional capabilities. Furthermore, due to national legal and criminal justice systems that require states to cooperate with the international law and a variety of rule-of-law based counter-terrorism initiatives, many criminal justice systems are faced with constraints and a weakened ability to function within basic rule of law and human rights principles (Cassese, 2009).

Conclusion

This chapter explored historical trends in terrorism within the United States from the past 50 years. The discussion also informs counter-terrorism decisions and the process of delineating enhanced homeland security policies for the future while applying the criminal justice model to analyze strategies toward prevention and response to acts of terrorism.

Over the past 5 decades, terrorism in the United States has acquired different shapes and menacing proportions. One or another terrorist incident may cause a massive loss of life, exerting significant psychological pressure on societies and its citizens. Almost three decades after the 9/11 terrorist attacks, looking back is as important as looking forward to learn from the past and to examine the current and future threats facing the United States. Terrorism has become the most violent form of psychological warfare and a means of asserting power. Terrorism has remained a part of human history and continues to be a major concern for the international community (Barghothi, 2005; Laqueur, 1999; Pelfrey, 2009). The threat environment has transformed significantly since 9/11 and will continue to evolve. Law enforcement's role is to prevent, deter, and disrupt terrorist activities. To position itself to respond to these threats, U.S. law enforcement agencies are constantly undergoing transformation in the way they collect and use intelligence.

The FBI, for instance, has implemented a new, proactive, intelligence-driven model that enables it to develop a comprehensive threat analysis and enhances its ability to prioritize resources to address and mitigate terrorist threats. The United States and its allies must work harder to meet the challenges posed by the constantly changing acts and threats of terrorism. Strategies must be encompassing and include intelligence gathering, technological advancement, and capabilities to confront new scourges of self-directed terror groups. The nation must constantly assess vulnerabilities and anticipate new lines of attack, including domestic and international terrorists. Equally, governments must ensure laws, rules, and policies that mitigate against group grievances and reduce vulnerable populations in society.

Discussion Questions

1. What is the state of Al Qaeda today and what effects have nearly two years of unremitting war had on it?
2. What do broader current trends in terrorism today tell us about future potentialities?
3. How should we be thinking about terrorism today and tomorrow?
4. Terrorism has been one of the defining concepts of our age that poses challenges to governments, private organizations, and individuals. How do we define the concept? How can we prevent and respond?

References

Banks, W., de Nevers, R., & Wallerstein, M. (2008). *Combating terrorism: Strategies and approaches.* Washington, DC: CQ Press.

Barghothi, J. L. (2005). International terrorism in historical perspective. In C. B. Fields. & R. H. Moor (Eds.), *Comparative and international criminal justice: Traditional and nontraditional systems of law and control* (pp. 55–70). Longrove, IL: Waveland Press, Inc.

Brister, P. D. (2010). Patriotic enemies of the state: A cross comparison of the Christian Patriot Movement and the 1920s Ku Klux Klan, *The Homeland Security Review, 4*(3), 173.

Cable News Network. (2006). *The human cost of the war in Iraq: A mortality study, 2002–2006.* Retrieved from http://i.a.cnn.net/cnn/2006/images/10/11/human.cost.of.war.pdf.

Cooper, H. H. A. (2008). Terrorism: The problem of definition revisited. In S. Mahan & P. L. Griset (Eds.). *Terrorism in perspective* (2nd ed.) (pp. 15–23). Thousand Oaks, CA: SAGE.

Dekmejian, R. H. (1995). *Islam in revolution: Fundamentalism in the Arab world.* (2nd ed.). Contemporary issues in the Middle East. Syracuse University Press.

DeLone, G. J. (2007). Law enforcement mission statements post-September 11. *Police Quarterly, 10*(2), 218–235. doi:10.1177/1098611107300945.

Department of Homeland Security. (2007). *National preparedness guidelines.* Washington, DC: Government Printing Office. Retrieved from http://catalog.gpo.gov.

Faksh, M. A. (1997). *The future of Islam in the Middle East: Fundamentalism in Egypt, Algeria, and Saudi Arabia.* Praeger.

Federal Bureau of Investigation. (2006). *Terrorism in the United States 2002–2005.* Washington, DC: Author.

Fletcher, G. P. (2009). "The Influence of the Common Law and Civil Law Traditions on International Criminal Law." In Cassese, Antonio ed. *The Oxford Companion to International Criminal Justice.* Oxford: Oxford University Press, Part III, pp. 104–110.

Freilich, J. D., Pienik, J. A., & Howard, G. J. (2001). Toward comparative studies of US militia movement. *International Journal of Comparative Sociology, 42*(1), 163-210.

Gartenstein-Ross, D., & Grossman, L. (2009). *Homegrown terrorists in the US and U.K.: An empirical examination of the radicalization process.* (1st ed.). FDD's Center for Terrorism Research, FDD Press, Washington, D. C.

Gibbs, J. (1989). Conceptualizations of terrorism. *American Sociological Review, 54*(3), 329–340.

Hafez, M. M. (2003). *Why Muslims rebel: Repression and resistance in the Islamic World.* Lynne Rienner Publication.

Henry, V. (2002). The need for a coordinated and strategic local police approach to terrorism: A practitioner's perspective. *Police Practice and Research, 3*(4), 319–336. doi:10.1080/1561426022000032088.

Hewitt, C. (2003). *Understanding terrorism in America: From the Klan to Al-Qaeda.* New York, NY: Routledge.

Hoffman, B. (2006). *Inside terrorism* (2nd ed.). New York, NY: Columbia University Press.

Kushner, H. (1998) *Terrorism in America: A structured approach to understanding the terrorist threat.* Springfield, IL: Charles C. Thomas Publishers.

Lafree, G., & Hendrickson, J. (2007). Build a criminal justice policy for terrorism. Criminology & Public Policy, 6(4), 781–790.

Laqueur, W. (1999). The new terrorism: Fanaticism and the arms of mass destruction, Oxford: Oxford University Press, 40 and 82.

Leuprecht, P. (2007), "An International Perspective on Anti-Terrorism Laws and Academic Freedom", in J. Turk and A. Manson, eds, *Free Speech in Fearful Times: After 9/11 in Canada, the U.S., Australia and Europe,* 109-20. Toronto: James Lorimer & Company Limited.

Maggs, G. E. (2010). *Terrorism and the law: Cases and materials* (2nd ed.). Washington, DC: George Washington Law.

Mahan, S. & Griset, P. L. (2008). *Terrorism in perspective* (2nd ed.). Thousand Oaks, CA: SAGE

Manson, A. (2007). "The Rule of Law, and Academic Freedom in Fearful Times: Canada after Gouzenko", in J. Turk and A. Manson, eds, *Free Speech in Fearful Times: After 9/11 in Canada, the U.S., Australia and Europe,* 63-84. Toronto: James Lorimer & Company Limited.

Martin, G. (2006). *Understanding terrorism: Challenges, perspectives, and issues.* Thousand Oaks, CA: Sage.

McCulloch, J. & Pickering, S. (2009). Pre-crime and counter-terrorism: Imagining future crime in the war on terror. *British Journal of Criminology, 49*(5), 628–645.

McVey, P. M. (2003). The local role in fighting terrorism. In R. L. Kemp (Ed.), *Homeland security: Best practices for local government* (pp. 125–130). Washington, DC: International City/County Management Association.

Mouras, M. C. (2013). *Power, Law and Violence: Critical Essays on Hans Kelsen and Carl Schmitt.* LAP LAMBERT Academic Publishing.

Mullins, W. C. (1997). *A sourcebook on domestic and international terrorism: An analysis of issues, organizations, tactics and responses* (2nd ed.). Springfield, IL: Thomas.

Nemeth, S. P. (2017). *Homeland security: An introduction to principles and practice.* Boca Raton, FL: CRC Press.

Ogundiya, I. S. & Amzat, J, (2008). Nigeria and the threats of terrorism: myth or reality. *Journal of Sustainable Development in Africa, 10*(2), Clarion University of Pennsylvania, Clarion, PA.

Oliver, W. M. (2006). The fourth era of policing: Homeland security. *International Review of Law Computers & Technology, 20*(1–2), 49–62. doi:10.1080/13600860600579696.

Pelfrey, W. V. (2009). An exploratory study of local homeland security preparedness: Findings and implications for future assessments. *Criminal Justice Policy Review, 20*(3), 261–273. doi:10.1177/0887403408330637.

Plous, S., & Zimbardo, P. (2004). How social science can reduce terrorism. *Chronicle of Higher Education, 51*(3), B9.

Precht, R. E. (2007). *Defending Mohammad: The unfinished story of the 1993 World Trade Center bombing trial and why it matters today*. Justice Labs Press, New York, NY.

Qutb, S. (1965). *Milestones*. Reprint, Indianapolis: American Trust Publications.

Reese, S. (2013). Defining homeland security: Analysis and congressional considerations. *Congressional Research Service*, 7-5700, 1–18.

Rehm, M. K. (2000). Terrorism preparedness calls for proactive approach. *Police Chief, 12*, 38–43.

Scaparroti, C. M. (2007). U.S. Department of Defense Homeland defense. Joint Publications, 3-27, Washington, D. C.

Silber, M. D. & Bhatt, A. (2007). *Radicalization in the West: The homegrown threat*. Retrieved from https://sethgodin.typepad.com/seths_blog/files/NYPD_Report-Radicalization_in_the_West.pdf.

Spindlove, J. R. & Simonsen, C. E. (2010). *Terrorism today: The past, the players, the future* (5th ed.). Upper Saddle River, N.J.: Pearson Prentice-Hall, Inc.

Tham, J. (2007), "Australian Terror Laws and Academic Freedom", in J. Turk and A. Manson, eds, *Free Speech in Fearful Times: After 9/11 in Canada, the U.S., Australia and Europe*, 234-52. Toronto: James Lorimer & Company Limited.

Thomas, P. (2002). Legislative responses to terrorism. *The Guardian*. Retrieved from https://www.theguardian.com/world/2002/sep/11/september11.usa11.

United Nations, GA. (2005). "World Summit Outcome Document." *Resolution adopted by the General Assembly, A/RES/60/1* 24.

Vavrenyuk, S. A. (2018). International terrorism and the basic ways to deal with it at the present stage. *CES Working Papers, (X)*2 213–233.

Wilner, A. S., & Dubouloz, C. J. (2010). Homegrown terrorism and transformative learning: An interdisciplinary approach to understanding radicalization. *Global Change, Peace, and Security, 22*(1), 33–51. doi:10.1080/14781150903487956.

Appendix

FIGURE 6.1 A litany of terrorist attacks in the United States from 1960 to Present

Date	Method	Death	Injured	Location	Detail	Perpetrator
Oct 2, 1960	Bombings	1	51	New York City, NY	The Sunday Bomber detonated a series of bombs in the New York City Subway and ferries.	Unknown
Nov 22, 1963	Assassination, shooting	2	2	Dallas, TX	Assassination of President John F. Kennedy and Dallas police officer J.D. Tippit by communist Lee Harvey Oswald.	Lee Harvey Oswald
Jun 16 & 21, 1964	Burning, Murder	3	0	Mississippi	Mt. Zion Baptist Church was burnt. Michael (Mickey) Schwerner, James Chaney, and Andrew Goodman were detained by police then abducted and murdered for their work with CORE.	KKK
Apr 23, 1968	Hostage-taking	1	0	Hartford, CT	Students at Trinity College hold the board of trustees captive until their demands were met	Trinity College students
Apr 4, 1968	Assassination, shooting	1	0	Memphis, TN	Martin Luther King Jr. was assassinated.	James Earl Ray
Jun 5, 1968	Assassination, shooting	1	5	Los Angeles, CA	Assassination of Senator Robert F. Kennedy.	Sirhan Sirhan
Feb 26, 1969	Bombing	0	2	Claremont & SF, CA	Secretary at Pomona College severely injured by bomb; Students injured at SF College classroom	Left-wing student radicals
Aug 20, 1969	Bombing	0	20	New York City, NY	Twenty injured by radical leftist in a bombing of the Marine Midland Building.	Sam Melville

111

Date	Method	Death	Injured	Location	Detail	Perpetrator
Apr 15, 1970	Bombing	5	69+	New York City/ Chicago, IL	Terrorism attacks by Fuerzas Armadas de Liberacion Nacional (FALN), a Puerto Rican separatist group, the Jewish Defense League (JDL), the Independent Armed Revolutionary Commandos (CRIA), and Omega 7, an anti-Castro Cuban organization.	Fuerzas Armadas de Liberacion Nacional (FALN)
May 28; Sept 24; & Nov 21, 1970	Riot; Firebombing	0	1	Fresno, CA; Stanford, CA; Portland, OR	Student radicals set fires, break windows and throw rocks in reaction to the U.S. invasion of Cambodia; Bombing of the City Hall of Portland, Oregon in an attempt to destroy the state's bronze Liberty Bell replica.	Left-wing student radicals
Aug 24, 1970	Bombing	1	3	Madison, WI	Sterling Hall at the University of Wisconsin–Madison bombing in protest of the Army Mathematics Research Center and the Vietnam War.	Karleton Armstrong, Dwight Armstrong, David Fine, and Leo Burt
1970 & 1971	Bombing	0	0	New York City, NY	Bomb explosion outside of Aeroflot's New York City office in protest of the treatment of Soviet Jews; Bomb denotated outside of Soviet cultural offices in Washington, D.C. and rifle fire into the Soviet mission to the United Nations.	Jewish Defense League
Mar 1, 1971	Bombing	0	0	Washington, D.C.	The radical leftist group Weatherman exploded a bomb in the United States Capitol to protest the U.S. invasion of Laos.	Weatherman
Jun 1, 1973	Shooting	1	0	Chevy Chase, MD	Yosef Alon, the Israeli Air Force attaché in Washington, D.C., was shot and killed outside his home in Chevy Chase, Maryland.	Palestinian militant group Black September (suspected)

Date	Method	Death	Injured	Location	Detail	Perpetrator
Jun 13, 1974	Bombing	0	0	Pittsburgh, PA	The 29th floor of the Gulf Tower in Pittsburgh, Pennsylvania, was bombed with dynamite.	Radical leftist Weatherman
Aug 6, 1974	Bombings	3	36	Los Angeles, CA	The Pan Am Terminal at Los Angeles International Airport bombed.	"Alphabet Bomber" Muharem Kurbegovich
Jan 24, 1975	Bombing	4	50+	New York City, NY	A bomb exploded in the Fraunces Tavern of New York City. No one was ever prosecuted for the bombing.	The Puerto Rico nationalist group- FALN
Dec 29, 1975	Bombing	11	75	New York City, NY	LaGuardia Airport Bombing; killed 11 and injured 75. The bombing remains unsolved.	Unknown
Sep 11, 1976	Aircraft hijacking, bombing	1	3	United States Airspace	Croatian terrorists hijacked a TWA airliner and diverted it to Gander, Newfoundland and Labrador, and then Paris, demanding a manifesto be printed.	Zvonko Bušić and co-conspirators
Sep 21, 1976	Assassination, bombing	2	1	Washington, D.C.	Orlando Letelier, a former member of the Chilean government, was killed by a car bomb in Washington, D.C. along with his assistant Ronni Moffitt.	Members of the Chilean Intelligence Agency, DINA
Mar 9-11, 1977	Hijacking	2	149 hostages	Washington, D.C.	1977 Hanafi Siege involving three buildings in Washington, DC and held hostages for three days.	Hanafi Muslim gunmen
July 22, 1980	Shooting	1	0	Bethesda, MD	Ali Akbar Tabatabai, an Iranian exile and critic of Ayatollah Khomeni, was shot in his Bethesda, Maryland home.	American Muslim convert, Dawud Salahuddin Iran

Date	Method	Death	Injured	Location	Detail	Perpetrator
Mar 21, 1981	Lynching, Cross Burning	1	0	Mobile, AL	In response to a black man not being found guilty of murdering a white man, three members of the KKK burned a cross on the courthouse lawn. They then picked a black person at random, abducted, beat, strangled and killed Michael Donald. They left his body hanging from a tree.	KKK
Jan 28, 1982 & May 4, 1982	Assassination, shooting	1	0	Los Angeles, CA; Somerville, PA	Kemal Arkan, the Turkish Consul-General in Los Angeles, was killed; Assassination of Orhan Gündüz: Turkish Honorary Consul Orhan Gunduz.	Justice Commandos Against Armenian Genocide
Nov 7, 1983	Bombing	0	0	Washington, D.C.	U.S. Senate bombing: The Armed Resistance Unit, a militant leftist group, bombed the United States Capitol in response to the U.S. invasion of Grenada.	May 19th Communist Organization
June 18, 1984	Assassination, shooting	1	0	Denver, CO	Alan Berg, Jewish lawyer-talk show host was shot and killed in the driveway of his home on Capitol Hill, Denver, Colorado.	White Nationalist group called The Order
Aug 5- Oct 28, 1984	Food poisoning	0	751	The Dalles, OR	Rajneeshee bioterror attack: In what was believed to be the first incident of bioterrorism in the United States.	Rajneesh movement
Oct 11, 1985	Assassination, bombing	1	0	Santa Ana, CA	Alex Odeh, a prominent Arab-American, was killed by a bomb in his office in Santa Ana, California.	Jewish Defense League (suspected)
Dec 11, 1985	Bombing	1	0	Sacramento, CA	Computer rental store owner, Hugh Scrutton, was the first fatality of the Unabomber's neo-luddite campaign.	Ted Kaczynski (Unabomber)
Mar 1, 1989	Firebombing	0	0	New York City, NY	Firebombing of the Riverdale Press: The Riverdale Press, a weekly newspaper in the Bronx, New York.	Unknown
Nov 5, 1990	Assassination, shooting	1	0	New York City, NY	Assassination of Meir Kahane: El Sayyid Nosair, a member of an Islamist terror cell.	El Sayyid Nosair

Date	Method	Death	Injured	Location	Detail	Perpetrator
Jan 25, 1993	Shooting	2	3	Langley, VA	CIA Shooting - outraged by U.S. policy toward Palestinians, opens fire on cars stopped at a traffic signal outside CIA Headquarters in Langley, Virginia.	Pakistani Mir Qazi (a/k/a Mir Aimal Kansi)
Feb 26, 1993	Truck bombing	6	1042	New York City, NY	World Trade Center bombing.	Ramzi Yousef, a member of Al Qaeda
Mar 10, 1993	Shooting	1	0	Pensacola, FL	Murder of David Gunn, gynecologist.	Army of God member Michael F. Griffin
Mar 1, 1994	Shooting	1	3	New York City, NY	Brooklyn Bridge Shooting - ambushes and shoots up a van full of Jewish students returning from a visit with Rabbi Menachem M. Schneerson.	Lebanese-born Rashid Baz
Jul 29, 1994	Shooting	2	1	Pensacola, FL	Murder of gynecologist John Britton and Britton's bodyguard James Barrett outside the Ladies Center clinic in Pensacola, Florida.	Army of God member Rev. Paul Jennings Hill
Dec 10, 1994	Bombing	1	0	North Caldwell, NJ	Advertising executive Thomas J. Mosser killed by a mail bomb sent by the Unabomber (Ted Kaczynski).	Ted Kaczynski (Unabomber)
Dec 30, 1994	Shooting	2	5	Brookline, MA	Rampage attack at a Planned Parenthood clinic in Brookline, Massachusetts.	Anti-abortion activist John C. Salvi III
Dec 31, 1994	Shooting	0	0	Norfolk, VA	Salvi attacks the Planned Parenthood clinic in Norfolk, Virginia.	John C. Salvi III
April 19, 1995	Truck bombing	168	680+	Oklahoma City, Ok	Bombing of Alfred P. Murrah Federal Building, Oklahoma.	Timothy McVeigh and Terry Nichols
April 24, 1995	Bombing	1	0	Sacramento, CA	Timber industry lobbyist Gilbert P. Murray was killed in the third and final mailbomb attack by the Unabomber.	Ted Kaczynski (Unabomber)

Date	Method	Death	Injured	Location	Detail	Perpetrator
July 27, 1996	Bombing	1	111	Atlanta, GA	Centennial Olympic Park bombing.	Army of God member Eric Robert Rudolph
Jan 16, 1997	Bombing	0	6	Sandy Springs, GA	Bombing of women's health clinic in Sandy Springs, Georgia.	Eric Robert Rudolph
Feb 21, 1997	Bombing	0	5	Atlanta, GA	Bombing of the Otherside Lounge, a gay bar in Atlanta, Georgia.	Eric Robert Rudolph
Feb 23, 1997	Shooting	1	6	New York City, NY	Shooting on tourists from an observation deck atop the Empire State building.	Palestinian Ali Hassan Abu Kamal
July 31, 1997	Police raid, planned suicide bombings	0	3	New York City, NY	Brooklyn bombing plot: Two Palestinian illegal immigrants shot and arrested in a police raid that found two pipe bombs in a Brooklyn apartment.	Gazi Ibrahim Abu Mezer
Jan 29, 1998	Bombing	1	1	Birmingham, AL	A women's clinic in Birmingham, Alabama bombed.	Eric Robert Rudolph
June 7, 1998	Murder	1	0	Jasper, TX	Three white gang members, dragged James Byrd Jr. to his death behind their truck and left his body in front of an African-American church.	Shawn Berry, Lawrence Russell Brewer, John King
June 18, 1999	Arson	0	0	Sacramento, CA	Fires set to Congregation B'nai Israel, Congregation Beth Shalom, and Knesset Israel Torah Center in Sacramento, California. The fires cause more than $1 million in damage.	Brothers Matthew and Tyler Williams
Jul 1, 1999	Shooting	2	0	Happy Valley, CA	Murder of gay couple Gary Matson and Winfield Mowder in Happy Valley, California.	Matthew and Tyler Williams

Date	Method	Death	Injured	Location	Detail	Perpetrator
Jul 2, 1999	Arson	0	0	Sacramento, CA	Fire set to the Country Club Medical Building in Sacramento County, California, which houses an abortion clinic.	Matthew and Tyler Williams
Jul 2-4, 1999	Shootings	2 (+1)	9	Illinois and Indiana	A two-state shooting spree in Indiana and Illinois.	Benjamin Nathaniel Smith
Aug 10, 1999	Shootings	1	5	Los Angeles, CA	Los Angeles Jewish Community Center shooting.	Buford O. Furrow Jr
Dec 31, 1999	Arson	0	0	East Lansing, MI	Four members of the Earth Liberation Front start a fire in Michigan State University's Agriculture Hall causing $1 million in damage.	Earth Liberation Front
Oct 10, 2000	Firebombing	0	0	New York City, NY	Three young men of Arab descent hurled crude Molotov cocktails at a synagogue in The Bronx, New York to "strike a blow in the Middle East conflict between Israel and Palestine".	Mazin Assi and co-conspirators
Oct 13, 2000	Firebombing	0	0	Syracuse, New York	Firebombing of Temple Beth El (Syracuse)	Ramsi Uthman
May 21, 2001	Firebombing	0	0	Seattle, WA	The Center for Urban Horticulture at the University of Washington burned by the Earth Liberation Front. Replacement building cost $7 million ($9,674,000 today). Earth Liberation Front members pled guilty.	Earth Liberation Front

Date	Method	Death	Injured	Location	Detail	Perpetrator
Sep 11, 2001	Aircraft hijackings, suicide attacks	2,977 (+19)	6,000+	New York City, NY; Arlington County, Virginia Pennsylvania Shanksville, PA	9/11 attacks: Aircraft hijackings and suicide attacks carried out against the United States by the Al Qaeda Network. Four domestic commercial airliners were hijacked simultaneously while flying within the North-eastern United States; two flew directly into the Twin Towers of the World Trade Center in New York City, the third into the Pentagon in Arlington County, Virginia, and the fourth into a field near Shanksville, Pennsylvania, during a failed attempt to destroy its intended target in Washington, D.C	Al Qaeda
Sept 18 - Nov, 2001	Bioterrorism	5	17	United States	Letters tainted with anthrax killed five across the U.S., with politicians and media officials as the apparent targets.	Unknown
Dec 22, 2001	Bombing	0	1	Miami, FL	Failed shoe bomb attempt: An al-Qaeda operative attempted to detonate a bomb concealed in his shoes while on board a plane from Paris to Miami. He failed to detonate it and was apprehended by passengers and crew.	Al Qaeda operative Richard Reid
May 8, 2002	Dirty Bomb	0	0	Chicago, IL	Abdullah al-Muhajir was arrested for planning to use a radiological bomb.	Abdullah al-Muhajir
July 4, 2002	Shooting	2 (+1)	4	Los Angeles, CA	2002 Los Angeles International Airport shooting that killed two Israelis and wounded four others at the El Al ticket counter at Los Angeles International Airport.	41-year-old Egyptian national
Feb 16, 2002 - Oct 24, 2002	Shootings	17	10	Montgomery County, MD; Beltway, VA; Washington DC	Beltway sniper attacks; No motivation was given at the trial, but evidence presented showed an affinity to the cause of the Islamic Jihad	Betway snipers John Allen Muhammad and Lee Boyd Malvo

Date	Method	Death	Injured	Location	Detail	Perpetrator
Mar 19, 2003	Sabotage	0	0	New York City, NY	Iyman Faris was arrested for plotting to destroy the Brooklyn Bridge.	Iyman Faris
Aug 2003	Shootings	3	0	West Virginia	Three people were killed in a series of sniper shootings in West Virginia.	Shawn Lester
Dec 8, 2003	Shootout	2	0 (+1)	Abbeville, SC	Right-of-way standoff: Two police officers were killed in a shootout with three "sovereign citizens."	Arthur, Rita and Steven Bixby
Mar 5, 2006	Vehicle assault	0	9	Chapel Hill, NC	Mohammed Reza Taheri-azar drove an SUV into a group of pedestrians at UNC-Chapel Hill to "avenge the deaths or murders of Muslims around the world."	Mohammed Reza Taheri-azar
Mar 25, 2006	Shooting	6 (+1)	2	Seattle, WA	Capitol Hill massacre: Kyle Aaron Huff entered a rave afterparty in the southeast part of Seattle's Capitol Hill neighborhood and opened fire, killing six and wounding two.	Kyle Aaron Huff
Jul 28, 2006	Shooting, hostage taking	1	5	Seattle, WA	Seattle Jewish Federation shooting: Naveed Afzal Haq, an American citizen of Pakistani descent, killed one woman and shoots five others at the Jewish Federation building in Seattle. During the shooting, Haq told a 911 dispatcher that he was angry with American foreign policy in the Middle East.	Naveed Afzal Haq
Oct 26, 2007	Bombing	0	0	New York City, NY	A pair of improvised explosive devices were thrown at the Mexican Consulate in New York City. The fake grenades were filled with black powder, and detonated by fuses, causing very minor damage.	Unknown
Mar 3, 2008	Arson	0	0	Woodinville, WA	Four luxury woodland houses near Woodinville, Washington were torched, leaving behind a message crediting the Earth Liberation Front.	Earth Liberation Front

Date	Method	Death	Injured	Location	Detail	Perpetrator
Mar 6, 2008	Bombing	0	0	New York City, NY	A homemade bomb damaged an Armed Forces Recruiting Office in Times Square.	Unknown
May 4, 2008	Bombing	0	0	San Diego, CA	Multiple pipe bombs exploded at 1:40 am at the Edward J. Schwartz United States Courthouse in San Diego causing "considerable damage" to the entrance and lobby and sending shrapnel two blocks away, but causing no injuries.	Rachel Lynn Carlock and Danny Love Sr.
Jul 27, 2008	Shooting	2	6	Knoxville, TN	Knoxville Unitarian Universalist church shooting: 58-year-old Jim David Adkisson opened fire on a Universalist church because he wanted to kill Democrats and Liberals.	Jim Adkisson
Apr 8, 2009	Cyberattack, sabotage	0	0	United States	According to a report in the Wall Street Journal, intruders left malware in power grids, water, and sewage systems that could be activated at a later date.	Unknown
May 25, 2009	Bombing	0	0	New York City, NY	17-year-old Kyle Shaw sets off a crude explosive device at a Starbucks at East 92nd Street on the Upper East Side of Manhattan, shattering windows and destroyed a bench at the coffee shop.	Kyle Shaw
May 31, 2009	Assassination, shooting	1	0	Wichita, KS	Scott Roeder shoots and kills Dr. George Tiller, an abortion doctor in a Wichita, Kansas church. Roeder, an anti-abortion extremist who believes in justifiable homicide of abortion providers, was arrested soon afterward.	Scott Roeder
Jun 1, 2009	Shooting	1	1	Little Rock, AK	Abdulhakim Mujahid Muhammad shot and killed one military recruiter and seriously wounded another at a Little Rock, Arkansas Army/Navy Career Center in an act of Islamic extremism.	Abdulhakim Mujahid Muhammad

Date	Method	Death	Injured	Location	Detail	Perpetrator
Jun 1, 2009	Shooting	1	1 (+1)	Washington, D.C.	Elderly white supremacist James von Brunn, who had previously attempted to kidnap Federal Reserve employees in 1981, shot and killed a police officer at the United States Holocaust Museum before being wounded by other officers.	James Wenneker von Brunn
Nov 5, 2009	Shooting	13	32 (+1)	Killeen, TX	Nidal Malik Hasan, a US Army Major serving as a Psychiatrist, opened fire at Fort Hood, TX, killing 13 and wounding 29. His motive was jihad to fight "illegal and immoral aggression against Muslims".	Nidal Malik Hasan
Dec 25, 2009	Bombing	0	2 (+1)	Detroit, MI	Umar Farouk Abdulmutallab attempted to blow up Northwest Airlines flight 253 using plastic explosives sewn into his underwear while en route from Amsterdam to Detroit.	Umar Farouk Abdul-mutallab
Feb 18, 2010	Suicide attack	1 (+1)	13	Austin, TX	Andrew Joseph Stack III flying his single engine plane flew into the Austin Texas IRS building killing himself and one IRS employee and injuring 13 others. Stack left a suicide note online, comparing the IRS to Big Brother from the novel 1984.	Joe Stack
Mar 4, 2010	Shooting	0 (+1)	2	Arlington County, VA	John Patrick Bedell shot and wounded two Pentagon police officers at a security checkpoint in the Pentagon station of the Washington Metro rapid transit system in Arlington County, Virginia.	John Patrick Bedell
May 1, 2010	Bombing	0	0	New York City, NY	Faisal Shahzad ignited an explosive in Times Square. The bomb failed to go off, and he was later arrested on a flight leaving for Dubai.	Faisal Shahzad

Date	Method	Death	Injured	Location	Detail	Perpetrator
May 20, 2010	Shooting	2 (+2)	2	West Memphis, AK	Two West Memphis police officers were killed by a father and son who supported the sovereign citizen movement during a traffic stop. The suspects were later killed by other officers.	Jerry and Joseph Kane
Sept 1, 2010	Hostage taking	0 (+1)	0	Silver Spring, MD	James J. Lee, armed with two starter pistols and an explosive device, takes three people hostage in the lobby of the Discovery Communications headquarters in Silver Spring, Maryland before being killed by police.	James J. Lee
Oct 28, 2010	Bombing	0	0	Virginia	Farooque Ahmed conspired with law enforcement officials posing as al-Qaeda to bomb Arlington Cemetery, the Pentagon City subway station, Crystal City subway station, and Court House subway station.	Farooque Ahmed
Oct 29, 2010	Bombing	0	0	Chicago, IL	Two plastic explosive bombs were discovered on two cargo planes destined for two synagogues in Chicago. They were discovered at East Midlands Airport and Dubai International Airport while en route.	al-Qaeda in the Arabian Peninsula
Oct 17, 2010 - Nov 2, 2010	Bombing and Shooting	0	0	Virginia	A series of shootings took place at the five military buildings including the National Museum of the Marine Corps and the Pentagon. He also attempted to bomb and damage Arlington National Cemetery.	Yonathan Melaku
Nov 25, 2010	Bombing	0	0	Portland, OR	2010 Portland car bomb plot: Mohamed Osman Mohamud attempted to detonate what he thought was a car bomb at a Christmas tree lighting ceremony.	Mohamed Osman Mohamud
Jan 17, 2011	Attempted Bombing	0	0	Spokane, WA	Spokane bombing attempt: A radio-controlled-shaped pipe bomb was found and defused in Spokane, Washington along the route of that year's Martin Luther King Jr. memorial march.	

Date	Method	Death	Injured	Location	Detail	Perpetrator
May 25, 2011	Bombing	0	0	Bowling Green, KY	Two Iraqi immigrants were arrested for sending money and weapons to Iraq while residing in Bowling Green, Kentucky, as well as participating in attacks while in Iraq and plotting to kill American soldiers on their return.	Mohanad Shareef Hammadi and Waad Ramadan Alwan
Dec 6, 2011	Shooting	2	0	Fort Stewart, GA	19-year-old Michael Roark and his girlfriend, 17-year-old Tiffany York, were found by two fishermen near a rural road in southeastern Georgia. It was believed that Roark was killed for his part in giving information to Fort Bliss authorities in El Paso.	FEAR
Aug 5, 2012	Shooting	6 (+1)	4	Oak Creek, WI	Six people were killed and three others were injured, including a police officer who was tending to victims at a Sikh temple in Oak Creek, Wisconsin. The gunman, 40-year-old Wade Michael Page, killed himself after being shot by police.	Wade Page
Feb 3-12, 2013	Shootings	4 (+1)	6	California	Former LAPD officer Chris Dorner goes on a killing spree targeting police officers and their families throughout Southern California.	Chris Dorner
Apr 15, 2013	Bombings, shootout	5 (+1)	280 (+1)	Boston, MA	Two bombs detonated within seconds of each other near the finish line of the Boston Marathon. On the evening of April 18 in Cambridge, Massachusetts, an MIT campus police officer was shot and killed while sitting in his squad car. Two suspects then carjacked an SUV and fled to nearby Watertown, Massachusetts, a suburb of Boston.	Dzhokar Tsarnaev, Tamerlan Tsarnaev
Apr 16, 2013	Bioterrorism	0	0	Washington, D.C.	Two letters, sent to Mississippi Republican Senator Roger Wicker and president Barack Obama, were tested positive for ricin. Each letter contained the message "I am KC and I approve this message"	Evertt Dutschke

Date	Method	Death	Injured	Location	Detail	Perpetrator
Nov 1, 2013	Shooting	1	6)	Los Angeles, CA	Paul Anthony Ciancia entered the checkpoint at the Los Angeles International Airport and fired his rifle, killing one Transportation Security Administration officer and injuring six others. The motivation behind the attack was Paul's inspiration of the anti-government agenda of the New World Order conspiracy theory.	Paul Anthony Ciancia
Dec 13, 2013	Bombing attempt	0	0	Wichita, KS	58-year-old avionics technician, identified as Terry Lee Loewen, was arrested on December 13, 2013, for attempting a suicide bombing at Wichita Mid-Continent Airport, where he was employed.	Terry Lee Loewen
Apr 13, 2014	Shootings	3	0	Overland Park, KS	A pair of shootings committed by a lone gunman occurred at the Jewish Community Center of Greater Kansas City and Village Shalom, a Jewish retirement community, in Overland Park, Kansas.	Frazier Glenn Miller, Jr.
Apr 27, 2014	Shootings	1	0	Seattle, WA	Ali Muhammad Brown shot and killed a man who was walking home from a store. This killing was part of a series of terrorism related killings in the states of Washington and New Jersey.	Ali Muhammad Brown
Jun 1, 2014	Shootings	2	0	Seattle, Washington	Ali Muhammad Brown shot and killed two men outside a Seattle gay nightclub. These killings were part of a series of terrorism related killings in the states of Washington and New Jersey.	Ali Muhammad Brown
Jun 8, 2014	Shooting	3 (+2)	0	Las Vegas, Nevada	Two police officers and one civilian died in a shooting spree in the Las Vegas Valley committed by a couple who espoused anti-government views and were reportedly inspired by the outcome of the Bundy standoff.	Jerad and Amanda Miller

Date	Method	Death	Injured	Location	Detail	Perpetrator
Jun 25, 2014	Shootings	1	0	West Orange, NJ	Ali Muhammad Brown shot and killed a man who was driving home from college while stopped at a traffic light. This killing was part of a series of terrorism related killings in the states of Washington and New Jersey.	Ali Muhammad Brown
Sept 12, 2014	Shooting	1	1	Blooming Grove, PA	Two Pennsylvania State Policemen were shot in a sniper attack nearby a police barracks, one died. Eric Frein arrested after a 48-day manhunt.	Eric Frein
Sept 24, 2014	Stabbing	1	1 (+1)	Moore, OK	Vaughan Foods beheading incident: Alton Alexander Nolen aka "Jah'Keem Yisrael" attacked two employees at Vaughan Foods, beheading one and stabbing the other before being shot and injured by Vaughan Foods' Chief Operating Officer.	Alton Alexander Nolen "Jah'Keem Yisrael"
Oct 23, 2014	Melee attack	0 (+1)	3	New York City, NY	Zale Thompson injured two New York City Police Department (NYPD) officers, once critically at a Queens, New York City shopping district by striking them with a hatchet.	Zale Thompson
Dec 18, 2014	Cyberattack	0	0	United States	"The Guardians of Peace" linked by the United States to North Korea launched a cyberattack against SONY pictures. Embarrassing private emails were published and the organization threatened attacks against theaters that showed The Interview, a satire which depicted the assassination of North Korean leader Kim Jong Un.	North Korea
May 3, 2015	Shooting	0 (+2)	1	Garland, TX	Two gunmen opened fire outside the Curtis Culwell Center during an art exhibit hosted by an anti-Muslim group called the American Freedom Defense Initiative in Garland, Texas.	Elton Simpson, Nadir Hamid Soofi, and Abdul Malik Abdul Kareem

Date	Method	Death	Injured	Location	Detail	Perpetrator
Jun 2, 2015	Stabbing	0 (+1)	0	Boston, MA	Police investigating a planned Islamic terrorist attack on police confronted Usaama Rahim to question him. He pulled out a military knife, and was eventually shot and killed by police as he approached them with the knife. David Wright was later arrested and charged with planning a terrorist attack with Usaama Rahim.	Usaama Rahim and David Wright
Jul 16, 2015	Shootings	5 (+1)	2	Chattanooga, TN	Muhammad Youssef Abdulazeez opened fire on two military installations in Chattanooga, Tennessee. He first committed a drive-by shooting at a recruiting center, then traveled to a naval reserve center and continued firing.	Muhammad Youssef Abdulazeez
Nov 4, 2015	Stabbing	0 (+1)	4	Merced, CA	Faisal Mohammad, armed with a hunting knife, stabbed four people at the University of California before being shot and killed by police.	Faisal Mohammad
Nov 27, 2015	Shooting	3	9	Colorado Springs, CO	Robert L. Dear, armed with a semi-automatic rifle opened fire at a Colorado Springs Planned Parenthood clinic.	Robert Dear
Dec 2, 2015	Shooting	14 (+2)	24	San Bernardino, CA	A mass shooting occurred at the Inland Regional Center in San Bernardino, CA. Two suspects fled in an SUV, but were later killed.	Rizwan Farook and Tashfeen Malik
Jan 7, 2016	Shooting	0	1 (+1)	Philadelphia, PA	A man shot at a police officer in his cruiser multiple times, injuring him in the process. The officer returned fire injuring the assailant. The assailant later pledged allegiance to ISIL, citing it as his reason for the attack.	Edward Archer
Feb 11, 2016	Melee attack	0 (+1)	4	Columbus, OH	A man with a machete attacked them at random. After a car chase, the assailant, who was from the West African nation of Guinea, was killed by police.	Mohamed Barry

Date	Method	Death	Injured	Location	Detail	Perpetrator
Jun 12, 2016	Shooting, hostage taking	49 (+1)	58	Orlando, FL	Orlando nightclub shooting: 49 people were killed and 53 were injured in a terrorist attack at a gay nightclub in Orlando, Florida.	Omar Mateen, American-born citizen with Afghan immigrant
Aug 20, 2016	Stabbings	0	2	Roanoke, VA	Wasil Farooqui stabbed a man and a woman in a random attack at an apartment complex.	Wasil Farooqui
Sept 17, 2016	Stabbings	0 (+1)	10	St. Cloud, MN	Mass stabbing occurred at the Crossroads Center shopping mall in St. Cloud, Minnesota. ISIL claimed responsibility for the attack through its Amaq media agency, claiming Adan "was a soldier of the Islamic State".	ISIS member Dahir A. Adan
Sept 17 - 19, 2016	Bombings	0	34 (+1)	New Jersey and New York City	Four bombings or bombing attempts occurred in the New York metropolitan area, specifically in Seaside Park, New Jersey; Manhattan, New York; and Elizabeth, New Jersey. The attacker was motivated and inspired by the extremist Islamic ideology espoused by al-Qaeda founder Osama bin Laden and al-Qaeda chief propagandist Anwar al-Awlaki.	Ahmad Khan Rahimi
Nov 28, 2016	Vehicle attack, stabbing	0 (+1)	13	Columbus, OH	A car ramming attack and mass stabbing occurred at Ohio State University (OSU)'s Watts Hall in Columbus, Ohio by attacker, Somali refugee Abdul Razak Ali Artan, who was inspired by terrorist propaganda from the Islamic State of Iraq and the Levant and radical Muslim cleric Anwar al-Awlaki.	Abdul Razak Ali Artan

Date	Method	Death	Injured	Location	Detail	Perpetrator
Mar 20, 2017	Stabbing by sword	1	0	New York City, NY	Timothy Caughman, 66, was attacked in Midtown Manhattan with a sword, killing him. Police allege ties to White Supremacist hate groups.	White Supremacist James Harris Jackson
Aug 12, 2017	Vehicle-ramming attack	1	28	Charlottesville, VA	James Alex Fields Jr. intentionally drove his car into a group of counter-demonstrators at the Unite the Right rally in Charlottesville, Virginia.	White Supremacist James Alex Fields Jr.
Aug 5, 2017	Bombing	0	0	Bloomington, MN	An explosive device shattered windows and damaged an office at the mosque, which primarily serves people from the area's large Somali community.	Unknown
Oct 31, 2017	Vehicle-ramming attack	8	11 (+1)	New York City, NY	An ISIS-inspired man drove a rented Home Depot flatbed pickup truck in a vehicle-ramming attack on cyclists and runners along 1 mile (1.6 km) of a bike path alongside West Street in Lower Manhattan,	Sayfullo Saipov
Feb 16, 2018	Assault with vehicle	0	3	New Jersey East Orange,	A man crashed a stolen truck into a Planned Parenthood clinic, injuring a pregnant woman and two others.	Marckles Alcius
Oct 22, 2018	Bombing	0	0	United States Several states	In late October 2018, at least twelve packages containing pipe bombs were mailed within the U.S. Postal Service system to several prominent critics of U.S. President Donald Trump, including various Democratic Party politicians (Hillary Clinton, Barack Obama, Joe Biden, Eric Holder, Debbie Wasserman Schultz, Maxine Waters, Cory Booker), actor Robert De Niro, billionaire investor George Soros, former CIA Director John O. Brennan, and former Director of National Intelligence James Clapper.	Cesar Sayoc Jr.

Source: Collated from National Consortium for the study of terrorism and responses to terrorism (2016). Global terrorism database, University of Maryland (globalterrorismdb_0616dist.xlsx, Retrieved from https://www.start.umd.edu/gtd/).

Corrections

Chapter 7

Punishment in the Latter Half of the 20th Century

Examining Empiricism and Its Role in Assessing Correctional Policy

Ricky S. Gutierrez

"The degree of civilization in a society can be judged by entering its prisons."

—Fyodor Dostoevsky (1917)

Introduction

The penal system contributes heavily to the permanent marginalization of economically disadvantaged people of color, an outcome magnified by the scale of the penal system since the early 2000s. Prison population growth may be explained in part as resulting from the abolition of parole and related statutes in the 1970s; drug-reform laws that began under Reagan in the 1980s; and tough-on-crime reforms for certain types of offenders and mandatory sentencing laws in the 1990s. As a result of more than a quarter century of growth, in 2003 the scale of the penal population exceeded its historic average by a factor of nearly five (Western, 2006). Furthermore, a clear pattern emerges when we consider the greatly inflated incarceration rates among minority males who are statistically less educated, have fewer work skills, and who tend to reside in communities and live in families that are economically disadvantaged. Social inequality, permanent marginalization, inescapable poverty, and the associated barriers to healthcare, education, work, and civil rights are part of the nexus of collateral damage suffered by those reentering their communities after serving penal sentences.

Politics and Policies in the 20th Century Approaching Punishment in the Pre- and Post-Civil Rights Era

In the 1950s and 1960s, the prevailing belief among academics and practitioners alike was that offenders could be reformed through education, counseling, and job training, and the correctional system was seen as a way to prepare offenders to rejoin society (Loury, 2008; Pager, 2007). Empirical studies in the late 1960s and early 1970s countered this optimistic outlook in revealing the questionable efficacy of prison and parole services during this time. As crime rates rose in the 1960s and continued to rise through the 1970s, public opinion polls consistently registered high anxiety regarding the issue of crime. At the outset of the 1970s, political progressives viewed the irrelevance of prisons in crime policy while conservatives were convinced that prisons were instrumental to the war on crime—and as such, penal policy should view prisons as key institutes of punishment and retributive justice (Clear, 2007; Zimring and Hawkins, 1991). Conservative politicians espousing the "law and order" platform in the 1960s and 1970s used their influence to target and focus blame on street crime as the primary cause for the increase in crime, as well as insinuate that the major culprit in the increased crime rate was African American criminality (Western, 2006). Rising crime rates prompted changes in state penal codes that reflected increases in the frequency and duration of prison terms for those convicted of felonies. At the same time, an influential review by Robert Martinson concluded that the rehabilitation of offenders was not an efficacious practice (Martinson, 1974). This led to the retributive policy emphasis on punishment and containment that followed, as well as escalation of policing, prosecution, and imprisonment of offenders. Felons were no longer viewed as persons to be supported through rehabilitative efforts, but were instead regarded as risks that needed to be contained within the penal system (Loury, 2008). In the late 1970s and early 1980s, conservative politicians offered a new public framework of crime as being a problem of moral order (Phillips, 1969). Crime was not viewed as an indicator of the failings of a social system, but rather as a symptom of moral corruption (Bennett, DiIulio, & Walters, 1996). Federal drug laws in the Ronald Reagan and George H. W. Bush administrations provided for mandatory prison sentences of 5 years for possession of extremely small amounts of drugs when they were presumed to be "for distribution." These policy reforms were intended to reduce judicial discretion in sentencing, and by the end of the decade, a dozen states had passed sentencing guidelines to enable more stringent standards (Clear, 2007).

The effect of the shift in penal policy focus and the populations who were most impacted are critical considerations when constructing an accurate account of the pre- and post-civil rights eras. The first consideration is that the multitudes of the impoverished are essentially invisible to the middle class and more affluent social strata. This has been the case for many years, but we will focus on the early 1960s when the veil separating the "haves" from the "have nots" was intact and when sustained economic growth seemed assured long into the future. While the ranks of the economically disadvantaged continued to swell, their needs were essentially "off the beaten path" for policy makers (Harrington, 1962). Incarceration makes the economically disadvantaged invisible due to the fact that prison populations are omitted from the data source used to track economic trends. The penal system also influences the distribution of labor by reducing the number of mostly young, able-bodied men engaging in productive employment. Therefore the public was virtually unaware that significant numbers of the poor were not enjoying the "fair weather" times in the early 1960s. There was, however, a building storm that would target and place blame for crime on economically disadvantaged, marginalized populations.

Research on criminal punishment reveals that the shift in focus to vilifying the economically disadvantaged and marginalized populations tends to occur in three ways. First, the political platform of associating economically disadvantaged and marginalized populations with the perpetuation of crime and racial threat prompts the design of laws that will target and contain the perceived threat. Residential segregation, one factor of social inequality, had a significant impact in the negative labeling of economically disadvantaged people of color. Vagrancy laws are another example of how poverty was criminalized (Dubber, 2001). Second, there is a tendency for police to target, investigate, and arrest the economically disadvantaged more frequently than the affluent. Ethnographers suggest that the purchase and use of drugs, drunkenness, and domestic disturbance are more easily tracked in public urban settings than in private suburban homes (Western, 2006). Thus, the impoverished are treated with more suspicion as a result of their higher incidence of arrest. Third, once they are adjudicated in court, economically disadvantaged defendants who have few social and economic support systems may be viewed as more worthy of blame, and, significantly, as having decreased potential for rehabilitation.

Examining Punishment During the Drug War

Musto (1989) described a cyclical pattern of American tolerance and intolerance of drug and alcohol use. The prevalent attitude of personal choice and autonomy concerning alcohol use during the early part of the 19th century, and marijuana use during the 1960s, was followed by periods of uncompromising prohibition and punitive legislation. By 1850, a dozen states legislated the prohibition of alcohol and eventually the temperance movement late in the 19th century led to national alcohol prohibition. Although use of cocaine and opium was initially treated with indifference in the 1890s, intolerance of drug use gradually built and eventually produced the Harrison Act of 1914, the first major federal narcotics legislation. During the Great Depression, White families had to compete for scarce jobs with Mexican immigrant and Mexican-American families. In response, White labor leaders, politicians, and publishers created a false narrative demonizing Mexicans as marijuana users and that the use of marijuana caused violence. These actions placed Mexicans and Mexican-Americans at a disadvantage in the labor market and led to the first federal marijuana law, the Marijuana Tax Act of 1937 (Bertram, Blachman, Sharpe, & Andreas, 1996; Musto, 1999). Demonizing the use of marijuana, demonstrably less harmful than tobacco or alcohol, had far-reaching consequences in the 1990s when nearly 8% of the growth in drug arrests were charged with possession of marijuana (King & Mauer, 2005).

The more current period of drug use intolerance began in the early 1970s with Nixon's declared war on drugs. Prior to this time, crime and criminal justice policy had largely been regarded as an issue of state and local jurisdiction. The new policy emphasis on law and order marked the beginning of the politicization of criminal justice (Pager, 2007). The temporal relevance of promoting more stringent anti-drug laws was given a boost by conditions in the Vietnam War. Drug use was prevalent among American military personnel serving in Vietnam (Baum, 1997) and it was feared that returning military personnel, an estimated 20% of whom were addicted to heroin, would fuel a crime wave in the United States. Thus, Richard Nixon's crime-fighting platform in 1968 resulted in his declaring a war on drugs in 1971 (Terkel, 1997). The Drug Enforcement Administration created in 1973 in due course became permanent—one of the results of a retributive-oriented policy design.

Policy initiatives introduced by both the Nixon and Reagan administrations resulted in the dramatic increase of drug enforcement during the 1970s and 1980s. The number of arrests associated with drug crimes increased by 170% from 1980–2001, and prison admissions for each arrest increased six-fold, from 2 to 12% (Western, 2006). Time served for drug-related offenses increased sharply as well. Considering the multiple factors of the significant increase in drug-related arrests, the likelihood of imprisonment that accompanied a drug-related conviction, the risk of parole revocation in these cases, and increase in time served due to mandatory sentencing, together produced more than a ten-fold increase in the incarcerations based on drug-related offenses between 1980 and 2001 (Western, 2006). An additional factor that contributed to the prison boom was a draconian resurgence in mandatory prison sentences of 10, 20, and 30 years issuing from drug-related convictions, as well as life imprisonment without hope of parole.

Drug-related offenses constituted approximately 24%, 20%, and 55% of the offenses for which jail, state, and federal inmates, respectively, were incarcerated in 2001 (Harrison & Beck, 2003). Importantly, irrespective of the offense category, many inmates indicate that they committed the offense to obtain money for drugs (24% of jail inmates, 19% of state prisoners, and 16% of federal inmates). Significantly, 36%, 33%, and 22% of jail, state, and federal inmates, respectively, reported being under the influence of drugs when they committed their current offense (Harlow, 1998; Mumola, 1999; Wilson, 2000).

The generally held notion is that drug users are presumed to be harmed by their drug use and that their drug use harms others. Although first-time offense candidates are usually referred for rehabilitation treatment, repeat offenders viewed as having a serious affliction generally receive a more severe form of punishment. Alternatively, drug abuse may be more accurately viewed as an illness, and punishing the ill is inhumane, or worse, barbaric (Sterling, 2004). A more effective, evidence-based corrections policy would be a shift of focus from viewing drug use as a criminal justice issue to that of drug use as an issue of public health, thus a redirection to treatment and prevention. In 2006, the National Institute on Drug Abuse (NIDA) published a research-based guide outlining 13 principles of substance abuse treatment for criminal justice–involved populations. The conclusion of the NIDA report is that drug addiction is a brain disorder that affects behavior. However, a policy shift from drug use as an issue of criminal justice to one of public health would be a heavy lift in many areas, not the least of which is a monetary loss to local law enforcement agencies. Worrall's (2001) research of the budgetary practices of over 1,400 local law enforcement agencies across the United States revealed that many of these agencies depended significantly on the revenue generated from civil asset forfeiture, which is the seizure and forfeiture of property connected with drug crimes, and constitutes a major source of annual budgets for many law enforcement agencies (Worrall, 2001). Coherent with this line of reasoning, there may be disincentive to adopt more progressive drug policies not inclusive of civil asset forfeiture practices since these policies would represent a significant monetary loss to law enforcement agency budgets.

Due to several factors, the increase in drug-related convictions led to exacerbated disparity in the prison population. Poor urban areas are the prime markets for drug activity, and street-level distribution is predominantly occupied by men of color (Clear, 2007). In addition, although there was widespread use of cocaine across income levels during the 1980s, the structure of penalties favored those of middle- and upper-income levels. The minimum amount of powder cocaine required to trigger mandatory sentencing under federal drug laws is *100 times greater* than for the crack cocaine equivalent. Given that the crack form of cocaine is cheaper, its use is more prevalent among the economically disadvantaged. Thus, these drug laws that impact communities in disparate ways ensure that the prevalent demographics of who gets locked up are the economically disadvantaged, and given urban policing departments' tactical focus on disadvantaged minority neighborhoods, they are persons of color. There is tactical advantage to making arrests in impoverished, socially disorganized neighborhoods wherein many routine activities of life, including drug dealing, take place out of doors. In working-class and middle-income neighborhoods, these same activities may occur, but it is more likely that they will occur indoors (Tonry, 1995). The legal sanctions and rules adopted by the Supreme Court virtually guarantee that those who are imprisoned and ultimately permanently disenfranchised are overwhelmingly Black and Brown. There is an additional consideration in the complex issue of drug use and who goes to prison. While there was focus on crack cocaine abuse among the African American population during the 1980s in particular, in 1991 nearly 2.5 million Whites reported lifetime use of crack cocaine compared with 999,000 Blacks (Alcohol, Drug Abuse, and Mental Health Administration (ADAMHA), 1992). The fact that there was a significantly higher number of White crack users than Black crack users reported did not factor into public awareness or opinion.

There is no evidence that more severe penalties and increased drug-related convictions lowered the level of drug use in the United States. Drug use had been on the decline for years before the war on drugs was re-emphasized by Reagan in the late 1980s, and this policy cannot claim credit for the continuation of preexisting trends (Zimring & Hawkins, 1991; Tonry, 1995). A well-documented historical record demonstrates that policy makers tend to overreact in the design and implementation of antidrug policies during times when social mores are becoming less accepting of the use of drugs, and this was certainly the case during this timeframe. The tough-on-crime policies and associated prison boom continued to grow unfettered through succeeding administrations. The platform justifying increased incarceration was a surge in crime exemplified in the 1992 U.S. Department of Justice report titled "The Case for More Incarceration." However, official crime and victimization statistics do not support this conclusion. While crime rates continue to fall, incarceration has played some role in the decline, but the magnitude of the effect, as well as the cost effectiveness compared to other possible interventions (Pager, 2007), does not justify incarceration as the primary policy and practice. There are other, even less visible costs in supporting the needs of an overinflated prison system. In response to the prison boom in California between 1984 and 1994, the Department of Corrections increased its workforce by more than 25,000, while the burden of this increase was borne by education. During this same timeframe, there was a decline of more than 8,000 employees in higher education (Chambliss, 1999; Currie, 1998). This is yet another example of collateral damage in shifting state funding allocations in response to ongoing retributive model of corrections policies and practice.

The "get-tough-on-crime" political agenda is appealing to stakeholders, including policy promoters in general because empirical evidence of its effectiveness cannot be used to completely negate it. Irrespective of the fact that this policy stance appears to have little to no impact on crime reduction rates, and is responsible for the uptick of convictions and extreme overcrowding of prisons, supporters of "three-strikes" laws and other enhanced sentences invariably insist we need to get tougher to appreciate greater results (Clark, Austin, & Henry, 1997; Cullen, Pratt, Miceli, & Moon, 2002; Pratt, 2009; Pratt & Cullen, 2005).

Changes in Sentencing in the Obama Era

By the time President Barack Obama was elected, the war on drugs had become institutionalized. It was no longer a special program or politicized platform; it was business as usual in the prosecution of drug-related offenses. African Americans are six to seven times more likely than Whites to be incarcerated in jail or prison. There are more African American adults under current correctional control in prison, jail, or on probation or parole, than were in enslaved in 1850 (Alexander, 2010). This is a major contributing factor in the circumstances that a Black child born today is less likely to be raised by both parents than a Black child born during times of slavery (Cherlin, 1992). In 1991, the rate of African Americans incarcerated in jails or prisons was 6.47 times higher than Whites (Tonry, 1995). There is an especially high percentage of African American males in prison, a population which has expanded continually since 1980. This high rate of imprisonment does not correspond to increases in the proportion of serious crimes committed by African Americans. While African Americans comprise 13% of the United States population, they comprise nearly one half of those incarcerated in jails and prisons. More African American men are imprisoned today than in any other time in our nation's history.

President Obama was deeply concerned about criminal justice reform, sentencing practices, and policing. He acted on those concerns and was the first sitting president to personally visit a federal corrections facility. While there, he engaged in dialogue with the inmates so as to gain further insight and become better informed on the issues that most concern inmates, and with this added perspective, develop alternative policies. Barack Obama was the first president in over half a century to orchestrate a sustained reduction in the rate of incarceration nationwide. During his two terms in office, President Obama granted pardon, commutation of sentence, remission of fine or restitution, or reprieve to 1,927 individuals convicted of federal crimes. He was also concerned about the disparate sentencing regarding possession of cocaine versus crack cocaine and the issues of racial inequity. The U.S. Sentencing Commission recommended to Congress twice that the penalties for possession of cocaine and crack cocaine be equalized in 1995 and again in 2002. However, Congress did not approve sentencing changes as were recommended. President Obama lobbied for and signed the Fair Sentencing Act of 2010, a statute that eliminated the mandatory minimum sentence for possession of crack cocaine as well as reducing the sentencing disparity between possession of cocaine versus crack cocaine. He launched initiatives promoting community policing and alternatives to incarceration. Through an executive order, President Obama also terminated the use of solitary confinement for juvenile inmates in federal penal institutions.

On May 23, 2011, the U.S. Supreme Court upheld an order requiring the state of California to reduce its state prison population to no more than 137.5% of its designed capacity within a period of 2 years. This was California's Safety Realignment Initiative, an attempt to reduce the state prison population by shifting much of that population to county jails. The history of the conditions that prompted the initiative was that the state prison population had risen to approximately 180% of the designed capacity, and the consequences of the extreme overcrowding included the inability for inmates to receive routine medical and mental health care. The Supreme Court held in a 5:4 decision that the California Department of Corrections and Rehabilitation had violated inmates' Eighth Amendment rights protecting them from cruel and unusual punishment. In response to the Supreme Court decision, the governor and state legislature passed Assembly Bill 109 and Assembly Bill 117, which became law on October 1, 2011. Under these laws, new offenders with nonviolent, non-serious, and nonsexual felonies with sentences longer than 1 year would be housed in county jail facilities, placing them under county-directed supervision rather than state parole. These laws provided new funding for county facilities for the management of the increase in inmate population. Each county created a Community Corrections Partnership to oversee implementation of the realignment.

After 15 months, approximately 24,000 inmates who would have served time in state prison were moved to county jails. In April of 2013, Governor Jerry Brown asked the federal court to rescind the order, citing a reduced prison population and improved healthcare provision. However, the Court rejected Governor Brown's challenge to which he responded in his May 2013 declaration that the state would not be able to fully meet the court order. He proposed a series of measures to continue to reduce prison overcrowding and achieve the goal of being within 2,570 inmates of the 137.5% goal. The measures included sending more inmates to firefighting camp, housing state inmates out of state, the issuance of medical parole, and leasing some private prisons. The underlying causes of mass incarceration and overcrowding remain largely unchanged, however, in that overcrowding has been instead transferred to county jails.

Anticipating Changes in the Trump Era

In the United States which comprises just 5% of the world's population, our prison system houses 25% of the world's inmate population (Loury, 2008). In our present configuration and for the foreseeable future, the aggregation of prisoners at any given time is a function of human flows between the prison system and the community. The retributive philosophy that underpins the criminal justice system sanctions relatively onerous sentences for a broad range of offenses and results in accelerating the massive expansion and overpopulation of prisons and associated institutions. The average duration of incarceration in state prison is roughly 28 months (Pager, 2007), a fact which results in a steady flow of individuals transitioning between prisons and their respective communities. Given the statistics associated with mass incarceration and resulting flow of ex-offenders into communities, there are previously unanticipated consequences that impact and heighten inequalities. There is a dearth of systematic research on the success with which ex-offenders are able to secure work, and the few existing studies reveal disturbing results. Controlled studies reveal seriously detrimental and lasting economic penalties, as well as a significant negative impact on subsequent job attainment and job security, for those who have a record of incarceration (Sampson & Laub, 1993). Returning inmates are faced with substantial legal and social barriers in their quest to secure employment and become self-sustaining. The "tough-on-crime" stance of the Trump administration will most assuredly result in the creation of more prisons (including for-profit prisons) and more rigid penalties, resulting in longer sentencing. The negative effects of incarceration result in a wide range of legal and social restrictions on employment and substantial barriers to reintegration into society. Assumptions about the criminality of young African American males based on false associations may intensify negative reactions to this group in particular. Surveys of employer groups have revealed that two-thirds of employers would not knowingly hire an ex-offender (Holzer, 2006). Given the annual 600,000–700,000 ex-offenders who return to home communities (Pager, 2007), this factor alone has dire implications for communities, community support agencies, and issues of homelessness. The California Department of Corrections estimates that on any given day, 10% of parolees are homeless, and in Los Angeles and San Francisco, the percentage of homeless parolees is between 30 to 50% (Pager, 2007).

Research on Recidivism and Prisoner Reentry

In 1974, Robert Martinson's "nothing works" article had a devastating effect on rehabilitative efforts and steered policy makers toward more punitive and retributive goals for the prison system. More recently, Jans (2002) argues that rehabilitation is not a subject that garners much support in American debates on crime. Leaving aside the more controversial topic of rehabilitation, assessing the efficacy of prisoner reentry programs should be an important area of contemporary concern for policy makers since so many offenders are being released annually. According to Schwarzfeld, Weiss, Plotkin, and Draper (2008), close to 700,000 ex-offenders are released from prison each year, and more than 9 million are released annually from local jails. An estimated 95% of all those incarcerated in state-run facilities will return to the community at some point in time. However, recent data on released offenders leads us to anticipate that two-thirds of offenders will be rearrested within

3 years of release (Mears, Wang, Hay & Bales, 2008). Decker (2007) reiterates the theme, reporting that the most troubling aspect of recidivism is that 52% of released offenders are returned to prison within this 3-year time window. Research by Johnson-Listwan, Cullen, and Latessa (2006) examined ways to enhance the effectiveness of reentry programs. They purport that rehabilitation can work for offenders, assuming that evidence-based and widely known principles of effective intervention are implemented.

There are relevant demographic considerations in developing an informed understanding of recidivism and reentry. Demographic data indicate that prison populations are undereducated and underemployed prior to incarceration. Findings published by the Bureau of Justice Statistics cite that approximately 41% of federal, state, and county inmates 18 years and older did not complete high school or a GED, compared with 18% of the general population (Harlow, 2003). The data further indicate that less educated inmates are more likely to recidivate than more educated inmates. Research focused on isolating the most critical risk factors associated with criminal behavior has identified personal education, vocational achievement, and post-secondary correctional education as being significantly associated with the reduction of recidivism (Andrews, 2001; Chappell, 2004). Closely associated with this paradigm is wage disparity, as it does not end with exiting the criminal justice system and those with felony conviction records find it extremely difficult to secure well-paid jobs. Research has demonstrated that men released from prison or jail earn less and are employed less than those who have not been incarcerated (Grogger, 1995; Kling, 1999; Lott, 1990; Waldfogel, 1994).

Given the high rate of substance and alcohol abuse among inmates, the term of incarceration can provide a focused opportunity for the screening, assessment, detoxification, and treatment of offenders with substance abuse problems. The provision of these services, especially when continued in the community setting upon release, has been demonstrated to reduce recidivism and substance abuse as documented in numerous studies of corrections-based treatment for substance abuse disorders (De Leon, 1985; De Leon, Melnick, Thomas, Kressel, & Wexler, 2000; Pearson & Lipton, 1999). There is evidence that substance abuse treatment provided to inmates while incarcerated reduces recidivism rates by approximately 6%, and substance abuse treatment provided in the community to which the ex-offenders are released has been shown to reduce recidivism by roughly 12% (Aos, Miller, & Drake, 2006). Inmates over 25 years of age are significantly more likely to remain in penal institution-based substance abuse treatment programs (Klein & Moeschberger, 1997; Krebs, Brady, & Laird, 2003; Saxon, Wells, Fleming, Jackson, & Calsyn, 1996) and length of time spent in these substance abuse programs is a strong predictor of success and greatly reduces recidivism as well.

Following a period of incarceration, the primary agencies charged with supervision of the reentry processes are state departments of parole. Early criminal justice policies viewed parole as integral to the corrections process. Accordingly, upon release parole officers facilitated every step of the reintegration process including helping ex-offenders secure housing, locating community resources, securing employment, and developing a social network that together supported desistance from crime. However, along with disillusionment in the ideal of rehabilitation of ex-offenders came the disbelief that parole was an effective policy and practice and, as a result, parole budgets were significantly reduced. The current parole paradigm is focused on surveillance and detection rather than efforts to support successful reintegration. It is hardly surprising that these shifts in policy and practice have manifested in roughly three fourths of ex-offenders remaining unemployed 1 year after release (Pager, 2007).

Community Research

The experience of incarceration primarily instructs inmates in coping behaviors that facilitate their survival while imprisoned rather than how to handle the complexities of being part of a community (Halsey, 2008). Examination of empirical research reveals a dearth of relevant factors of the impact of communities to which former offenders are returned. Instead, the community context is held as a constant and thus the influence of community on reentry not visible in the research. A notable exception is a study conducted in 2006, which examined the impact of community on recidivism and found that ex-offenders who return to disadvantaged communities recidivate at a greater rate than those who return to resource rich communities (Kubrin & Stewart, 2006). In our efforts to reduce recidivism, a focal point for future research should be the neighborhood structure–recidivism relationship in general, and to increase our understanding of the community-level processes that most impact recidivism (Sampson, Morenoff, & Gannon-Rowley, 2002).

Community effects were impacted by the war on drugs in multiple ways. In the late 1980s congressional anti-drug laws were intended to achieve a solution to the problem of drug users. The Anti-Drug Abuse Act of 1988 provided that anyone convicted of a state or federal drug offense would be ineligible for most federal benefits (P.L. 100-690, sec. 5301). The collateral damage of a retributive criminal justice stance regarding drug use goes far beyond that. In 2002, the U.S. Supreme Court upheld a provision of the Anti-Drug Abuse Act of 1988 that permitted families of drug users to be evicted from public housing. The consequences are that a person convicted or suspected of using drugs can be barred from visiting his or her parents if he or she lives in public housing (Sterling, 2004). Congress permanently denied welfare and food stamps to families when a parent has a felony drug conviction (P.L. 104–193, sec. 115; 42 U.S.C. 862a; August 22, 1996). The right to vote is lost upon a felony conviction in most states; thus, another consequence of the drug war is that the deprivation of voting rights has spread throughout the U.S. population.

Programmatic Research

A meta-analysis conducted by Lipton, Pearson, Cleland, and Yee, (2002) examined the effects of therapeutic communities (TCs) on recidivism. The findings indicated that TCs are effective strategies in reducing recidivism and that in particular increased time spent in treatment appears to be associated with significant reductions in recidivism. Lipton and colleagues (2002). indicate that the length of TC treatment should be measured "from onset in the penal institution, through the transition to community-based TC treatment, to discharge from the community-based TC" (p. 65). Related to this finding, Inciardi, Martin, Butzin, Hooper, and Harrison (1997) developed and tested the effectiveness of a multistage TC. The three stages of the TC continuum of care include the following:

+ Prison-based TC
+ Community-based work release TC (e.g., inpatient treatment)
+ Community-based aftercare component (e.g., outpatient treatment)

Analysis of 3- and 5-year post-release outcomes of this multistage TC treatment for substance abuse–involved offenders indicates that there is long-term support for the continuum model of TC treatment (Martin, Butzin, Saum, & Inciardi, 1999). Three years after release, offenders who received the full continuum of care were seven times more likely to be drug free and over twice as likely to be arrest free as compared with the control group who did not participate in the continuum of TC treatment (Martin, et al. 1999). Similarly, 5 years after release, analyses indicated that 42% of those who completed the continuum of care returned to custody compared to 86% of those who completed only the in-prison program (Prendergast, Hall, Wexler, Melnick, & Cao, 2004).

Correctional facility-based treatment models that produce more consistently positive outcomes include a comprehensive scope of services including the following: therapeutic communities (e.g., participative, group therapy approach); cognitive-behavioral treatment; correctional education programs; and, where available, segregation from the remainder of the inmate population while in treatment (Aos et al., 2006; Krebs et al., 2003; Peters, Kearns, Murrin, Dolente, & May,1993; Petersilia, 2003; Shrum, 2004). Therapeutic communities (TC) generally require that the inmates in treatment are segregated from the general inmate population through completion of the program. This factor complicates implementation of TC programs as institution resources such as space and personnel are frequently quite limited. Cognitive-behavioral treatment with an emphasis on relapse prevention is an option that does not require separation of those who are in treatment. As much as is practicable, individualized programs designed to be suited to the specific needs of the offender promote program completion as well as successful outcomes (NIDA, 2006). The provision of educational services while inmates are incarcerated is another important factor, especially in terms of successful reentry into ex-offenders' communities wherein employment opportunities and general labor market conditions require a technologically mediated skill-set base as well as facility with abstract thinking and innovative planning skills (Helms, Costanza, & Gutierrez, 2016). In addition, Kunitz, Woodall, Zhao, Wheeler, Lillis, and Rogers, (2002) found that the offender outcomes success rates increased when corrections-based substance abuse treatment programs were both culturally and individually relevant. In addition, it is important to recognize that offenders with co-occurring substance abuse and mental health issues most often require an integrated treatment approach. A synthesis of the foregoing underscores the importance of a holistic approach in community reentry (Helms et al., 2016). The linkages between community contexts and the reentry process is a necessary focus of ongoing empirical research, especially in terms of its impact on corrections and rehabilitative services (Gutierrez, 2003).

Policy Research

An organizing principle to understand current criminal justice policy, specifically the numerous noteworthy failures of policies pursued, is to view it from three focal points. The first of these is a failure to institute policies that are effective in reducing crime and the corollary of reducing the damage to the community that it causes. The second is failure to identify crimes as harmful acts perpetuated by those in positions of power and wealth. The third is failure to eliminate economic bias in the criminal justice system (Reiman, 2001). As has been argued in this chapter, and as demonstrated in empirical studies, effective control of crime cannot be accomplished by simply adding to the police force and incarcerating ever greater numbers of citizens. There are other programmatic solutions focused on rehabilitation and prevention of reoffending that empirical evidence demonstrates as being effective in reducing recidivism. In addition, the support needed to rehabilitate offenders is a continuum that begins within correctional facilities and upon completion of sentence and release, extends seamlessly into the community with effective reentry educational programs aligned with the results of empirical research.

The second factor in this trifecta of rationale as to why criminal justice policy is not working in some key areas may be more difficult to comprehend because conceptual impairments have been purposefully erected to obscure our societal view. We have, as a society, "bought in" to the paradigm that crime is caused by individuals, usually members of the lower echelons of society, who would seek to do us harm for their personal gain. If we can leave that assumption aside and instead consider the bigger picture in assessing the dangers of the workplace, the medical profession, the environmental issues such as pollution and air quality, and the all-encompassing effects of poverty, we can appreciate the societal rather than individual factors at play. Consider for a moment that these factors cause more human suffering and death and have an astronomically higher cost differential than the annually reported thefts, aggravated assaults, and murders documented by the FBI (Reiman, 2001). A government that is truly intent on protecting its citizens could enforce workplace safety regulations as well as proactively legislate new protections as the need arises; it could police the medical profession and put an end to malpractice as well as overprescribing pharmaceuticals such as opioids as a panacea to medical ills; it could require that environmental laws are stringently enforced and routinely scrutinized and reviewed; and it could stem poverty and its many deleterious effects by ensuring that income-based supplemental funding is robust so that no family must suffer the multiple disabilities associated with poverty and generational income deprivation.

The third factor has to do with economic class structure, as well as the benefits afforded to those who have the financial means to subvert the intentions of democratic principles in favor of protecting the wealthy or privileged class. As evidence of this bias, a substantial number of studies comparing economically disadvantaged offenders with those of middle- to upper-income offenders, including the racial disparity statistics, were reviewed. For the same crime, the criminal justice system is more likely to investigate and detect, arrest and charge, convict and sentence, and sentence to prison for a longer timeframe, a marginalized person of color without adequate means of financial support than a White middle- or upper-class person (Alexander, 2010; Clear, 2007; Pager, 2007; Reiman, 2001).

The devastating power of this trifecta of criminal justice policy is that while we were focused on the economically disadvantaged as being the perpetrators of crime, the truly criminal acts committed by the corporate well-to-do have continued unabated and unseen by the majority of our citizens. It is time to expose the truth on a wide basis beyond the criminal justice professional community.

Future Directions for Corrections

The philosophical foundations that inform our present criminal justice system are grounded in a theory of retribution (Judah & Bryant, 2004) which, in terms of practice, means simply that punishment is demanded as proportionate repayment for crimes committed. As we have seen throughout this chapter, this grounding philosophy is not effective in the prevention or reduction of criminal behavior and is disruptive and destructive to not only the lives, livelihood, and security of ex-offenders, but has far-reaching and deleterious consequences for families, communities, and social order in general. Though the term has been defined and redefined, an alternative to "retribution" as the cornerstone of criminal justice is "restorative justice." This conceptualization focuses on the repair of the damage done rather than the archaic focus on punishment for "sins" committed. Restorative justice is expansive and offers offenders, victims, and the community a new pathway forward to help heal the trauma of much crime. Restorative justice offers a method for using education to reduce reoffending (Consedine & Bowen, 1999). It calls on the government to exercise responsive regulation in determining the degree of interventional response necessary to respond effectively to the needs of the citizenry (Ayres & Braithwaite, 1992). A more effective focus in crime reduction would be policy development that mobilizes social support efforts to ameliorate the effects of economic deprivation and family disruption (Pratt, 2009). Among these programs (which could be supported through private-public partnerships) designed to bring stability to families that face financial hardship could be early intervention programs for at-risk families and youth; emergency financial, housing, and transportation assistance; quality health care (Currie, 1998); and public educational programs based on specific needs of the community.

Beyond a philosophical shift of focus, there are implications for a more equitable and effective paradigm in criminal justice professional practice. This begins with each type of correctional agency determining which programs or interventions will be applied in its institutions. Critical to the process for determining the organizing principles and practices that will be applied is an initial review of existing research on evidence-based practices that demonstrate program effectiveness. Research has revealed three bodies of knowledge central to the design of effective correctional interventions. First, a grounded understanding of empirically established predictions of offender recidivism is needed (Cullen & Gendreau, 2000; MacKenzie, 2000; Welsh & Farrington, 2001). This understanding must be inclusive of antisocial values, antisocial peers, poor self-control and self-management, lacking prosocial problem solving skills, family dysfunction, and past criminality. Successful programs will incorporate specifically designed interventions that target each of these factors and that facilitate positive change. In practice, however, widespread continuing ignorance of the sound research literature and empirical evidence of efficacious practices continues to be a major problem. Falsely based assumptions regarding the causes of crime tend to continue to dominate institutional practices and as a consequence too often doom many correctional programs to failure (Latessa, Cullen, & Gendreau, 2006).

Second, given the body of knowledge focused on interventions of policies that do not work in practice, it is important to avoid the pitfalls such as punishment-oriented programs, intensive supervision programs, wilderness programs, and nondirective psychological interventions (Cullen, 2002; Cullen & Gendreau, 2000; Gendreau, 1996; Lipsey & Wilson, 1998; MacKenzie, 2000). Sadly, a comprehensive review of prison programs reveals that these types of ineffective practices continue to prevail.

Third, there is a growing body of evidence-based practices that demonstrates effective offender treatment protocols (Andrews & Bonta, 1998; Cullen, 2002; Cullen & Gendreau, 2000; MacKenzie, 2000). The principles that form a nexus of effective correctional clinical practice are comprised of eight primary constructs (Latessa, Cullen, & Gendreau, 2006):

+ Organizational culture: Exemplified by having well-defined goals; efficiency in responding to issues that may have impact on treatment facilities; staff cohesion; service training; self-evaluation; and effective use of outside resources
+ Program implementation and maintenance: Empirically defined needs that are consistent with organizational values; fiscal responsibility; program design grounded in empirical research; implementation that relies on pilot research and is professionally staffed

- Management/staff characteristics: Experienced and professionally trained staff and management teams who are focused on rehabilitative practices, relationship skills, and effective therapies
- Client risk/need practices: Use of psychometric instruments with proven prediction validity in the assessment of client risk; changes in risk level over time is routinely assessed so that authentic measurement of change will inform intervention and practice
- Program characteristics: The program is grounded in empirically valid behavioral, social learning, and cognitive behavioral therapies. Relapse prevention strategies are developed and applied following formal treatment phase
- Core correctional practices: Program therapists implement the following practices: anti-criminal modeling; effective reinforcement and disapproval; problem-solving techniques; structured learning; effective use of authority; cognitive self-change; relationship building practices; and motivational interviewing
- Inter-agency networking and referral: Program structure is inclusive of staff and management relationships with community support providers. An essential and integral program element of offender reentry is advocacy for and referral to the community support network.
- Evaluation: Utilization-focused program evaluation is conducted on a routine basis; qualitative and quantitative data resulting from evaluation inform program change and ongoing practice with the intent to inform evidence-based policies and practices

Conclusion

High levels of incarceration damage social networks and reduce social capital, as well as increase disorganization by impeding other, more humanistic forms of social control. Elevated incarceration rates can contribute to high rates of criminal violence through fostering inequality, corroding family life, creating economic and political alienation, and adding to social disorganization. Communities with high rates of incarcerated individuals experience an undermining of the social, economic, and political systems that are already in a weakened state in human and social capital due to having high rates of poverty, unemployment, and criminal activity. The outcome of this deleterious process is a reduction in social cohesion that reduces the community's capacity for self-regulation.

Prisons have become a bottomless receptacle of people who are constantly battling with the turmoil associated with being a person of color, a poor person, a person who was failed by the education system, and/or one who struggles with mental illness. Once oriented to the prison system and branded as a criminal, the unending procession of court appearances and collateral damage inhibit those who might otherwise attempt to repair a troubled life. For Latinos, the incarceration rate is 831 in 100,000, and for African Americans the corresponding number is 2,306 per 100,000. In contrast, the incarceration rate for Whites is 450 in 100,000. Additionally, the Bureau of Justice Statistics report for 2011–2012 reveals that 37% of prison inmates had been told in the past by a mental health professional that they had a diagnosable mental disorder (Bronson & Berzofsky, 2017). If policy entrepreneurs continue discounting social scientific research, we are destined to continue on the same path of punishment in lieu of rehabilitation, and a serious violation of human rights and human dignity will likely become reality for many people of color. After working in corrections for a number of years, teaching, and researching the correctional industry, I have concluded that if Americans were aware of how taxpayer dollars were being spent in their name, the brutality and dehumanization present in our correctional institutions would compel them speak out in unison for correction system reform. If we view mass incarceration as a form of social control, then we must step back and examine the living conditions that some are forced to endure in their pursuit of the American dream. It will be interesting to document the next phase of our penal institutions as a movement toward greater humanity; while it does not appear to be an eminent change, in the more distant future it *must* be a goal of American society to live up to Dostoyevsky dictum of how societies are judged by history. Recent evidence strongly suggests that rather than using empirical research to guide policy design, strident organizations such as the American Legislative Exchange Council (ALEC) have entered into the dialogue related to meaningful criminal justice reform, wresting away evidence found in social science research from the discussion and substituting vitriol and misinformation that reflects a retributive mantra. Their influence can be found in policies related to stand-your-ground laws, limiting judicial discretion, modifying juvenile status and detention standards, limiting Constitutional rights, privatizing prisons, securing revenue for the commercial bail bond issue (a legislative issue currently under review), and supporting reforms that benefit corporate backers.

Discussion Questions

1. Break into groups and discuss the principal components involved with the policy-making process as it relates to corrections. Identify major stakeholders and provide a broad description of how stakeholders affect the development of correctional policies in America.

2. Find research related to the evaluation of programs designed to assist inmates with the transition from life in prison to life in the community. Provide a list of the programmatic components that are linked to reductions in recidivism.

3. Discuss the factors that have affected the major changes in correctional policy taking place since the 1970s.

4. Conduct investigative research related to testimony provided by interests during local, state, and federal government policy debates related to criminal justice issues.

References

Alcohol, Drug Abuse, and Mental Health Administration. (1992). *National household survey on drug abuse: Population estimates 1991*. Rockville, MD: National Institute on Drug Abuse.

Alexander, M. (2010). *The new Jim Crow: Mass incarceration in the age of colorblindness*. New York, NY: New Press.

Andrews, D. A. (2001). Principles of effective correctional programs. In R. C. Serin (Ed.), *Compendium 2000 on effective correctional programming*. Ottawa, Canada: Correctional Service Canada.

Andrews, D. A., & Bonta, J. (1998). *Psychology of criminal conduct (2nd ed)*. Cincinnati, OH: Anderson.

Aos, S., Miller, M., & Drake, E. (2006). *Evidence-based adult corrections program: What works and what does not*. Olympia, WA: Washington State Institute for Public Policy.

Ayres, I., & Braithwaite, J. (1992). *Responsive regulation: Transcending the deregulation debate*. New York, NY: Oxford University Press.

Baum, D. (1997). *Smoke and mirrors: The war on drugs and the politics of failure.* Boston, MA: Little, Brown and Company.

Bennett, W. J., DiIulio, J. J., Jr., & Walters, J. P. (1996). *Body count: Moral poverty and how to win America's war against crime and drugs.* New York, NY: Simon and Schuster.

Bertram, E., Blachman, M., Sharpe, K., & Andreas, P. (1996). *Drug war politics: The price of denial.* Berkeley, CA: University of California Press.

Bronson, J. and Berzofsky, M. (2017). *Indicators of mental health problems reported by prisoners and jail inmates.* Washington, DC: Bureau of Justice Statistics.

Chambliss, W. J. (1999). *Power, politics, and crime.* Boulder, CO: Westview Press.

Chappell, C. A. (2004). Post-secondary correctional education and recidivism: A meta-analysis of research conducted 1990–1999. *Journal of Correctional Education, 55*(2), 148–169.

Cherlin, A. J. (1992). *Marriage, divorce, remarriage.* Cambridge, MA: Harvard University Press.

Clark, J., Austin, J., & Henry, D. H. (1997). Three strikes and you're out: A review of state legislation. *NIJ Research in Brief.* Washington, DC: National Institute of Justice.

Clear, T. R. (2007). *Imprisoning communities: How mass incarceration makes disadvantaged neighborhoods worse.* New York, NY: Oxford University Press.

Consedine, J., & Bowen, H. (1999). *Restorative justice: Contemporary themes and practice.* Lyttleton, New Zealand: Ploughshares Publications.

Cullen, F. T. (2002). Rehabilitation and treatment programs. In J. Q. Wilson & J. Petersilia (Eds.), *Crime: Public policies for crime control* (pp. 253–289). Oakland, CA: ICS Press.

Cullen, F. T., & Gendreau, P. (2000). From nothing works to what works: Changing professional ideology in the 21st century. e *Prison Journal, 81*(3), 313–338.

Cullen, F. T., Pratt, T. C., Miceli, S. L., & Moon, M. M. (2002). Dangerous liaison? Rational choice theory as the basis for correctional intervention. In A. R. Piquero & S. G. Tibbetts, (Eds.), *Rational choice and criminal behavior: Recent research and future challenges.* New York, NY: Routledge.

Currie, E. (1998). *Crime and punishment in America.* New York, NY: Henry Holt.

Decker, S. (2007). The relationship between street and prison. *Criminology and Public Policy, 6*(2), 183–186.

De Leon, G. (1985). The therapeutic community: Status and evolution. *International Journal of Addiction, 20*(6–7), 823–844.

De Leon, G., Melnick, G., Thomas, G., Kressel, D., & Wexler, H. K. (2000). Motivation for treatment in a prison-based therapeutic community. *American Journal of Drug and Alcohol Abuse, 26*(1), 33–46.

Dostoevsky, F. (1917). *Crime and punishment*, Vol. XVIII. New York, NY: P. F. Collier & Son.

Dubber, M. D. (2001). Policing possession: The war on crime and the end of criminal law. *Journal of Criminal Law and Criminology, 91*, 829–996.

Gendreau, P. (1996). The principles of effective intervention with offenders. In A. T. Harland (Ed.), *Choosing correctional options that work: Defining the demand and evaluating the supply* (pp. 117–130). Newbury Park, CA: SAGE.

Grogger, J. (1995). The effect of arrests on the employment and earnings of young men. *Quarterly Journal of Economics, 110*(1), 51–71.

Gutierrez, R. S. (2003). *Social equity and the funding of community oriented policing.* New York, NY: LFB Scholarly Publications.

Halsey, M. (2008). Assembling recidivism: The promise and contingencies of post-release life. *Journal of Criminal-Law and Criminology, 97*(4), 1209–1260.

Harlow, C. W. (1998). *Profile of jail inmates 1996* (NCJ 164620). Washington, DC: Bureau of Justice Statistics.

Harlow, C. W. (2003). *Education and correctional populations* (NCJ 195670). Washington, DC: Bureau of Justice Statistics.

Harrington, M. (1962). *The other America: Poverty in the United States.* New York, NY: Macmillan.

Harrison, P. M., & Beck, A. J. (2003). *Prisoners in 2002* (NCJ 200248). Washington, DC: Bureau of Justice Statistics.

Helms, R., Costanza, S. E., & Gutierrez, R. S. (2016). Social inequality and county-level correlates of state prison releases and releases from community supervision. *International Journal of Social Science Research, 4*(1), 167–197.

Holzer, H. J. (2006). Perceived criminality, criminal background checks, and the racial hiring practices of employers. *Journal of Law and Economics, 49*(2), 451–480.

Inciardi, J. A., Martin, S. S., Butzin, C. A., Hooper, R. M., & Harrison, L. D. (1997). An effective model of prison-based treatment for drug involved offenders. *Journal of Drug Issues, 27*(2), 261–278.

Jans, N. (2002). *Too many convicts.* Anchorage, AK: Alaska Northwest Books.

Johnson-Listwan, S., Cullen, F. T., & Latessa, E. J. (2006). How to prevent prisoner re-entry programs from failing: Insights from evidence-based corrections. *Federal Probation, 70*(3), 19–25.

Judah, E. H., & Bryant, M. (2004). Rethinking criminal justice: Retribution vs. restoration. In E. H. Judah & Rev. M. Bryant, (Eds.), *Criminal justice: Retribution vs. restoration* (pp. 1–6). Binghamton, NY: Haworth Social Work Practice Press.

King, R., & Mauer, M. (2005). *The war on marijuana: The transformation of the war on drugs in the 1990s.* New York, NY: Sentencing Project.

Klein, J., & Moeschberger, M. (1997). *Survival analysis: Techniques for censored and truncated data.* New York, NY: Springer.

Kling, J. R. (1999). The effect of prison sentence length on the subsequent employment and earnings of criminal defendants. *Woodrow Wilson School Discussion Papers in Economics No. 208.* Princeton, NJ: Princeton University Press.

Krebs, C. P., Brady, T., & Laird G. (2003). Jail-based substance user treatment: An analysis of retention. *Substance Use and Misuse, 38*(9), 1227–1258.

Kubrin, C. E., & Stewart, E. A. (2006). Predicting who reoffends: The neglected role of neighborhood context in recidivism studies. *Criminology, 44*(1), 165–197.

Kunitz, S., Woodall, W., Zhao, H., Wheeler, D., Lillis, R., & Rogers, E. (2002). Rearrest rates after incarceration for DWI: A comparative study in a southwestern U. S. county. *American Journal of Public Health, 92*(11), 1826–1831.

Latessa, E. J., Cullen, F. T., & Gendreau, P. (2006). Beyond correctional quackery: Professionalism and the possibility of effective treatment. In R. Tewksbury (Ed.), *Behind bars: Readings on prison culture* (pp. 358–371). Upper Saddle River, NJ: Pearson.

Lipsey, M. W., & Wilson, D. B. (1998). Effective intervention for serious juvenile offenders. In R. Loeber and D. P. Farrington (Eds.), *Serious and violent juvenile offenders: Risk factors and successful intervention* (pp. 313–345). Thousand Oaks, CA: SAGE.

Lipton, D. S., Pearson, F. S., Cleland, C. M., & Yee, D. S. (2002). The effects of behavioral/cognitive-behavioral programs on recidivism. *Crime and Delinquency, 48*(3), 476–496.

Lott, J. R. (1990). The effect of conviction on the legitimate income of criminals. *Economics Letters, 34*(4), 381–385.

Loury, G. C. (2008). *Race, incarceration, and American values.* Cambridge, MA: Massachusetts Institute of Technology Press.

MacKenzie, D. L. (2000). Evidence-based corrections: Identifying what works. *Crime and Delinquency, 46*(4), 457–471.

Martin, S. S., Butzin, C. A., Saum, C. A., & Inciardi, J. A. (1999). Three-year outcomes of therapeutic community treatment for drug-involved offenders in Delaware: From prison to work release to aftercare. *Prison Journal, 79*(3), 294–320.

Martinson, R. (1974). What works? Questions and answers about prison reform. *Public Interest, 35,* 22–54.

Mears, D., Wang, X., Hay, C., & Bales, W. (2008). Social ecology and recidivism: Implications for prisoner reentry. *Criminology, 46*(2), 301–340.

Mumola, C. J. (1999). *Substance abuse and treatment, state and federal prisoners, 1997* (NCJ 172871). Washington, DC: Bureau of Justice Statistics.

Musto, D. (1989). How America lost its first drug war. *Insight, 20,* 8–17.

Musto, D. (1999). *The American disease: Origins of narcotic control (3rd ed.).* New York, NY: Oxford University Press.

National Institute of Drug Abuse (2006). Principles of drug abuse treatment for criminal justice populations: A research-based guide. Washington, DC: United States Department of Health and Human Services.

Pager, D. (2007). *Marked: Race, crime, and finding work in an era of mass incarceration.* Chicago, IL: University of Chicago Press.

Pearson, F. S., & Lipton, D. S. (1999). A meta-analytic review of the effectiveness of corrections-based treatments for drug abuse. *Prison Journal, 79*(4), 384–410.

Peters, R., Kearns, W., Murrin, M., Dolente, A., & May, R. (1993). Examining the effectiveness of in-jail substance abuse treatment. *Journal of Offender Rehabilitation, 19*(3), 1–39.

Petersilia, J. (2003). *When prisoners come home: Parole and prisoner reentry.* New York, NY: Oxford University Press.

Phillips, K. (1969). *The emerging republican majority.* New Rochelle, NY: Arlington House.

Pratt, T. C. (2009). *Addicted to incarceration: Corrections policy and the politics of misinformation in the United States.* Thousand Oaks, CA: SAGE.

Pratt, T. C., & Cullen, F. T. (2005). Macro-level predictors and theories of crime: A meta-analysis. In M. Tonry (Ed.), *Crime and justice: An annual review of research.* Chicago, IL: University of Chicago Press.

Prendergast, M., Hall, E., Wexler, H., Melnick, G., & Cao, Y. (2004). Amity prison-based therapeutic community: Five-year outcomes. *Prison Journal, 84*(1), 36–60.

Reiman, J. (2001). *The rich get richer and the poor get prison: Ideology, class, and criminal justice (6th ed.).* Needham Heights, MA: Allyn & Bacon.

Sampson, R. J., & Laub, J. H. (1993). *Crime in the making: Pathways and turning points through life.* Cambridge, MA: Harvard University Press.

Sampson, R. J., Morenoff, J. D., & Gannon-Rowley, T. (2002). Assessing neighborhood effects: Social processes and new directions in research. *Annual Review of Sociology, 28,* 443–478.

Saxon, A. J., Wells, E. A., Fleming, C., Jackson, T. R., & Calsyn, D. A. (1996). Pre-treatment characteristics, program philosophy, and level of ancillary services as predictors of methadone maintenance treatment outcome. *Addiction, 91*(8), 1197–1209.

Schwarzfeld, M., Weiss, D. M., Plotkin, M., & Draper, L. (2008). *Planning and assessing a law enforcement reentry strategy.* New York, NY: Council of State Governments Justice Center.

Shrum, H. (2004). No longer theory: Correctional practices that work. *Journal of Correctional Education, 55*(3), 225–235.

Sterling, E. (2004). Drug policy: A challenge of values. In E. H. Judah & Rev. M. Bryant, (Eds.), *Criminal justice: Retribution vs. restoration* (pp. 51–81). Binghamton, NY: Haworth Social Work Practice Press.

Terkel, S. N. (1997). *The drug laws: A time for change?* New York, NY: Franklin Watts.

Tonry, M. (1995). *Malign neglect: Race, crime, and punishment in America.* New York, NY: Oxford University Press.

Waldfogel, J. (1994). The effect of criminal conviction on income and the trust "reposed in the workmen." *Journal of Human Resources, 29*(1), 62–81.

Welsh, B. C., & Farrington, D. P. (2001). Toward an evidence-based approach to preventing crime. *Annals of the American Academy of Political and Social Science, 578*(1), 158–173.

Western, B. (2006). *Punishment and inequality in America.* New York, NY: Russell Sage Foundation.

Wilson, D. J. (2000). *Drug use, testing, and treatment in jails* (NCJ 179999). Washington, DC: Bureau of Justice Statistics.

Worrall, J. D. (2001). Addicted to the drug war: The role of civil asset forfeiture as a budgetary necessity in contemporary law enforcement. *Journal of Criminal Justice, 29*(3), 171–87.

Zimring, F. E., & Hawkins, G. (1991). *The scale of imprisonment.* Chicago, IL: University of Chicago Press.

Chapter 8

Restorative Justice

Processes and Promises

Ernest Uwazie

Introduction

The contemporary restorative justice (RJ) movement in the United States can trace its origins to the popular revolt against the government and civil rights movement in the 1960s, particularly challenging the effectiveness of the formal justice system (Zehr, 1990) as too costly and alienating of crime victims, slow or unable to provide racial justice, and ineffective in achieving the rehabilitation needs of the offenders and reduction of recidivism (Johnstone & Van Ness, 2007). Equally, the civil justice system was deemed ineffective due to the excessive court backlogs and protracted litigation that caused trial delays, hence "denial of justice" in the court system.

Accordingly, restorative justice emerged as a paradigm shift toward the view of crime as a personal violation of rights with real victims versus definition of crime as an offense against the government or "public wrong" (Zehr, 1990). In the civil justice arena, alternative dispute resolution (ADR) was proposed to mitigate the justice delays through the multi-door court house as well as private mediation and arbitration in civil disputes (Sander, 1976). Since the 1980s and from the lessons of the various alternative justice initiatives in the 1970s, restorative justice has taken center stage in the reform of the U.S. criminal justice system, from crime prevention strategies to rethinking of the view of crime or its causation and social response, to the inevitability of crime as well as the development of an influential victim's right movement (Johnstone & Van Ness, 2007). Often, the RJ applications have been influenced by experiences from other countries, including Native American or Indian tribal justice processes in Canada and New Zealand.

Restorative justice can be defined as a philosophy of justice that refers to a variety of balanced responses to crime intended to meet the needs of the victims, offenders, and community in the justice process (see also Zehr, 1990). In its application, restorative justice process focuses on the harm done to the person or victim and community, as well as its underlying causes, seeks offender accountability to make things right as far as possible; engages stakeholders (both community and government) to achieve healing or restoration of the victim, community, and offender; and prevents future harm.

Restorative justice is founded on the moral or theoretic view of positive humanity and the inevitability of crime/conflict in society. Hence, public response to crime shall be guided by the moral imperatives or principles of nonviolence; individual repentance and redemption, forgiveness, interpersonal reconciliation; and social reintegration/rehabilitation (Johnstone & Van Ness, 2007; Zehr, 1990).

Over the past 50 years, particularly since the U.S. informal justice movement of the 1970s, various restorative justice adaptations and rationale have emerged to challenge traditional justice systems' responses to crime and civil conflicts. Over time, RJ has expanded to examine specific policies and practices in juvenile justice diversion, rehabilitation, and treatment models in adult correctional services and alternative dispute resolution (ADR) in civil justice (Johnstone & Van Ness, 2007). More recently in the United States, RJ is being developed in schools as a mechanism to improve school climate and student academic performance to and reduce school violence and student misconduct and bullying (Skiba & Losen, 2016). There is an ongoing campaign for compassionate cities (Charter for Compassion, 2009), aimed at building or nurturing more human connections in diverse cultures and at more commitment to social justice and a peaceful world. Although the restorative justice movement has its roots and popular use elsewhere, it has become pronounced in various U.S. community policing models, alternative criminal sentencing policies, innovations in court processing of cases involving vulnerable populations, and creation of access to justice for the poor or marginalized groups. RJ has also created a heightened social consciousness about the interconnections of equity and fairness and the environment and has expanded from its application from minor property crimes to even the most serious felonies and gross human rights violations (Johnstone & Van Ness, 2007).

The modern global appeal to RJ is influenced by the applications of various RJ processes in such mass atrocity crimes as the Gacaca in the aftermath of the Rwanda genocide, the Truth and Reconciliation Commission in post-apartheid South Africa, collectivist cultures of Asia, and the institution of formal legal provisions and structures for diversion in juvenile offenses and mediation in Europe. While the RJ practices may vary across countries and regions of the world, they rely on the common core principle of rehabilitation and comparative experiences of healing or restoration from the application of each process as adaptable to the needs and circumstances of the disputants and community. Overall, RJ is a promising alternative to traditional conceptions and applications of justice, with the recognition of the inevitable linkages and complementarity of the formal and informal justice systems, both in the developed world and developing communities.

The Common Promises of Restorative Justice

1. Give victims, offenders, and community members a chance to share their perspectives about the incidents/crimes, especially where "talk" is beneficial
2. Offer the possibility of reconciliation, restitution, and reparation
3. Provide victims with an active role in the justice process
4. Divert cases away from more costly court proceedings
5. Provide a holistic approach to crime response
6. Provide victims with an opportunity to seek and receive explanations (e.g., "Why me?")
7. More actively and meaningfully engage the community in crime prevention and maintaining public safety
8. Reduce the risk of recidivism
9. Cause the community to re-examine its perceptions of crime and offenders

The goals and objectives of restorative justice may be achieved through its many processes and designs, depending on the availability of programs or resources, victim needs, and offenders' background. The various RJ processes may be applied or beneficial before (as diversion), during, and after trial as well as post incarceration. Many restorative justice processes are consensual between the victim and offender as well as their support-ers, even if or when those processes result in partial agreements or final resolution. The overriding principle of any restorative justice process is to "do no harm." Assessment of any RJ process should consider the extent of its resultant benefits and infliction of any harm to any of the parties involved in the case.

Victim Offender Mediation

Victim-offender mediation (VOM), sometimes called the "Elmira Case" of informal mediation of teenage vandalism in Ontario, Canada, in 1974 (Johnstone & Van Ness, 2007), is a process that brings the victim and the offender together to engage in a dialogue with the help of a third-party mediator or facilitator, regarding the injury caused to the victim. This dialogue will allow each side to explain his or her own understanding of the circumstances and impact of the harm and how to "make things right." Rather than retribution, victim-offender mediation seeks to reha-bilitate and reintegrate the victim and offender, possibly allowing them to reconcile (Dhami, 2016). Apology is the key outcome of the VOM, from the offender to the victim, directly or indirectly, verbally or written. Most victims find apology to be more effective than the criminal trial process and welcome a sincere, genuine, and unconditional apology from the offender (Dhami, 2016). VOM may also be denied if the victim is unwilling to forgive (Abdul & Bagshaw, 2015). Restitution may also be part of the agreement of the VOM, including the amount, date and manner or terms of payment. Such an encounter may also provide the victim the opportunity to seek answers from the offender that could help in the healing or recovery process, as well as provide a humanizing experience for both the victim and offender.

Victim-offender mediation is an alternative that seeks reconciliation and repentance and may be effective even in cases of mass crimes. For example, it was used in a clergy sexual abuse of a minor by a priest in Milwaukee, Wisconsin, with the victim and offender (priest) as well as the Catholic Archbishop engaging in the encounter that resulted in an apology and restitution (Geske, 2007); this experience also contributed to the development of the use of VOM in serious crimes in the state's correctional system. In an earlier case of mass alleged abuse of over 700 students/orphans that spanned 30–60 years at the Mount Cashel Orphanage in Newfoundland involving about 10 members of the Order of the Catholic Christian Brothers, the parties agreed to (Barnes, 2013) the following:

1. Facilitation of apologies by those responsible for physical and sexual abuse
2. Reasonable financial compensation for pain and suffering
3. Financial advances for medical services, vocational rehabilitation, educational upgrading and literacy training
4. Provision of counseling services
5. Payment to ex-students who had not been paid for farm work and menial work while at the schools
6. Participant commitment to work toward the eradication of child abuse

In the standard court system, the victim will use the court process to punish the offender. VOM allows the victim to heal from his or her loss or harm rather than the pyrrhic victory of inflicting retributive punishment. More importantly, VOM allows the offender the option of repairing the damage he or she has done and possibly gain forgiveness. Offenders can also use this opportunity to remain a part of the community. While VOM is a formal process within the legal system, it can be heavily influenced by cultural norms and institutional arrangements, which can complicate its implementation, especially if it occurs while the offender is under incarceration.

Conferencing

Group or family group conferencing (FGC) originated in 1989 under New Zealand's Children, Young Persons and Family Act, with the goal of adopting holistic response to the welfare of the delinquent-child and related justice issues (Johnstone & Van Ness, 2007); sometimes FGC is used in place of the court as a formal diversionary system. Later, the FGC process spread to Australia (town of Wagga Wagga in New South Wales) in 1991, with direct police involvement as facilitators, and in supervision of the process as well as development of the rules of the facilitation. Today, FGC processes exist in many parts of the world, especially the United States, Canada, and Britain, at varying degrees of case application, formal justice participation, and flexibility of victim participation.

The FGC process was intended to give direct voice to the Maori aboriginal families with disproportionate presence in the justice system and to enable them seek familiar solutions to problems with the joint participation of the victims and offenders with the assistance of a facilitator. Hence, the key difference between the FGC and VOM is the participation of family members, supporters, and possibly other criminal justice officials, school authority, and social welfare agencies in the process as a "wrap-around" program. FGC can be used as a diversion, post-trial and post-sentence, and is often used in child welfare or minor cases as well as in schools and employment.

Sentencing Circles

Sentencing circles, also known as community or peacemaking circles, emphasize the inclusion of the victim, offender, community, criminal justice officials, and other stakeholders necessary for a holistic response to any crime and its impact (Stuart, 1998). Sentencing circles are common in the Native American tribal justice system where the focus is on rehabilitation and reintegration of both the victim and offender, as well as restoration of the balance of peace in the community. Everyone in the circle is affected by the crime and has some level of responsibility for repairing the harm. The circle aims to promote understanding of the crime on all sides for any resolution to occur, including the reasons for the crime and other circumstances of the victim and offender. It can also be used prior to release from incarceration to develop necessary arrangements and manage expectations for successful re-entry into the community or to facilitate family reunification. The Huikahi Circles in Hawaii illustrate an effective reentry program in the community (Van Womer & Walker, 2013), with the following principles:

1. Prepare for reentry
2. Build bridges between prisons and communities

3. Seize the moment of release
4. Strengthen the concentric circles of support
5. Promote successful reintegration

Another key aspect of sentencing circles is the emphasis on community empowerment rather than deferring to governmental authority. This emphasis originates from the history of peace circles to an aboriginal system of treatment of offenders (Lilles, 2002). By seeking justice through the formal Western-based court system, victims see the system exact retribution on their behalf. However, sentencing circles seek ownership of the process of conflict resolution and avoid deferring sentencing decisions to the courts or outside alien power (Fitzgerald, 2008). Sentencing circles tend to utilize probation effectively, are amenable to integration of the offender into the community, and attempt to humanize the offender, his or her relationship to the community, and means of prevention. Through this process, the offender is viewed as a symptom of the problems in the community rather than treated as a threat or risk. As in the VOM, the outcome of the sentencing is an agreement of specific actions by the parties in the circle as well as an exchange of apologies and forgiveness.

Sentencing circles bring victims, offenders, and all other involved parties together. They give the justice system a useful insight into community problems, which the trial process may not reveal. While the emphasis is on community and reintegration, they may be limited in what crimes they may be able to resolve, particularly violent crimes, and be limited in different cultural and sociopolitical dynamics or conditions (Cameron, 2006).

Reparative Board

A reparative board is a formal process where an offender appears before a panel of local community representatives or a lay justice panel to discuss remedies or sanctions after determination of criminal liability. The decision of the panel is often informed by the relevant information about the offender, victim, and the nature as well as circumstances of the criminal act. Membership of the panel varies from three to 19 people, depending on location and availability of volunteers. They discuss the specifics of the crime with the offender and his or her willingness or capability to fulfill its decision or sanctions. The decision process is by consensus of the board, and the goal remains to arrive at a restorative outcome. The outcome is the creation of a contract with the offender's specific actions and timeline to repair the harm (Lyons, 2006) as part of the sentencing process. The offender may also reject the proposed contract and opt for traditional criminal sentencing. Board members may also accept some responsibility for monitoring compliance and provide some support to the offender and may revise the contract as the need arises in the monitoring or implementation phase. The victim(s) may attend the meeting or hearing and provide input, which the board may consider at its discretion, and the process may be open to the public (Bazemore & Schiff, 2016). Reparative process may be used as part of the probation or parole, with the goal of facilitating rehabilitation and reintegration.

The boards seek to tailor individual programs to suit the circumstances and capability of each offender as well as any mitigating conditions, with special focus on educating the offender on how his or her crime impacted the victim and community, the need to restore the victim, providing reparation to the community, and learning how to avoid reoffending in the future (Bazemore & Schiff, 2016). The board engages the offender in a discussion of the crime and solutions for making amends and ascertains if the offender is prepared to accept responsibility for his or her actions, as well as be held accountable. The process is not meant to be punitive or exact "a pound of flesh," but rather to promote understanding of the offender's situation and how to deter him or her from future crime as well as make him or her a functional, positive member of the community. The board usually commends the offender in a final meeting for successful completion of the contract but may void the contract for noncompliance.

Victim-Offender Panels (VOP)

A VOP is a process of encounter between crime victims and groups of offenders who are not necessarily connected to same crime or each other's victims or offenders (Van Ness & Strong, 2015). VOP seeks to impress upon offenders how their actions affect their victims. The process is not about monetary or physical compensation, but to educate the offenders about the damage they have caused to the individual(s), or co-victims in homicide situations. In other words, VOPs have a unique emphasis on expressing the victim's true, raw feelings of harm due to the crime, not necessarily mutual understanding, and the sessions can vary by location, type of crime, group size, and duration. Some of the sessions may also include role plays between the victims and offenders or story telling by the victims to the offenders about the dangerous impact of the offenders' behavior. Selection of participants in the sessions is usually voluntary and carefully done to ensure fit, although some offenders participate as part of the sentencing or probation condition.

An example of VOPs are drunk driving panels implemented by Mothers Against Drunk Driving (MADD), also called victim impact panels (Lord, 1990). During a single session, usually 60–90 minutes, the offender(s) will sit and listen to the stories of victims of drunk driving incidents. The offender does not need to hear from his or her victim specifically, and the panel can include victims, families who have been hurt by drunk driving, and other offenders (Lord, 1990). A key requirement is that offenders need to hear directly from people who have suffered due to drunk driving, not necessarily to chastise or harm the offender. The offenders are carefully screened to ensure that they have fully accepted their criminal responsibility and are sincere in their altruistic participation in the session. If the victims on the panel agree, there may be a question-and-answer session with the offenders. The process forces the offender to confront his or her actions and face the damage he or she has or could have caused and possibly change their perception or behavior about drunk driving; this change could also help victims heal.

Victim-offender panels also can benefit the victim. Being able to tell his or her story and share his or her pain can be important to emotional healing. Hearing the stories of other victims can help victims heal from their trauma. Further, victims may gain a sense of purpose or fulfillment from helping deter future offenses (Van Ness & Strong, 2015). These benefits are tangible for the emotional restoration of victims, especially as the process creates an emotional connection between the victim, the offender, and the offense. However, this emotional connection can make both parties vulnerable, depending on the type of offense, how the victim suffered, and the offender's mental state and interaction with the victim. Voluntary participation, careful selection of participants, proper orientation of the rules of engagement, and effective facilitation of the process will provide safeguards for the VOP process (see also Lord, 1990).

TABLE 8.1 Timeline of Key RJ Developments

1972 Minnesota Restitution Center: Community-based corrections facility, operated by the state's Department of Corrections and later fused into the state's current Department of Corrections RJ services.

1976 San Francisco community boards: Oldest community mediation/conflict resolution center in United States for business, individual, family, community, and school conflicts.

1976 First victim-offender reconciliation program in Canada: Kitchener, Ontario.

1976 U.S. Prison Fellowship: Trains churches and communities to assist in the restoration of those impacted by incarceration.

1978 First victim-offender reconciliation program in United States: Elkhart, Indiana, among estimated over 2,000 worldwide.

1983 Genesee Justice, Batavia, New York: First U.S. sheriff department–based restorative justice/conflict resolution program.

1985 First multi-door court house: Washington, DC, District of Columbia Resolution Program, in civil and domestic relations cases.

1986 California Dispute Resolution Programs (Garamendi) Act: Provides for the creation and funding of local mediation and conciliation programs and services.

1989 Drug Court in Miami Dade, Florida, is established: The first in the country to integrate treatment as an alternative to incarceration in drug offenses.

1993 Victim-Offender Mediation Association (formerly from the U.S. Association for Victim-Offender Mediation): Now an international organization.

1994 American Bar Association Endorsement of the victim-offender mediation programs: With recommendations for their consideration at all levels of the justice system.

1999 U.S. Department of Justice Office of Community-Oriented Policing publishes _A Toolbox for Implementing Restorative Justice and Advancing Community Policing_.

2000 University of Colorado, Boulder, establishes the first university campus restorative justice program for handling a variety of conflicts and certain crimes.

2001	Rwanda Gacaca courts: Resolve certain low-mid level categories of offenders in the 1994 genocide that killed over 800,000 Tutsis, aimed at reconciliation and establishment of truth now transformed into the Abunzi in 2004 for resolution or mediation of regular conflicts in the community with lay participation.
2005	Huikahi Restorative Circle: Developed in collaboration with the Waiawa Correctional Facility in Hawaii.
2010	Virginia legislation on the right of the crime victim to meet their offender in prison.
2006	UN Office of Drugs Crime's Criminal Justice Reform Unit publishes landmark *Handbook of Restorative Justice Programs*.
2009	The Charter for Compassion is established, with the inspiration and leadership of Karen Armstrong, urging the global community to be compassionate in all aspects of public policy and action toward creating a peaceful world; charter now in over 300 communities and 45 countries.
2011	Miami Dade County Public Schools adopts RJ as alternative to "zero tolerance."
2013	Colorado passes legislation mandating judges to offer RJ options to every crime victim and offender.

Limitations of Restorative Justice: Programming and Policy

Despite the obvious and potential benefits of RJ, persistent practical and philosophical challenges or areas of scholarly inquiry remain:

1. Political realities: How to ensure a supportive leadership at the local, state, and national leadership
2. Perceptions that restorative justice interventions are unrealizable, utopian, or irreconcilable in a society of retributive justice
3. Practical difficulties of implementation (e.g., criminal justice officials' concerns about diverting cases to a "soft" approach); perceived inappropriateness of victims interacting with offenders; overcoming the challenge of a reluctance of victims and offenders to participate in restorative justice encounters; public's receptivity to a perceived "soft" approach to law violators; application of multiple communication

competencies (i.e., ability to articulate oneself and listen to others, be rational during meetings or any encounters, and be receptive to creative options)

4. Perceived violation of due process, especially when cases are diverted or RJ process used in post-sentence decisions
5. Methodology: Limited access to quality information or quantitative as well as qualitative data about RJ impact in the community and overall crime in society, sometimes driven by the lack of reliable funding and program sustainability

Conclusion

Although myriad in its definition, restorative justice views crime as an inevitable human condition in society that requires recognition and proper response in order to satisfy the needs of healing of the victim, rehabilitation of the offender, and maintenance of peace in community. Although most studies demonstrate the effectiveness or positive influence of a variety of RJ processes on victim satisfaction, payment of restitution, reduction of recidivism and transactional costs of justice system, and improvement in school climate, there are questions or concerns about reliability in a heterogeneous, urban society, cultural differences over collective versus individual rights or interests, fair treatment of racial or gender minorities, and due process. As each crime, victim, and offender is different in his or her needs and complex circumstances, multiple processes are desired to achieve the goals of reducing the rate of reoffending, satisfy the emotional and physical needs of the victim, rehabilitate and reintegrate the offender, and maintain resiliency of the community. In this regard, there is need to seek, create, and promote the use of alternative and more effective responses to crime and reduce the current heavy reliance on punitive ideology and mass incarceration practices. A one-size-fits-all approach neither fits nor is sustainable. Given the circumstances of the offense, victim, and offender as well as social conditions, the VOM, VOP, peace circles, FGC, and reparative board processes hold psychological, physical, social, and criminogenic promises for a better, effective response to crime in society. They could be carefully applied at all stages of the justice procedure: pre-trial or diversion, at trial or adjudication, post-adjudication, sentencing, and post-sentencing, both as an alternative or addition to the formal justice procedures.

Box 8.1 Letters of Apology (from select letters of the inmates in my RJ class of the 10P program at the California State Prison, Sacramento)

"Mr ... (Victim),

I am sure that just seeing my name may cause some discomfort, which is not my intention. ... Matter of fact I am hoping and praying that my words will find you and your [f]amily in the very best of health and spirits with God watching over all of you.

I almost want to ask you for your permission to do what's right in apologizing for the harm I caused you and those who care about you. Simply, I just want to say that I "apologize" and "[t]hank you."

Our paths crossed because you were told that someone had been shot and you were coming to assist that person ... me. I was shot and out of an act of criminality I altered both our lives and those of our [f]amilies. That is what I take away from the tragic events I caused that morning. I harmed not just a human being who did me no harm[,] but someone who was carrying out his duties as a police officer. I regret my actions of that morning.

I am not sure if 28 years is punishment enough for the courts or you[,] but I owe a lifetime to anyone I have harmed. I am nowhere near that person now that I was when I committed my crime against you. Old age, time, and self-work have transformed me in many ways. Two of my major changes would be changing my criminal lifestyle and being nonviolent. I thought like a criminal so I acted like one. Through hard work, assistance from people and self-help groups, I transformed that part of my life. I believe in honest work and effort. I realize I have a lot more to offer myself and society. Equally, violence is a thing of the past for me. I was out of control and I don't want to ever be that violent dangerous person again. No person has the right to harm another human being if they themselves are not being harmed. I understand this now and I am committed to living this way.

Again I deeply apologize for the senseless crime I committed against you. I am deeply sorry for all the hurt and pain I caused you, your [f]amily, my [f]amily and community, and society as a whole.

In closing, I will understand if you choose not to accept this letter or my apology.

Sincerely,
Anonymous (Inmate)

Box 8.1   Letters of Apology (Continued)

Anonymous (Victim),

I hope that this letter reaches you in the best of health of spirit. I know that you may not know me personally[,] but I would like to take this time to apologize for all the pain that I caused you and your family. I didn't think about the results of my selfish actions and how my actions would forever alter your life. I ask that you bear with me and take the time to read this letter. It is not my intention to hurt you; I just want to be honest and transparent. My name is [Anonymous] and I am the man that killed your father. ... I am sorry. I am ashamed to have to write those words[,] but I know that my shame cannot compare to all of the pain that you feel inside. I want you to know that I take accountability for my actions and that I have taken numerous steps to see what was going on inside of me at the time so that I never make that mistake again. I know that your father loved and adored you. At times I think about the relationship that you and your father had and I think about the milestones that you were deprived of because of my numerous stupid decisions, like you going to prom and him not being able to send you off, you graduating from high school and him not being there in the crowd. I think about the love that only he could have genuinely given to you[;] I think about the fatherly guidance that he never had the opportunity to share with you. I write, speak, and advocate for healthy family relationships especially pertaining to family structure of blacks, and other minorities that are heavily represented in downtrodden communities. I speak about the importance of having fathers in the household and how the absence of productive fathers in these communities contributes to poverty, crime, plight, and despair ... and then reality sets in. I think about how I personally contributed to this issue that I vehemently advocate against and I get disgusted every time I think about it. I am ashamed every time I think about the way that I hurt you. I hope that you can find it in your hurt to forgive me and I pray that all of your dreams, hopes, aspirations, and ambitions are realized in the most positive manner. Thank you for taking the time out to read this letter. I admire your strength and perseverance and I am truly sorry for all the pain that I caused you and your family and I sincerely apologize to you from the bottom of my heart. If you have any questions I will try to answer them to the best of my ability. I accept full accountability for my actions and I will continue to make amends by sharing my true feelings and trying to help individuals avoid the mistakes that I made. I will volunteer to be the ear that listens to those who need to vent, the mouth that speaks to those who need encouragement, and the heart that understands that so many of us have areas within ourselves that crave compassion and healing.

Sincerely,
Anonymous (Inmate)

Discussion Questions

1. In your own words and in one sentence, define restorative justice.
2. Explain the key objectives of restorative justice.
3. Compare key differences and similarities of VOM, VOP, Peace Circle, and Reparative Board. Are there any limitations or implications for racial/ethnic and gender groups?
4. Think of one serious and one nonserious crime and select one of the processes for resolution. Justify your choice. Does your choice have any limitations for achieving justice?
5. Assess the effect or effectiveness of the select letters of apology. In your assessment, focus on each writer's or offender's sincerity, acceptance of responsibility, acknowledgment of harm, willingness to make amends, empathy, vulnerability, and change. If you were the victim, which of the letters do you find more satisfactory and why?
6. Review and critique three original case studies in current peer-reviewed scholarly journals about any of the RJ processes or promises discussed in the USA and/or elsewhere, with particular focus on the theses, methodology, findings, and conclusions of the studies.

References

Abdul Syukur, F., & Bagshaw, D. M. (2015). Victim-Offender Mediation with Youth Offenders in Indonesia. *Conflict Resolution Quarterly, 32*(4), 389–411. doi:10.1002/crq.21120

Barnes, B. (2013). An overview of restorative justice programs. *Alaska Journal of Dispute Resolution, 2013*(1) 17–26.

Bazemore, S. G., & Schiff, M. (2016). *Restorative community justice: Repairing harm and transforming communities.* London, UK: Routledge.

Cameron, A. (2006). Sentencing circles and intimate violence: A Canadian feminist perspective. *Canadian Journal of Women & The Law,* 18(2), 479–512. doi:10.3138/cjwl.18.2.479

Charter for Compassion. (n.d.). Retrieved from https://charterforcompassion.org

Dhami, M. K. (2016). Apology in victim–offender mediation. *Contemporary Justice Review,* 19(1), 31–42. doi:10.1080/10282580.2015.1101686

Fitzgerald, J. (2008). Does circle sentencing reduce aboriginal offending? *Crime and Justice Bulletin: NSW Bureau of Crime Statistics and Research,* 115, 1–11. Retrieved from http://www.bocsar.nsw.gov.au/Documents/CJB/cjb115.pdf

Geske, J. (2007). Restorative justice and the sexual abuse scandal in the Catholic Church. *Journal of Conflict Resolution's 2006 Symposium,* 8, 651–658.

Johnstone, G. & Van Ness, D. (Eds.) (2007). *Handbook of restorative justice.* Portland, OR: William Publishing.

Lilles, H. (2002, August 9). Circle sentencing: Part of the restorative justice continuum. *International Institute for Restorative Practices.* Retrieved from https://www.iirp.edu/eforum-archive/circle-sentencing-part-of-the-restorative-justice-continuum

Lord, J. H. (1990). *A how-to guide for victim impact panels: A creative sentencing opportunity.* Irving, TX: MADD.

Lyons, C. L. (2016). Restorative justice. *CQ Researcher,* 26(6), 121–144.

Sander, F. (1976). *The Pound Conference: Perspectives on justice in the future.* Roscoe Pound Conference, Minneapolis, Minnesota.

Skiba, R., & Losen, D. (2016). From reaction to prevention turning the page on school discipline. *American Educator,* 39(4) 4–12.

Stuart, B. D. (1998). Key differences: Courts and community circles. *Justice Professional,* 11(1–2), 89–116.

Van Ness, W., & Strong, K. (2015). *Restoring justice: An introduction to restorative justice.* New York, NY: Routledge.

Van Wormer, K., & Walker, L. (2013). *Restorative justice today: Practical applications.* Thousand Oaks, CA: SAGE, 173–183.

Zehr, H. (1990). *Changing lenses: A new focus for crime and justice.* Scottsdale, PA: Herald Press.

Law and Courts

Chapter 9

Justice Through Science

The Transformational Impact of DNA Evidence in Criminal Justice

Laurie Kubicek

Introduction

Deoxyribonucleic acid—DNA—is a self-replicating material present in nearly all living organisms. It is the main building block of chromosomes and the carrier of genetic information in human beings. DNA can be obtained from biological material such as blood, saliva, hair, bone, semen and urine. DNA is typically found in the cell's nucleus. An individual's complete set of genetic material, more than 3 billion DNA base pairs, is present in every cell and is called a genome. DNA's famous double-helix structure is a visual representation of the sequence of nucleotide bases (adenine, thymine, guanine, and cytosine, abbreviated A, T, G and C). It looks much like a twisted or spiraling ladder. Through complex processes, forensic scientists are able to obtain snapshots of individuals' DNA, differentiating them from the rest of the population. Humans share 99.1% of their DNA profile with each other, leaving only a .1% difference in genomes among individuals (with the exception of identical twins). Its capacity to identify individuals with scientific certainty led many to declare it the most important evidentiary discovery since fingerprint identification.

Understanding the History of DNA Evidence in Criminal Justice

The use of DNA evidence to identify suspects first came into use in the mid to late 1980s. Almost immediately after its initial applications in criminal justice, DNA was hailed as a cure for many ills that plague criminal trials: It provides scientific proof of identity of both the perpetrator and the innocently accused in criminal investigations. The first reported appellate opinion concerning DNA evidence was a 1988 Florida case, *Andrews v. State*. The federal government quickly realized the importance and utility of DNA identification and almost immediately began preparing to share information among states. The National Combined DNA Index System or CODIS went online in 1990. State law enforcement agencies can access two databases: one that indexes convicted offenders and one that contains DNA profiles from crime scene evidence (Kaye & Sensabaugh, 2011).

In an extensive report on the use of DNA in criminal trials, David Kaye and George Sensabaugh (2011) articulate a five-phase historical process through which courts developed standards for admitting DNA evidence in criminal trials. They explain that courts readily embraced DNA evidence in the early cases—rarely questioning its validity or the scientific processes concerned with its use (Kaye & Sensabaugh, 2011). Within 10 years, United States courts had critically questioned the process of DNA extraction and the evaluation and reading of DNA testing results and had come full circle by the late 1990s, once again widely accepting DNA evidence as scientifically sound. Courts have settled on the validity of PCR-based methods. Forensic scientists "have settled on one type of DNA variation known as 'short tandem repeats' or STRs to include or exclude individuals as the source of DNA at a crime scene" (Kaye & Sensabaugh, 2011, p. 133).

DNA evidence has multiple potential applications. It can be used by law enforcement agencies to identify suspects. The use of DNA testing to identify suspects in cold cases—those cases where law enforcement has no suspects or initial leads—is highly desirable. Successful cold case arrests and prosecutions generate significant media attention and public praise. In addition to identifying suspects' DNA, evidence can be used at trial to establish the defendant's guilt. Equally important is the potential for DNA evidence to exonerate wrongly accused suspects or innocent individuals convicted of crimes.

The Use of DNA Evidence Used to Prosecute Offenders

DNA evidence is used in criminal trials to identify perpetrators by matching their DNA profile with DNA evidence found at a crime scene to prove their presence or their contact with victims. This identification can provide convincing proof of guilt to the judge or jury. DNA evidence might serve to confirm existing probable cause already developed by law enforcement through investigation; this is called a confirmatory case. It might instead be a "cold hit" identification through database analysis alone. A common application for DNA evidence is in sexual assault cases. Alec Jeffreys, an English researcher, is credited with discovering the methods for extracting vaginal cells from sperm cells, as well as obtaining DNA profiles from old stains in 1985. Where hair, semen, or saliva is present on the body or clothing of a victim, it may prove the suspect's participation in a sexual assault. The dramatic impact of the availability of scientific proof to connect a rape suspect and victim has had a profound impact in sexual assault cases. DNA evidence can also exclude individuals from a crime scene by ruling them out as suspect, preventing the conviction of innocent suspects.

How common is the use of DNA evidence in identifying suspects? While the perception might be that it is used in every case, this is not true. In the United Kingdom, where the first murderer was convicted through the use of DNA fingerprinting and screening in 1988, "DNA matches from the national database help solve as few as one crime in every 1,300. ... Figures published in a Home Affairs Select Committee report suggest just 3,666 crimes are detected every year with links to an existing DNA profile. That is one in every 1,300 of the 4.9 million crimes carried out, and just one in 350 of the 1.3 million crimes solved by police" (Home Affairs Select Committee, 2010).

DNA evidence is scientific in nature, and its complexity requires expert testimony in the majority of cases. In criminal trials, judges have the latitude to evaluate and determine the credibility of a scientific expert before allowing their testimony in a trial. The process of qualifying expert witnesses is governed by the Federal Rules of Evidence § 702 and by state statutes for use in state criminal cases. Experts must meet specific criteria to qualify—which allows them to "assist" the jury to either "understand the evidence or determine a fact in issue." Attorneys who call expert witnesses will present the judge and jury with background to establish the expert's qualification to provide interpretation and opinion regarding their evaluation of the evidence. Attorneys typically exercise great care to choose experts they believe will be convincing to the judge and jury and whose professional opinions mirror their desired outcome in the case.

How important is DNA or scientific evidence to jurors in criminal trials? Some scholars have argued for the existence of a "CSI effect," whereby members of the public have a higher expectation that prosecutors present scientific evidence to convict in rape and other circumstantial cases. An extensive study of over 1,000 jurors found the reality in terms of impact regarding the CSI effect to be mixed (Barak, 2006). Considering juror expectations and demands about scientific evidence in relationship to other types of evidence, such as circumstantial or eyewitness, the study found that it did not always work in the direction hypothesized by complaining prosecutors and judges (Barak, 2006). While the study did find significant expectations and demands for scientific evidence, there was little or no indication of a link between those inclinations and watching particular television shows (Barak, 2006).

The Use of DNA Evidence to Protect and Exonerate the Innocent

According to the Innocence Project (2018), over 350 convicted offenders have been exonerated through DNA evidence. In 1989, Illinois man Gary Dotson served 10 years in prison before successfully securing his release through the use of DNA evidence to exclude him as the perpetrator in a rape case (Innocence Project, 2018). In 2015, the FBI was the focus of a widespread scandal centering on their laboratory handling of hair samples. In the FBI's April 20, 2015 press release, they indicated that their investigation involved the U.S. Department of Justice, the FBI, the Innocence Project and the National Association of Criminal Defense Lawyers. The FBI concluded that at least 90% of the trial transcripts they reviewed as part of their audit and investigation contained erroneous statements by the FBI agents or analysts who participated.

Twenty-six of the 28 FBI agents or analysts who offered trial testimony offered erroneous statements (FBI, 2015).

This scandal shed light on the differences between DNA testing being conducted in the context of medical science and DNA testing done in crime labs. The reality is that while DNA research and testing done in the medical context is often performed in sterile conditions where uniformity is the norm, crime laboratories may be very different. Often the individuals hired to perform testing in crime lab settings are not always educated or trained as scientists. Dr. Fred Whitehurst, a self-proclaimed FBI whistleblower, asserted that agents performing these tests in the FBI's crime labs failed to meet even minimal standards of education or training and were not genome experts (Whitehurst, 2017).

In addition to errors resulting from misapplied forensic science or failure to follow best practices in testing of DNA samples, there may also be a risk of psychological contamination of DNA evidence. Vanessa Meterko (2016), analyst for the Innocence Project explains that

> [o]ne strategy to protect evidence from psychological contamination is based on the idea that there is some information that a forensic analyst never needs. For instance, a fingerprint analyst does not need to know the race of the victim in order to do her job of analyzing a print recovered from the crime scene; likewise, a hair analyst never needs to know whether or not the suspect confessed in order to perform his job. This type of information is irrelevant and analysts should be insulated from it. Of course, sometimes an analyst *does* need to be exposed to potentially biasing information (e.g., a fingerprint analyst may need to compare an unidentified print with a known suspect's print, which could potentially bias the analyst). In situations like these, laboratories could employ a technique dubbed Linear Sequential Unmasking. Essentially, this means providing analysts with all the information needed, but doing it as late in the analysis process as possible. (p. 649)

Reformers continue to advocate for changes to the way DNA testing is conducted and for best practices in scientific testing for criminal trials.

The Future of DNA Evidence: Expanded Database Construction and Searches

In recent years, law enforcement has moved toward utilizing familial DNA charting to identify suspects. Where law enforcement does not find a match in any DNA database for a suspect, they can run the DNA profile from the evidence obtained for matches to close relatives. Investigators develop family trees and locate potential suspects from among the relatives of a DNA match. To date, familial DNA matching is not widely used in the United States, but it is gaining traction as high-profile cases are solved using the technique. In the spring of 2018, an Arizona cold murder case was solved through familial matching when the database picked up a closely matching DNA profile to the brother of the man eventually convicted for the murder of Allison Feldman (Rainey, 2018). Soon after came the celebrated arrest of Joseph James DeAngelo in Sacramento—the notorious Golden State Killer and East Area Rapist—also the result of familial DNA matching (Rainey, 2018).

The affidavit for probable cause for the arrest of DeAngelo was released to the press by the Sacramento County Superior Court in June 2018 and revealed details about investigator's use of DNA in cracking the case. DNA from the 1980 murders of Lyman and Charlene Smith in Ventura County, California, was matched to earlier Golden State Killer cases. In early 2018, DNA evidence from the Smith rape/murder produced a familial match to a close relative of Joseph James DeAngelo. Subsequent investigation—including collecting discarded DNA samples from DeAngelo's curbside trash and fingerprints from his vehicle's door handle—led to the confirmation of him as a suspect and his subsequent arrest. This cold case, dating back to June of 1976, may finally be solved, although his trial on charges in Sacramento and Ventura counties may take years to complete (*Los Angeles Times*, 2018).

In the United States there is a movement to prevent and rectify wrongful convictions based on DNA evidence. Nonprofit organizations such as the Innocence Project provide support and legal resources to inmates claiming innocence. Read and analyze the U.S. Supreme Court's decision in *DA et al. v. Osborne* (2009) regarding post-conviction access to new DNA testing. This defendant, convicted in Alaska state court, was unsuccessful in securing new DNA testing on due process grounds.

READING 9.1

District Attorney's Office for the Third Judicial District et al. v. William G. Osborne

Argued March 2, 2009, Decided June 18, 2009, 129 S.Ct. 2308

Chief Justice Roberts delivered the opinion of the Court.

DNA testing has an unparalleled ability both to exonerate the wrongly convicted and to identify the guilty. It has the potential to significantly improve both the criminal justice system and police investigative practices. The Federal Government and the States have recognized this, and have developed special approaches to ensure that this evidentiary tool can be effectively incorporated into established criminal procedure—usually but not always through legislation.

Against this prompt and considered response, the respondent, William Osborne, proposes a different approach: the recognition of a freestanding and far-reaching constitutional right of access to this new type of evidence. The nature of what he seeks is confirmed by his decision to file this lawsuit in federal court under 42 U.S.C. § 1983, not within the state criminal justice system. This approach would take the development of rules and procedures in this area out of the hands of legislatures and state courts shaping policy in a focused manner and turn it over to federal courts applying the broad parameters of the Due Process Clause. There is no reason to constitutionalize the issue in this way. Because the decision below would do just that, we reverse.

I

A

This lawsuit arose out of a violent crime committed 16 years ago, which has resulted in a long string of litigation in the state and federal courts. On the evening of March 22, 1993, two men driving through Anchorage, Alaska, solicited sex from a female prostitute, K.G. She agreed to perform fellatio on both men for $100 and got in their car. The three spent some time looking for a place to stop and ended up in a deserted area near Earthquake Park. When K.G. demanded payment in advance, the two men pulled out a gun and forced her to perform fellatio on the driver while the passenger penetrated her vaginally, using a blue condom she had brought. The passenger then ordered K.G. out of the car and told her to lie face-down in the snow. Fearing for her life, she refused, and the two men choked her and beat her with the gun. When K.G. tried to flee, the passenger beat her with a wooden axe handle and shot her in the head while she lay on the ground. They kicked some snow on top of her and left her for dead. K.G. did not die; the bullet had only grazed her head. Once the two men left, she found her way back to the road, and flagged down a passing car to take her home. Ultimately, she received medical care and spoke to the police. At the scene of the crime, the police recovered a spent shell casing, the axe handle, some of K.G.'s clothing stained with blood, and the blue condom. ...

Other evidence also implicated Osborne. K.G. picked out his photograph (with some uncertainty) and at trial she identified Osborne as her attacker. Other witnesses testified that shortly before the crime, Osborne had called Jackson from an arcade, and then driven off with him. An axe handle similar to the one at the scene of the crime was found in Osborne's room on the military base where he lived.

The State also performed DQ Alpha testing on sperm found in the blue condom. DQ Alpha testing is a relatively inexact form of DNA testing that can clear some wrongly accused individuals, but generally cannot narrow the perpetrator down to less than 5% of the population. See Dept. of Justice, National Comm'n on the Future of DNA Evidence, The Future of Forensic DNA Testing 17 (NCJ 183697, 2000) (hereinafter Future of Forensic DNA Testing); Dept. of Justice, National Comm'n on the Future of DNA Evidence, Post-conviction DNA Testing: Recommendations for Handling Requests 27 (NCJ 177626, 1999) (hereinafter Post-conviction DNA Testing). The semen found on the condom had a genotype that matched a blood sample taken from Osborne, but not ones from Jackson, K. G., or a third suspect named James Hunter. Osborne is [B]lack, and approximately 16% of [B]lack individuals have such a genotype. App. 117–119. In other words, the testing ruled out Jackson and Hunter as possible sources of the semen, and also ruled out over 80% of other [B]lack individuals. The State also examined some pubic hairs found at the scene of the crime, which were not susceptible to DQ Alpha testing, but which state witnesses attested to be similar to Osborne's. App. to Pet. for Cert. 117a.

B

Osborne and Jackson were convicted by an Alaska jury of kidnaping, assault, and sexual assault. They were acquitted of an additional count of sexual assault and of attempted murder. Finding it "nearly miraculous" that K.G. had survived, the trial judge sentenced Osborne to 26 years in prison, with 5 suspended. His conviction and sentence were affirmed on appeal.

Osborne then sought post-conviction relief in Alaska state court. He claimed that he had asked his attorney, Sidney Billingslea, to seek more discriminating restriction-fragment-length-polymorphism (RFLP) DNA testing during trial, and argued that she was constitutionally ineffective for not doing so. Billingslea testified that after investigation, she had concluded that further testing would do more harm than good. She planned to mount a defense of mistaken identity, and thought that the imprecision of the DQ Alpha test gave her "very good numbers in a mistaken identity, cross-racial identification case, where the victim was in the dark and had bad eyesight." Because she believed Osborne was guilty, "insisting on a more advanced ... DNA test would have served to prove that Osborne committed the alleged crimes." The Alaska Court of Appeals concluded that Billingslea's decision had been strategic and rejected Osborne's claim. ... The court relied heavily on the fact that Osborne had confessed to some of his crimes in a 2004 application for parole—in which it is a crime to lie. In this statement, Osborne acknowledged forcing K.G. to have sex at gunpoint, as well as beating her and covering her with snow. He repeated this confession before the parole board. Despite this acceptance of responsibility, the board did not grant him discretionary parole. ...

Meanwhile, Osborne had also been active in federal court, suing state officials under 42 U.S.C. § 1983. He claimed that the Due Process Clause and other constitutional provisions gave him a constitutional right to access the DNA evidence for what is known as short-tandem-repeat (STR) testing (at his own expense). This form of testing is more discriminating than the DQ Alpha or RFLP methods available at the time of Osborne's trial. ...

On cross-motions for summary judgment after remand, the District Court concluded that "there *does exist, under the unique and specific facts presented,* a very limited constitutional right to the testing sought." <u>445 F.Supp.2d 1079, 1081 (2006)</u>. The court relied on several factors: that the testing Osborne sought had been unavailable at trial, that the testing could be accomplished at almost no cost to the State, and that the results were likely to be material. It therefore granted summary judgment in favor of Osborne. ...

The court declined to decide the details of what showing must be made to access the evidence because it found "Osborne's case for disclosure ... so strong on the facts" that "[w]herever the bar is, he crosses it." While acknowledging that Osborne's prior confessions were "certainly relevant," the court concluded that they did not "necessarily trum[p] ... the right to obtain post-conviction access to evidence" in light of the "emerging reality of wrongful convictions based on false confessions."

We granted certiorari to decide whether Osborne's claims could be pursued using § 1983, and whether he has a right under the Due Process Clause to obtain post-conviction access to the State's evidence for DNA testing. We now reverse on the latter ground.

II

Modern DNA testing can provide powerful new evidence unlike anything known before. Since its first use in criminal investigations in the mid–1980s, there have been several major advances in DNA technology, culminating in STR technology. It is now often possible to determine whether a biological tissue matches a suspect with near certainty. While of course many criminal trials proceed without any forensic and scientific testing at all, there is no technology comparable to DNA testing for matching tissues when such evidence is at issue. Post-conviction DNA Testing 1–2; Future of Forensic DNA Testing 13–14. DNA testing has exonerated wrongly convicted people, and has confirmed the convictions of many others.

At the same time, DNA testing alone does not always resolve a case. Where there is enough other incriminating evidence and an explanation for the DNA result, science alone cannot prove a prisoner innocent. See *House v. Bell,* <u>547</u>

U.S. 518, 540–548, 126 S.Ct. 2064, 165 L.Ed.2d 1 (2006). The availability of technologies not available at trial cannot mean that every criminal conviction, or even every criminal conviction involving biological evidence, is suddenly in doubt. The dilemma is how to harness DNA's power to prove innocence without unnecessarily overthrowing the established system of criminal justice.

That task belongs primarily to the legislature. "[T]he States are currently engaged in serious, thoughtful examinations," *Washington v. Glucksberg*, 521 U.S. 702, 719, 117 S.Ct. 2258, 138 L.Ed.2d 772 (1997), of how to ensure the fair and effective use of this testing within the existing criminal justice framework. Forty-six States have already enacted statutes dealing specifically with access to DNA evidence. ... The Federal Government has also passed the Innocence Protection Act of 2004, § 411, 118 Stat. 2278, codified in part at 18 U.S.C. § 3600, which allows federal prisoners to move for court-ordered DNA testing under certain specified conditions. That Act also grants money to States that enact comparable statutes, § 413, 118 Stat. 2285, note following 42 U.S.C. § 14136, and as a consequence has served as a model for some state legislation. At oral argument, Osborne agreed that the federal statute is a model for how States ought to handle the issue. Tr. of Oral Arg. 33, 38–39; see also Brief for United States as Amicus Curiae 19–26 (defending constitutionality of Innocence Protection Act).

These laws recognize the value of DNA evidence but also the need for certain conditions on access to the State's evidence. A requirement of demonstrating materiality is common, *e.g.*, 18 U.S.C. § 3600(a)(8), but it is not the only one. The federal statute, for example, requires a sworn statement that the applicant is innocent. § 3600(a)(1). This requirement is replicated in several state statutes. *E.g.*, Cal.Penal Code Ann. §§ 1405(b)(1), (c)(1) (West Supp. 2009); Fla. Stat. § 925.11(2)(a)(3) (2006); N.H. Rev.Stat. Ann. 651–D:2(I) (b) (2007); S.C. Code Ann. 17–28–40 (Supp.2008). States also impose a range of diligence requirements. Several require the requested testing to "have been technologically impossible at trial." Garrett, *supra*, at 1681, and n. 242. Others deny testing to those who declined testing at trial for tactical reasons. *E.g.*, Utah Code. Ann. § 78B–9–301(4) (2008).

Alaska is one of a handful of States yet to enact legislation specifically addressing the issue of evidence requested for DNA testing. But that does not mean that such evidence is unavailable for those seeking to prove their innocence. Instead, Alaska courts are addressing how to apply existing laws for discovery and post-conviction relief to this novel technology.

See *Osborne I*, 110 P.3d, at 992–993; *Patterson v. State*, No. A–8814, 2006 WL 573797, *4 (Alaska App., Mar.8, 2006). The same is true with respect to other States that do not have DNA-specific statutes. *E.g.*, *Fagan v. State*, 957 So.2d 1159 (Ala.Crim.App.2007). Cf. Mass. Rule Crim. Proc. 30(c)(4)(2009).

First, access to evidence is available under Alaska law for those who seek to subject it to newly available DNA testing that will prove them to be actually innocent. Under the State's general post-conviction relief statute, a prisoner may challenge his conviction when "there exists evidence of material facts, not previously presented and heard by the court, that requires vacation of the conviction or sentence in the interest of justice." Alaska Stat. § 12.72.010(4) (2008). Such a claim is exempt from otherwise applicable time limits if "newly discovered evidence," pursued with due diligence, "establishes by clear and convincing evidence that the applicant is innocent." § 12.72.020(b)(2).

Both parties agree that under these provisions of § 12.72, "a defendant is entitled to post-conviction relief if the defendant presents newly discovered evidence that establishes by clear and convincing evidence that the defendant is innocent." *Osborne I, supra,* at 992 (internal quotation marks omitted). If such a claim is brought, state law permits general discovery. See Alaska Rule Crim. Proc. 35.1(g). Alaska courts have explained that these procedures are available to request DNA evidence for newly available testing to establish actual innocence. See *Patterson, supra,* at *4 ("If Patterson had brought the DNA analysis request as part of his previous application for [post-conviction] relief … he would have been able to request production of evidence").

In addition to this statutory procedure, the Alaska Court of Appeals has invoked a widely accepted three-part test to govern additional rights to DNA access under the State Constitution. *Osborne II,* 163 P.3d, at 974–975. Drawing on the experience with DNA evidence of State Supreme Courts around the country, the Court of Appeals explained that it was "reluctant to hold that Alaska law offers no remedy to defendants who could prove their factual innocence." *Osborne I,* 110 P.3d, at 995; see *id.*, at 995, n. 27 (citing decisions from other state courts). It was "prepared to hold, however, that a defendant who seeks post-conviction DNA testing … must show (1) that the conviction rested primarily on eyewitness identification evidence, (2) that there was a demonstrable doubt concerning the defendant's identification as the perpetrator, and (3) that scientific testing would likely be conclusive on this issue." *Id.*, at 995. Thus, the Alaska courts have suggested that even those who do not get discovery under the State's criminal rules have available to them a safety valve under the State Constitution.

This is the background against which the Federal Court of Appeals ordered the State to turn over the DNA evidence in its possession, and it is our starting point in analyzing Osborne's constitutional claims.

III

The parties dispute whether Osborne has invoked the proper federal statute in bringing his claim. He sued under the federal civil rights statute, 42 U.S.C. § 1983, which gives a cause of action to those who challenge a State's "deprivation of any rights ... secured by the Constitution." The State insists that Osborne's claim must be brought under 28 U.S.C. § 2254, which allows a prisoner to seek "a writ of habeas corpus ... on the ground that he is in custody in violation of the Constitution."

While Osborne's claim falls within the literal terms of § 1983, we have also recognized that § 1983 must be read in harmony with the habeas statute ... the State says, "Osborne's § 1983 action is nothing more than a request for evidence to support a hypothetical claim that he is actually innocent. ... [T] his hypothetical claim sounds at the core of habeas corpus."

Osborne responds that his claim does not sound in habeas at all. Although invalidating his conviction is of course his ultimate goal, giving him the evidence he seeks "would not necessarily imply the invalidity of [his] confinement." Brief for Respondent 21. If he prevails, he would receive only *access* to the DNA, and even if DNA testing exonerates him, his conviction is not automatically invalidated. He must bring an entirely separate suit or a petition for clemency to invalidate his conviction. If he were proved innocent, the State might also release him on its own initiative, avoiding any need to pursue habeas at all. ...

While we granted certiorari on this question, our resolution of Osborne's claims does not require us to resolve this difficult issue. Accordingly, we will assume without deciding that the Court of Appeals was correct that *Heck* does not bar Osborne's § 1983 claim. Even under this assumption, it was wrong to find a due process violation.

IV

A

"No State shall ... deprive any person of life, liberty, or property, without due process of law." U.S. Const., Amdt. 14, § 1; accord Amdt. 5. This Clause imposes procedural limitations on a State's power to take away protected entitlements. See, *e.g., Jones v. Flowers* <u>547 U.S. 220, 226–239, 126 S.Ct. 1708, 164 L.Ed.2d 415 (2006)</u>. Osborne argues that access to the State's evidence is a "process" needed to vindicate his right to prove himself innocent and get out of jail. Process is not an end in itself, so a necessary premise of this argument is that he has an entitlement (what our precedents call a "liberty interest") to prove his innocence even after a fair trial has proved otherwise. We must first examine this asserted liberty interest to determine what process (if any) is due.

In identifying his potential liberty interest, Osborne first attempts to rely on the Governor's constitutional authority to "grant pardons, commutations, and reprieves." <u>Alaska Const., Art. III, § 21</u>. That claim can be readily disposed of. We have held that noncapital defendants do not have a liberty interest in traditional state executive clemency, to which no particular claimant is *entitled* as a matter of state law. Osborne therefore cannot challenge the constitutionality of any procedures available to vindicate an interest in state clemency.

Osborne does, however, have a liberty interest in demonstrating his innocence with new evidence under state law. As explained, Alaska law provides that those who use "newly discovered evidence" to "establis[h] by clear and convincing evidence that [they are] innocent" may obtain "vacation of [their] conviction or sentence in the interest of justice." <u>Alaska Stat. §§ 12.72.020(b)(2), 12.72.010(4)</u>. This "state-created right can, in some circumstances, beget yet other rights to procedures essential to the realization of the parent right." *Dumschat, supra,* <u>at 463, 101 S.Ct. 2460</u>. ...

The Court of Appeals went too far, however, in concluding that the Due Process Clause requires that certain familiar pre-conviction trial rights be extended to protect Osborne's post-conviction liberty interest. After identifying Osborne's possible liberty interests, the court concluded that the State had an obligation to comply with the principles of *Brady v. Maryland,* <u>373 U.S. 83, 83 S.Ct. 1194, 10 L.Ed.2d 215</u>. ... Osborne does not claim that *Brady* controls this case and with good reason.

A criminal defendant proved guilty after a fair trial does not have the same liberty interests as a free man. At trial, the defendant is presumed innocent and may demand that the government prove its case beyond reasonable doubt. But "[o]nce a defendant has been afforded a fair trial and convicted of the offense for which he was charged, the presumption of innocence disappears." *Herrera v. Collins,* 506 U.S. 390, 399, 113 S.Ct. 853, 122 L.Ed.2d 203 (1993). "Given a valid conviction, the criminal defendant has been constitutionally deprived of his liberty." *Dumschat, supra,* at 464, 101 S.Ct. 2460. ...

Instead, the question is whether consideration of Osborne's claim within the framework of the State's procedures for post-conviction relief "offends some principle of justice so rooted in the traditions and conscience of our people as to be ranked as fundamental," or "transgresses any recognized principle of fundamental fairness in operation." *Medina v. California,* 505 U.S. 437, 446, 448, 112 S.Ct. 2572, 120 L.Ed.2d 353 (1992) (internal quotation marks omitted); see *Herrera, supra,* at 407–408, 113 S.Ct. 853 (applying *Medina* to post-conviction relief for actual innocence); *Finley, supra,* at 556, 107 S.Ct. 1990 (post-conviction relief procedures are constitutional if they "compor[t] with fundamental fairness"). Federal courts may upset a State's post-conviction relief procedures only if they are fundamentally inadequate to vindicate the substantive rights provided.

We see nothing inadequate about the procedures Alaska has provided to vindicate its state right to post-conviction relief in general, and nothing inadequate about how those procedures apply to those who seek access to DNA evidence. Alaska provides a substantive right to be released on a sufficiently compelling showing of new evidence that establishes innocence. It exempts such claims from otherwise applicable time limits. The State provides for discovery in post-conviction proceedings, and has—through judicial decision—specified that this discovery procedure is available to those seeking access to DNA evidence. *Patterson,* 2006 WL 573797, at *4. These procedures are not without limits. The evidence must indeed be newly available to qualify under Alaska's statute, must have been diligently pursued, and must also be sufficiently material. These procedures are similar to those provided for DNA evidence by federal law and the law of other States, see, *e.g.,* 18 U.S.C. § 3600(a), and they are not inconsistent with the "traditions and conscience of our people" or with "any recognized principle of fundamental fairness." *Medina, supra,* at 446, 448, 112 S.Ct. 2572 (internal quotation marks omitted).

B

The Court of Appeals below relied only on procedural due process, but Osborne seeks to defend the judgment on the basis of substantive due process as well. He asks that we recognize a freestanding right to DNA evidence untethered from the liberty interests he hopes to vindicate with it. We reject the invitation and conclude, in the circumstances of this case, that there is no such substantive due process right. ... To suddenly constitutionalize this area would short-circuit what looks to be a prompt and considered legislative response. The first DNA testing statutes were passed in 1994 and 1997. In the past decade, 44 States and the Federal Government have followed suit, reflecting the increased availability of DNA testing. As noted, Alaska itself is considering such legislation. ... If we extended substantive due process to this area, we would cast these statutes into constitutional doubt and be forced to take over the issue of DNA access ourselves. We are reluctant to enlist the Federal Judiciary in creating a new constitutional code of rules for handling DNA.

Establishing a freestanding right to access DNA evidence for testing would force us to act as policymakers, and our substantive-due-process rulemaking authority would not only have to cover the right of access but a myriad of other issues. ... DNA evidence will undoubtedly lead to changes in the criminal justice system. It has done so already. The question is whether further change will primarily be made by legislative revision and judicial interpretation of the existing system, or whether the Federal Judiciary must leap ahead—revising (or even discarding) the system by creating a new constitutional right and taking over responsibility for refining it.

Federal courts should not presume that state criminal procedures will be inadequate to deal with technological change. The criminal justice system has historically accommodated new types of evidence, and is a time-tested means of carrying out society's interest in convicting the guilty while respecting individual rights. That system, like any human endeavor, cannot be perfect. DNA evidence shows that it has not been. But there is no basis for Osborne's approach of assuming that because DNA has shown that these procedures are not flawless, DNA evidence must be treated as categorically outside the process, rather than within it. That is precisely what his § 1983 suit seeks to do, and that is the contention we reject.

The judgment of the Court of Appeals is reversed, and the case is remanded for further proceedings consistent with this opinion.

It is so ordered.

The Court's discussion of post-conviction relief for newly discovered DNA evidence illuminates the legal framework for defendants' rights in this area of law.

Discussion Questions

1. Do you believe that government maintenance of DNA databases presents a threat to individual freedom or privacy?

2. Do you agree with Meterko's contentions regarding the risk of psychological contamination of evidence? What practical ways do you believe courts can mitigate the risks associated with this phenomenon?

3. Explain whether you agree with the use of familial DNA charting to help law enforcement develop leads to suspects who are not in the database.

References

Andrews v. State, 533 So. 2d 841, Fla. Dist. Ct. App. (1988)

Barak, G., Kim, Y. S., & Shelton, D. E. (2006). A study of juror expectations and demands concerning scientific evidence: Does the "CSI effect" exist? *Vanderbilt Journal of Entertainment and Tech Law, Vol. 9 Pg. 331.*

Committee Office, & House of Commons. (2010, March 8). Home Affairs Select Committee. Retrieved from https://publications.parliament.uk/pa/cm200910/cmselect/cmhaff/222/22203.htm#a1

District Attorney's Office for the Third Judicial District, et al. v. Osborne, 129 S.Ct. 2308 (2009)

FBI. (2015, April 20). *FBI testimony on microscopic hair analysis contained errors in at least 90 percent of cases in ongoing review.* Retrieved from https://www.fbi.gov/news/pressrel/press-releases/fbi-testimony-on-microscopic-hair-analysis-contained-errors-in-at-least-90-percent-of-cases-in-ongoing-review

Innocence Project (2018, July 23). *DNA exonerations.* Retrieved from https://www.innocenceproject.org/dna-exonerations-in-the-united-states/

Kaye, D. H., & Sensabaugh, G. (2011). Reference guide on DNA identification evidence. In National Research Council of the National Academies (Ed.), *Reference Manual on Scientific Evidence* (3rd ed.) (pp. 129–210). Washington, D.C.: The National Academies Press.

Los Angeles Times. (2018, June 1). Affadavit in support of arrest of Golden State killer. Retrieved from http://documents.latimes.com/la-me-affidavit-warrant-suspectedgolden-state-killer/.

Meterko, V. (2016). Strengths and limitations of forensic science: What DNA exonerations have taught us and where to go from here. *West Virginia Law Review,* 119, 639–649.

Parliament (UK). (2010, March 15). *Memorandum submitted by GeneWatch UK.* Retrieved from https://publications.parliament.uk/pa/cm200910/cmselect/cmhaff/222/222we04.htm

Rainey, J. (2018, April 15). Familial DNA puts elusive killers behind bars. But only 12 states use it. *NBC.* Retrieved from https://www.nbcnews.com/news/us-news/familial-dnaputs-elusive-killers-behind-bars-only-12-states-n869711

Whitehurst, F. (2017). Whistleblower protection blog. *National Whistleblower Legal Defense and Education Fund.* Retrieved from https://www.whistleblowersblog.org/2017/11/articles/intelligence-community-whistleblowers/dr-whitehurst-and-the-fbi-lab-scandal/

Chapter 10

Child Pornography Offenses and Offenders

New Challenges for the Criminal Justice System

Alexa D. Sardina

Introduction

Child pornography offenses are sex crimes that involve the visual depiction of children involved in a sexual act. Although this offense was almost completely eradicated in the 1980s, the dawn of the Internet ushered the proliferation of online or virtual child pornography. The anonymity of the Internet and the ease of sharing digital images of children has contributed to the public's concern regarding child pornography and fear that child pornography offenders will use the Internet to commit contact sexual offenses against children. The emergence of increased numbers of child pornography offenders has led to the mobilization of legal and investigative resources toward identifying and prosecuting child pornography offenders, as well as a great deal of research into all aspects of online sexual offending in hopes of clarifying, reducing, and eliminating these kinds of offenses. This chapter examines the history of child pornography law, the characteristics of child pornography offenders and the threat they pose, and the challenges that police, prosecutors, and judges face when dealing with child pornography offenses/offenders. The impact of technology on an emergent concern regarding "sexting" is also discussed within the broader context of the challenges associated with defining child pornography and punishing child pornography offenders.

What Is Child Pornography?

Defining child pornography is challenging. Child pornography is broadly defined as the depiction of sexually explicit behavior involving a minor under the age of 18 years old. However, the definition of "child" and "pornography" vary by state and country. In the United States, child pornography includes actual or simulated vaginal intercourse, oral or anal intercourse, bestiality, masturbation, sexually sadistic or masochistic behavior, and exhibition of genitals of minors under the age of 18 (U.S. Code, Title § 2256). Images are also considered pornographic if the child is the central part of a sexually suggestive setting, the child is in an unnatural pose or in inappropriate attire, the depiction suggests willingness to engage in sexual activity, or the depiction is intended to elicit a sexual response in the viewer (Terry, 2013).

Federal law prohibits knowingly producing, manufacturing, distributing, or accessing with the intent to view child pornography (18 U.S.C. § 2552).

The History of Child Pornography in the United States

Concern over child pornography and legislation protecting children from sexual exploitation is relatively new (Adler, 2001). It was during the late 1970s and through the early 1980s that awareness of the necessity to protect children from sexual exploitation was growing. During this period, child sexual abuse became linked to a variety of other issues, including kidnapping, organized sex trafficking, and sex rings (Adler, 2001). This was the context for the unanimous decision of *New York v. Ferber* (1982). The decision in the *Ferber* case separated child pornography from other types of pornographic material and it became a separate category (Wortley & Smallbone, 2006). (At this time, legislation only applied to actual images. Virtual images were not given consideration under early legislation.) This decision was an important step in addressing the issue of child exploitation. However, it was limited to visual depictions of actual minors engaged in sexual conduct. Also, this ruling applied to individuals who produced, promoted, or distributed child pornography, not individuals who possessed it (Burke, 1997). But, in 1977, Congress passed the Protection of Children Against Sexual Exploitation Act, which prohibited using children to make pornographic material for financial gain (Vandiver, Braithwaite, & Stafford, 2017).

Throughout the 1970s and 1980s, child pornography trafficking in the United States decreased and had been almost eradicated due to the aforementioned legislation and successful campaigns by law enforcement agencies (Terry, 2013). At this time, production and reproduction of child pornography was risky and expensive. Prior to the widespread accessibility of the Internet, those interested in deviant acts with children had greater difficulty in networking. Purchase, distribution, and receipt of child pornography became near impossible because consumers of the material found it more challenging to find ways to interact with each other (Terry, 2013). However, the electronic environment provides a space in which potential sex offenders can engage in deviant behavior (Quayle & Taylor, 2002).

Child pornography has resurged as a serious offense in the United States and is now a multi-billion-dollar industry (Vandiver et al., 2017). In response to the discovery of a new way to promote illicit sexual activity with children, in 1998, the Office of Juvenile Justice and Delinquency Prevention began to label online sexual crimes directed toward children as Internet Crimes Against Children (ICAC). ICAC were defined as any computer-facilitated sexual exploitation of children, including online solicitation and child pornography (Babchishin, Hanson, & Hermann, 2011).

Child Pornography Offenders: Demographics and Typologies

In a study conducted for the National Center for Missing and Exploited Children, Wolak, Finkelhor, and Mitchell (2005) found that more than 90% of those arrested for possessing child pornography were male, most were White, age 26 or older, about equally likely to be single or married, and most were employed. Forty-six percent had access to a child in their home, through work, or through an organized activity (Wolak et al., 2005). The demographics of the average possessor of child pornography are very similar to the demographics of the average child pornography producer. Most of the offenders who produced child pornography were male, White, age 26 or older, single, employed, were not registered sex offenders, and possessed other child pornography in addition to what they had produced (Wolak et al., 2005).

Child pornography offenders can be broadly separated into four categories: (a) those who access child pornography to satisfy a curiosity or an impulse but lack a sexual interest in children, (b) those who access child pornography and have a sexual interest in children but do not commit contact sexual offenses, (c) those who use the Internet to commit contact sexual offenses, and (d) those who produce and distribute child pornography for financial gain only (Krone, 2004).

Possessors of child pornography that have a sexual interest in children may consciously create digital images of children for their private use, actively seek materials via peer-to-peer networks (P2P) (peer-to-peer networking is an approach to computer networking through which all computers are equally responsible for data processing; peer-to-peer workgroups allow the sharing of files and other resources and as the network increases, the power of the P2P network also increases (Mitchell, 2018), or actively seek material but only through secure networks (Krone, 2004). Overall, the risk of contact offending posed by possessors of child pornography is unknown. However, research suggests that child pornography offenders with a greater number of images, a higher ratio of child-to-adult images, images of younger children, and images including male and female children are at a greater risk for seeking sexual contact with children in the future (Seto, Cantor, & Blanchard, 2006).

The third group of child pornography offenders is made up of individuals who access child pornography *and* sexually abuse children. Some expose their victims to child pornography to desensitize them and lower their sexual inhibitions (Krone, 2004). Others initiate sexual acts with children they find online and record their encounters for personal use. According to research conducted by Alexy, Burgess, and Baker (2005) there may be a group of Internet offenders, called combination trader-travelers, who trade child pornography and travel across states or internationally to sexual abuse children.

The final grouping of offenders includes individuals who produce and distribute child pornography. Distributers and producers are motivated by profit and not necessarily a sexual interest in children (Vandiver et al., 2017). But, some studies have found rare cases in which a distributer or producer may also consume child pornography (Mitchell & Jones, 2013). Producers of child pornography are typically involved in the recruitment and/or solicitation of child victims and the filming or photography of sexually explicit material (Krone, 2004). Distributers are not usually involved in production but distribute child pornography to consumers (Krone, 2004).

Child Pornography Offenders and Contact Child Sexual Abuse Offenses

An important question regarding child pornography offenders is whether they are likely to commit a contact sexual offense against a child. Research into sexual offenses involving the Internet is in its infancy, is not fully developed, and has produced differing results (Briggs, Simon, & Simonsen, 2011). There are two main reasons for the challenge of identifying the overlap of the two offenses. First, official statistics report low rates for child pornography and contact sex offenses. In other words, many offenders who have admitted to viewing child pornography have not be convicted of a contact sexual offense against a child. Conversely, contact offenders who view child pornography have often not been convicted of child pornography offenses (Terry, 2013). Second, when both types of offending are present, it is difficult to establish the chronology of the behaviors and therefore it is difficult to estimate the risk that child pornography offenders will eventually commit contact child sexual abuse offenses (Terry, 2013).

Generally, research suggests that there is some overlap between child pornography offenses and contact sex offenses (Bourke & Hernandez, 2009; Seto & Eke, 2005). Using several methods to determine if an individual arrested for possession of child pornography had also committed a contact sex offense, Bourke and Hernandez (2009) conducted a study comparing two groups of child pornography offenders in a prison treatment program. The first group's self-reported history included possession, receipt, and/or distribution of child pornography. The second group had a criminal history that included child pornography offenses and contact sexual offenses. The offenders' self-reported histories were recorded at two times, before and after the treatment program. At the end of treatment, Bourke and Hernandez (2009) found that 91 of the child pornography-only offenders admitted to sexually abusing an average of 8.7 children. This challenges the belief that child pornography offenders are impulsive or stumble on child pornography accidently and are not likely to commit a contact sexual offense against a child (Vandiver et al., 2017).

There is also research that suggests that child pornography use may predict hands-on offenses. Seto and Eke (2005) studied a sample of 201 adult child pornography offenders. They found that 4% committed a new contact sexual offense within an average of 2.5 years. Furthermore, offenders with a criminal history were significantly more likely to offend within a year, and offenders who committed prior and concurrent sex crimes were the most likely to reoffend (Seto & Eke, 2005). This research suggests that recidivism rates among child pornography offenders is low, but the risk increases for offenders with a prior criminal history and is especially heightened among offenders with a history of prior sexual offenses. This study was replicated in 2011 and included a larger sample with a longer follow-up period (Eke, Seto, & Williams, 2011). Five hundred and forty-one child pornography offenders were followed over a 4.1-year period. Eke and colleagues (2011) found that 4% of offenders committed a new contact sexual offense within an average of 4.1 years and 7% were charged with a new child pornography offense. Furthermore, Eke and colleagues (2011) identified criminal history and younger offender age as predictors of new violent offending. This research highlights the important risk factors for recidivism. Risk factors for recidivism among child pornography offenders include lower education, being single, prior sex offender treatment, and possession of collections of child pornography (Eke et al., 2011). Overall, sex offenders as a group rarely re-offend by committing another sex offense. Most often, sex offenders who re-offend commit a variety of offenses. The research on child pornography offenders suggests the same (Vandiver et al., 2017).

The Criminal Justice Response to Child Pornography

Today, child pornography is a digital and virtual industry nationally and internationally. Investigating the possession, production, and distribution of child pornography is difficult because of the anonymity and global reach of the Internet. Recent technological innovations have given offenders easy, fast, and anonymous access to child pornography.

Justice statistics suggest that the number of child pornography investigations is increasing (Finkelhor & Ormrod, 2004). Because of the rapid technological advances, law enforcement agencies and prosecutors have had to update their investigative procedures and courts must engage in continuous review to ensure that search and seizures are constitutional (Wells, Finkelhor, Wolak, & Mitchell, 2007).

Investigating Child Pornography

There are significant hurdles to investigating the misuse of the Internet by child pornography offenders, and many law enforcement agencies, especially at the state and local levels, are not well-equipped to deal with high-tech crimes (Franqueria, Bryce, Al Mutawa, & Marrington, 2018). Yet, despite the challenges associated with investigating online child pornography, computer technology can give law enforcement agents powerful tools and forensic evidence, which is often lacking in conventional, contact child sex crimes (Norland & Bartholet, 2001). Most activity that takes place on the Internet leaves a digital trail. Thus, it can aid the police in their investigations by allowing agencies with access to computer forensic equipment to collect valuable digital evidence (Norland & Bartholet, 2001). The advanced technological expertise necessary to target these crimes comes at a high price. In 2008 alone, state and local law enforcement agencies received more than $17 million to combat Internet crimes against children (Motivans & Kyckelhahn, 2008).

Despite these emerging investigative techniques, law enforcement investigations of Internet child pornography possession present specific challenges. Not only do they require digital evidence collection and undercover operations, they may also involve multiple law enforcement jurisdictions when child pornography is distributed via the Internet (Wells et al., 2007). Another challenge for law enforcement is proving that images fit statutory definitions of child pornography. Wolak and colleagues (2003) reported that 92% of offenders arrested for possessing child pornography had images of minors engaged in explicit sexual activity. Such images fit within most states' definitions of child pornography. Although an image that shows sexually explicit conduct between an adult and a child can be easily categorized as child pornography, images of nude children may be viewed as artistic (Lanning, 1992). Generally, images of nude children would only be considered child pornography if they focus on the genital area (Lanning, 1992). However, law enforcement agents are encouraged to consider questionable material in the context of an offender's entire collection (Lanning, 1992). Law enforcement agents may also have difficulty determining the age of children depicted in pornographic material (Wells et al., 2007). Consideration of a child's age can be problematic in these cases, especially since offenders most often collect images produced by others (Wells et al., 2007). Some jurisdictions utilize medical experts to testify that the children in pornographic images are minors (Rosenbloom & Tanner, 1998).

The challenges of investigating child pornography cases are further complicated by the stressors that are unique to child pornography cases (Krause, 2009). Child pornography investigators' roles are multi-faceted, but a central aspect of their duties involves accessing, preserving, collating, and presenting evidence in a format that meets legal requirements (Powell, Cassematis, Benson, Smallbone, & Wortley, 2014). In most cases, each image or video must be categorized by severity and catalogued so appropriate charges can be made against the offender (Powell et al., 2014). Child pornography investigators' roles are also unique because they must repeatedly expose themselves to disturbing images of child victims during investigations (Krause, 2009). Thus, they may experience various emotional and behavioral symptoms stemming from work-related stress, including behavioral changes, absenteeism, fatigue, anxiety, and feelings of worthlessness (Bourke & Craun, 2014; Edelmann, 2010; Violanti & Gehrke, 2004). Research suggests that the risk for negative personal and professional outcomes for these investigators is influenced by five factors: the frequency of exposure to disturbing images, the duration of the exposure, the type and intensity of the exposure, the perceived control of the stress, and the coping strategies an investigator may possess (Krause, 2008). Although based on limited data, researchers have found that several safeguards are successful in managing and mitigating these risks to child pornography investigators. These safeguards may include organizational support, informal networks promoting well-being and communication, lateral transfer options without penalty, and program-specific training (Krause, 2008).

Prosecuting Child Pornography Offenders

Over the course of the past 15 years, the federal government has increased the prosecution of child exploitation cases. In 2006, child pornography cases constituted 69% of the total amount of child exploitation cases referred for federal prosecution. From 2006 to 2007, there was a 27.8% increase in the number of child pornography indictments filed (Motivans & Kyckelhahn, 2008). This is most likely due to advancement in law enforcement methods that have brought a greater number of offenders under criminal investigation.

There is no single way to prosecute a child pornography case, and prosecutors often use a mix of complex strategies to try a case (Howard, 2004). Some prosecutors may charge one count per image. Other prosecutors determine a saturation point, at which there is no reason to go beyond a certain number of images (Howard, 2004). Prosecuting child pornography crimes can also be challenging, especially with respect to establishing *mens rea*. It is the duty of the prosecutor to prove that the defendant *knowingly* possessed illegal images. The results of the National Juvenile Online Victimization (N-JOV) Prosecutor Study indicate that several defenses are encountered by prosecutors of child pornography (Walsh, Wolak, & Finkelhor, 2013). These defenses include unknowingly downloading images, addiction or mental illness, not perceiving downloaded images as child pornography, and claiming downloaded images were used for research purposes (Walsh et al., 2013). One way federal and state statutes have construed knowing possession of child pornography has to do with images found on the defendant's computer cache. (A cache is a storage mechanism designed to speed up the loading of Internet displays, including pictures and movies. When a webpage is viewed, the web browser saves a copy of the page in a folder on the computer's hard drive. This folder is known as the cache (Walsh et al., 2013).) The majority of courts take the position that the images or movies on a hard drive as sufficient evidence to demonstrate possession of child pornography (Walsh et al., 2013).

Sentencing Child Pornography Offenders

Regarding sentencing, child pornography offenses are typically divided into two groups: production offenses and non-production offenses, including distribution, transportation, receipt, and possession (U.S.

Sentencing Commission, 2009). The prosecution of non-production offenses account for approximately 90% of all federal child pornography prosecutions (U.S. Sentencing Commission, 2009). When Congress criminalized possession of child pornography and possession with intent to sell child pornography, the sentencing guidelines were amended to impose harsher punishments (Vandiver et al., 2017). Congress directed the U.S. Sentencing Commission to reduce the frequency of lesser sentences and to add enhancements for crimes with aggravated situations, such as (a) violent images, (b) sexual abuse of a minor, or (c) prior convictions for child exploitation (Vandiver et al., 2017). Furthermore, harsher punishments were permitted if the material is distributed for financial gain, depicts prepubescent children in a violent context, or is sent to minors (Hamilton, 2012). As a result, the length of child pornography sentences has increased. In 1994, the average sentence for child pornography offenders was 36 months; in 2002, the average sentence was 49.7 months, and in 2007, it was 109.6 months. This accounts for a 300% increase (Stabenow, 2009). This pattern is problematic because the sentencing enhancements, which were originally intended to provide proportional punishment for aggravating circumstances, are now applied to most child pornography offenders (U.S. Sentencing Commission, 2010).

Much controversy surrounds the sentencing of child pornography offenders. In a survey of federal trial court judges, 70% deemed the guidelines as "too high" as they applied to possession of child pornography and 69% believed that sentences for receipt of child pornography was excessive (U.S. Sentencing Commission, 2010). In response to this excess, federal judges began sentencing offenders below the guideline range when they deemed it appropriate. Thus, sentencing practices in child pornography non-production cases have shown significant increases in minimum and average sentence lengths and significant decreases in the rate of sentences within the applicable guideline ranges (U. S. Sentencing Commission, 2012).

In 2012, the United States Sentencing Commission published a report based on a multi-year study to aid in Congress' continual assessment of how child pornography offenders are handled in all phases of the criminal justice system. Specifically, the report focused on sentencing guidelines for non-production offenses. Ultimately, the commission's report recommended that the non-production child pornography sentencing scheme should be revised to account for recent technological changes in offense conduct, research regarding offenders' collecting behaviors and previous histories, and offenders' culpability and dangerousness when determining punishment (U.S. Sentencing Commission, 2012). The report suggested that in non-production child pornography cases the court consider the content of an offender's child pornography collection and the nature of his or her offending behavior, the degree of the offender's involvement with other offenders, and whether the offender has a history of predatory sexual behavior (U.S. Sentencing Commission, 2012). The commission also noted that the current guidelines do not adequately distinguish commercial distributors of child pornography from individuals who are determined to be in possession of pornographic material because the guidelines were enacted before the evolution of more sophisticated technologies, which are now commonly utilized for distribution purposes (U.S. Sentencing Commission, 2012).

An Emerging Issue: "Sexting"

New electronic means of communication (such as Facebook, Twitter, Snapchat, and text messaging) have spurred concern among parents, teachers, police, and legislatures in terms of how young people are using them (Vandiver et al., 2017). "Sexting" refers to sending sexual images, such as nude pictures, over cell phones or other electronic devices (Augustina & Gomez-Duran, 2012). Research shows that this is a fairly common practice among teenagers, with 28% of 16-year-olds and 31% of 17-year-olds having sent or received a nude image or video (Mitchell, Finkelhor, Jones, & Wolak, 2012).

"Sexting" among young people has ignited a national debate regarding the appropriate response to the trend. Among other concerns about this behavior is that youth under the age of 18 may be creating child pornography and distributing it by sending it to a romantic partner, who then also possesses child pornography (Mitchell et al., 2012). Part of the concern is that if the pictures involved in the offense meet the state's standard for child pornography, individuals engaging in "sexting" could be prosecuted under federal sex offender legislation (Vandiver et al., 2017). For example, a 14-year-old girl in Minnesota was charged with felony distribution of child pornography after she sent a revealing image of herself to a boy at her school. If convicted, she would be required to spend 10 years on the sex offender registry (Nelson, 2018). While these images may meet the legal definition of child pornography, they likely were not the intended targets of laws that were created before this type of technology proliferated. Thus, researchers remain skeptical about treating "sexting" as child pornography because the context of the image does not constitute the legal definition of child pornography (Mitchell et al., 2012). It remains to be seen how legislators, policymakers, and communities continue to come to terms with this issue in the future.

Conclusion

+ Though the scope of child pornography is unknown, studies show that it is a vast problem in the United States and worldwide.
+ The rise of the Internet has led to the growth of child pornography as one of the fastest growing online businesses with an estimated value of $20 billion.
+ There is a range of child pornography crimes, including production, distribution, and possession.
+ As with other types of offenders, child pornography offenders can be categorized by the nature and scope of their interests and activities.
+ As child pornography offenders rely on new technology, the police, prosecutors, and lawmakers have had to adapt how offenders are apprehended, prosecuted, and sentenced.
+ Child pornography investigators may experience emotional, social, and behavioral consequences due to their exposure to pornographic material.
+ Child pornography offenses are prosecuted as federal crimes, and convicted offenders are sentenced according to federal sentencing guidelines.
+ Technological advances have led to new offenses, such as "sexting," where (usually) adolescents text sexual images of themselves to others. "Sexting" presents a new and unique challenge for criminal justice professionals.

Discussion Questions

1. Is it appropriate to charge young people who sext child pornography with distribution, production, and/or possession? Why or why not?

2. Does possessing online child pornography make a person a sex offender? Why or why not?

3. Is someone who trades child pornography ONLY for profit a sex offender? Why or why not?

References

18 U.S.C. § 2252

18 U.S.C. § 2556

Adler, A. (2001). The perverse law of child pornography. *Columbia Law Review, 101*(2), 209–273.

Alexy, E. M., Burgess, A. W., & Baker, T. (2005). Internet offenders: Traders, travelers, and combination trader-travelers. *Journal of Interpersonal Violence, 20*(7), 804–812.

Augustina, J., & Gomez-Duran, J. (2012). Sexting: Research criteria of a globalized social phenomenon. *Archives of Sexual Behavior, 41*(6), 1325–1328.

Babchishin, K. M., Hanson, R. K., & Hermann, C. A. (2011). The characteristics of online sex offenders: A meta-analysis. *Sexual Abuse: A Journal of Research and Treatment, 23*(1), 92–123.

Bourke, M. & Hernandez, A. (2009). The "Butner study" redux: A report of the incidence of hands-on child victimization by child pornography offenders. *Journal of Family Violence, 24*(3), 183–191.

Bourke, M. L. & Craun, S. W. (2014). Coping with secondary traumatic stress: Differences between U.K. and U.S. child exploitation personnel. *Traumatology: An International Journal, 20*(1), 57–64.

Briggs, P., Simon W. T, & Simonsen, S. (2011). An exploratory study of Internet-initiated sexual offenses and the chat room sex offender: Has the Internet enabled a new typology of sex offender? *Sexual Abuse: A Journal of Research and Treatment, 23*(1), 72–91.

Burke, D. D. (1997). Criminalization of virtual child pornography: A constitutional question. *Harvard Journal on Legislation, 34*, 439–472.

Edelmann, R. J. (2010). Exposure to child abuse images as part of one's work: Possible psychological implications. *Journal of Forensic Psychology and Psychiatry*, *21*(4), 481–489.

Eke, A. W., Seto, M. C., & Williams, J. (2011). Examining the criminal history and future offending of child pornography offenders. *Law and Human Behavior*, *35*(6), 466–478.

Finkelhor, D., & Omrod, R. (2004, December). *Child pornography: Patterns from NIBRS* (Juvenile Justice Bulletin NCJ 204911). Washington, DC: U.S. Department of Justice, Office of Justice Programs, Office of Juvenile Justice and Delinquency Prevention.

Franqueria, V. N. L., Bryce, J., Al Mutawa, N., & Marrington, A. (2018). Investigation of indecent images of children cases: Challenges and suggestions collected from the trenches. *Digital Investigation*, *24*, 95–105.

Hamilton, M. (2012). The child pornography crusade and its net-widening effect. *Cardozo Law Review*, *33*(4), 1679–1732.

Howard, T. E. (2004). Don't cache out your case: Prosecuting child pornography possession law based on images located in temporary Internet files. *Berkeley Technology Law Journal*, *19*(4), 1227–1273.

Jenkins, P. (2001). *Beyond tolerance: Child pornography on the Internet*. New York: New York University Press.

Krause, M. (2008, August). Addressing the needs of undercover employees: A practical approach. *FBI Law Enforcement Bulletin*, 1–18.

Krause, M. (2009). Identifying and managing stress in child pornography and child exploitation investigators. *Journal of Police and Criminal Psychology*, *24*(1), 22–29.

Krone T. 2004. *A typology of online child pornography offending*. Trends & issues in crime and criminal justice No. 279. Canberra: Australian Institute of Criminology. https://aic.gov.au/publications/tandi/tandi279.

Lanning, K. V. (1992). *Child molesters: A behavioral analysis* (#98-MC-K002). Washington, DC: National Center for Missing and Exploited Children.

Mitchell, B. (2018, April 23). Introduction to peer-to-peer networks. *Lifewire*. Retrieved from https://www.lifewire.com/introduction-to-peer-to-peer-networks-817421

Mitchell, K. J., & Jones, L. M. (2013). *Internet-facilitated commercial sexual exploitation of children*. Durham, NH: Crimes Against Children Research Center, University of New Hampshire.

Mitchell, K., Finkelhor, D., Jones, I., & Wolak, J. (2012). Prevalence and characteristics of youth sexting: A national study. *Pediatrics*, *129*(1), 13–20.

Mitchell, K., Wolak, J., & Finkelhor, D. (2005). Police posing as juveniles online to catch sex offenders: Is it working? *Sexual Abuse: A Journal of Research and Treatment, 17*(3), 211–267.

Motivans, M., & Kyckelhahn, T. (2008). *Federal prosecution of child exploitation offenders.* Washington, DC: United States Department of Justice.

Nelson, T. (2018, January 5). Minnesota prosecutor charges sexting teenage girl with child pornography [Web log comment]. *ACLU.* Retrieved from https://www.aclu.org/blog/juvenilejustice/minnesota-prosecutor-charges-sexting-teenage-girl-child-pornography.

New York v. Ferber, 458 U.S. 747 (1982)

Norland, R., & Bartholet, J. (2001, March 19). The Web's dark secret. *Newsweek,* 44–51.

Office for Victims of Crime. (2001). *OVC bulletin: Internet crimes against children* (NCJ 184931). Washington, DC: National Institute of Justice Research Report.

Powell, M., Cassematis, P., Benson, M., Smallbone, S., & Wortley, R. (2014). Police officers' perceptions of their reactions to viewing Internet child exploitation material. *Journal of Police and Criminal Psychology, 30*(2), 103–111.

PROTECT Act of 2003 (Pub. L. 108-21, 117 Sat. 650, S. 151)

Quayle, E. & Taylor, M. (2002). Child pornography and the Internet: Perpetuating a cycle of abuse. *Deviant Behavior, 23*(4), 331–362.

Rosenbloom, A. L., & Tanner, J. M. (1998). Letter to the editor. *Pediatrics, 102*(6), 1494.

Seto, M. & Eke, A. (2005). The criminal histories and later offending of child pornography offenders. *Sexual Abuse: A Journal of Research and Treatment, 17*(2), 201–210.

Seto, M. C., Cantor, J. M., & Blanchard, R. (2006). Child pornography offenses are a valid diagnostic indicator of pedophilia. *Journal of Abnormal Psychology, 115*(3), 610–615.

Stabenow, Troy. (2009). Deconstructing the myth of careful study: A primer on the flawed progression of the Child Pornography Guidelines. Retrieved from: https://www.ussc.gov/sites/default/files/pdf/training/annual-national-trainingseminar/2016/report_stabenow.pdf

Terry, K. J. (2013). *Sexual offenses and offenders: Theory, practice, and policy.* Belmont, CA: Wadsworth.

U.S. Sentencing Commission (2009). *The history of child pornography guidelines.* Retrieved from https://www.ussc.gov/sites/default/files/

pdf/research-and-publications/research-projects-andsurveys/sex-offenses/20091030_History_Child_Pornography_Guidelines.pdf.

U.S. Sentencing Commission (2010). Results of survey of United States district judges: January 2010 through March 2010. *Federal Sentencing Report, 23*, 296.

U.S. Sentencing Commission (2012). *Federal child pornography offenses.* Retrieved from https://www.ussc.gov/sites/default/files/pdf/news/congressional-testimony-and-reports/sexoffense-topics/201212-federal-child-pornography-offenses/Full_Report_to_Congress.pdf.

Vandiver, D., Braithwaite, J., & Stafford, M. (2017). *Sex crimes and sex offenders: Research and realities.* New York, NY: Routledge.

Violanti, J. M. & Gehrke, A. (2004). Police trauma encounters: Precursors of compassion fatigue: *International Journal of Emergent Mental Health, 6*(2), 75–60.

Walsh, W., Wolak, J., & Finkelhor, D. (2013). *Prosecution dilemmas and challenges for child pornography crimes: The Third National Juvenile Online Victimization Study (NJOV-3).* Dunham, NI: Crimes Against Children Research Center.

Wells, M., Finkelhor, D., Wolak, J., & Mitchell, K. J. (2003). *Internet sex crimes against minors: Law enforcement dilemmas.* Washington, DC: US Department of Justice.

Wells, M., Finkelhor, D., Wolak, J., & Mitchell, K. J. (2007). Defining child pornography: Law enforcement dilemmas in investigations of Internet child pornography possession. *Police Practice and Research, 8*(3), 269–282.

Wolak, J., Finkelhor, D., Mitchell, K., & Jones, L. (2011). Arrests for child pornography production: Data at two points from a national sample of U.S. law enforcement agencies. *Child Maltreatment, 16*(3), 184–195.

Wolak, J., Finkelhor, D., & Mitchell, K. (2005). *Child pornography possessors arrested in Internet-related crimes: Findings from the National Juvenile Online Victimization Study.* Alexandria, VA: National Center for Missing and Exploited Children.

Wolak, J., Mitchell, K. J., & Finkelhor, D. (2003). *Internet sex crimes against minors: The response of law enforcement.* Washington, DC: National Center for Missing and Exploited Children.

Wortley, R. K., & Smallbone, S. (2006). *Child pornography on the Internet.* Washington, DC: U.S. Department of Justice, Office of Community Oriented Policing Services.

Chapter 11

A Nation Talking to Itself About Justice
Fifty Years of Media Coverage of Criminal Justice

Jennifer Noble

"A good newspaper, I suppose, is a nation talking to itself."

—Arthur Miller

Introduction

In early 2003, the small Central California city of Modesto played host to dozens of reporters from national and local news organizations to observe a tragic spectacle. Journalists were there to cover an ongoing search for Laci Peterson, a 27-year-old woman who was 8-months pregnant with her first child. She had been reported missing on December 23, 2002. Family and friends scoured parks and outlying areas and spoke with reporters who were eager for any new scrap of information to advance the story, which was growing more dire by the hour. The daily coverage continued over the next 2 years—with the nation watching as the bodies of Laci Peterson and her unborn child were recovered, as Laci's husband Scott Peterson was arrested, and then through his trial, where he was convicted and sentenced to death.

But why was there such a desire and a need to know those details about what was essentially a local crime story? What elevated Laci Peterson's disappearance, the discovery of her body, and the trial of her husband for murder to a news story of national importance? Did the coverage enlighten the public about the criminal justice system, about their own risk of harm, about the processes and protections and laws that would come into play while Scott Peterson's trial played out over the next 2 years?

Or was it merely a spectacle?

211

News coverage of crime and criminal justice can teach the public about important policy considerations, such as whether we should treat juveniles as adults, impose mandatory minimum sentences on convicted felons, or continue to institute a death penalty. It can educate the public on crime statistics. It can show the evidence of whether criminal justice policies are effective.

Or, it can entertain the viewer with tales of sordid crimes. By focusing a lens on murder and other violent crimes, media coverage can skew the perception of risk and can influence the public's desire for more punitive penalties and harsher police tactics. (Bjornstrom, Kaufman, Peterson, & Slater, 2010; Beale, 2006.) How the media covers crime, and how that has changed in recent history, affects criminal justice policies and can provide insight into how new media sources and technology will shape these issues in the future.

Evolution of Media Consolidation

Journalism, in the form of newspapers and broadcast media, has always sought to serve two masters. Journalists strive to serve the public interest by covering news of importance to the community, making the powerful accountable to everyday citizens and shining a light on injustices. But news is also a business. And, increasingly, it's an industry that is dominated by a fewer number of players that are increasingly corporate.

Media consolidation is what happens when the concentration of ownership of news outlets is in the hands of fewer corporate entities (Light, 2017). Newspapers and local television stations that used to have local owners are now increasingly owned by national media powerhouses. Changes in ownership rules for broadcast media have resulted in vast changes in who controls news sources.

When the Federal Communications Commission was created in 1934, it sought to prevent media consolidation. To preserve and promote media diversity, regulations discouraged a single corporation from owning too many newspapers or TV stations and limited the size of the market any one business could reach (Light, 2017). When President Ronald Reagan ushered in an era of deregulation in the 1980s, the FCC chairman rolled back some restrictions on ownership in a move to deregulate media ownership. In the following decade, President Bill Clinton signed the Telecommunication Act of 1996, which permitted corporations to own more local newspapers and television stations and raised the percentage of national audience a single company could reach. These and other changes to the Federal Communications Commission's oversight have resulted in fewer independent media owners. In 1983, 50 corporations controlled a majority of media sources. By 2012, that number was six (Light, 2017).

Corporations, no matter what sort of industry they operate in, must answer to shareholders and are largely profit-driven. When this conflicts with the public-goals of journalism, profits take precedent (Turner, 2015). Television stations have trimmed expensive investigative reports to the point that "[c]heap-to-produce traffic, weather, and sports updates comprise nearly half of all local news programming" (Turner, 2015). Because the same corporation may own multiple news outlets in one market, a report from one newsroom can be slightly repackaged to run on multiple stations. Reporters become redundant, and the news industry is beset by frequent reports of layoffs.

Combined with increasing competition from Internet news sources and social media, newsrooms are operating with a skeleton staff, in both TV and newspapers, across the country. With fewer resources, editors and producers have to do more with less—no matter how impossible that directive is. It results in more stories that are cheap to cover and fewer resources given to in-depth reporting on complicated issues.

Crime has always been a staple of news coverage. In part, this is due to public interest. Stories of murder and intrigue are popular with readers. Crime is also a fairly easy story to cover. Traditionally, rookie reporters were often assigned to cover the "cop shop," sometimes working out of offices within police precincts. Law enforcement agencies maintain public information offices and provide press releases and public information officers who are dedicated to answering questions from the media. Information on charges, suspects, and future court dates are therefore easy to find and verify.

Competition between news outlets drove reporters to gather facts and advance a story beyond what the police provided. Even smaller cities often had multiple newspapers and TV news operations that covered the local area. Until recently, newspapers often had robust coverage of courts, too (Policinski, 2014). Reporters in even medium-sized cities worked out of offices in local courthouses so they could cover whatever notable and newsworthy cases were on the docket. These reporters understood how courts worked, who the players were, and kept an eye on the system, not just individual cases (Policinski, 2014).

But in the last several decades, as the media landscape changed, the number of newspaper reporters has steadily shrunk. Many newspapers have disappeared altogether. Those that remain are working with far fewer reporters on staff. As newsrooms shrink, fewer reporters are available to cover news that readers need to know—and what they want to know. More newspapers began relying on wire services, such as the *Associated Press* and other syndicated services (Montross & Mulvaney, 2009). Reporters are more likely to parachute in to cover high-profile cases where a celebrity is charged with a crime or the trial is particularly compelling. (Polinscki, 2014).

Newspapers are no longer just competing with each other for readers. Increasingly, they're competing with every other distraction those readers have at their fingertips—TV news, Internet sites, and social media—any source that can provide headlines (if not much more) to inform the reader. Television news also began to focus on news that its viewers wanted most—because that results in the highest ratings and those ratings determine the price of advertising. Reporting on crime fits the directive that newsrooms have been given; the public has a great interest in crime stories, and reporting on the latest shooting or drug bust is easy when the police have provided a press release with the details. One study of 33,000 local news stories over 5 years found that over 90% of newscasts started with a story about crime or public safety and over 80% also covered crime in their second segment (Rosenstiel, Just, Pertilla, Dean & Chinni, 2007). It became more difficult for reporters to provide in-depth coverage of criminal justice issues and policies under these conditions. But it was still easy to cover crime.

So they did.

Criminal Justice Reporting vs. Crime Reporting

In a 2009 article, Montross and Mulvaney note the difference between criminal justice reporting and crime reporting in modern media. Criminal justice reporting covers the complex issues relating to crime, its causes, and the system that deals with it. This includes relevant criminal procedures and law, the trial process, appeals, conditions of incarceration, and effects on the victims. This type of reporting takes time and resources. But, it can effect change in attitudes or in legislation by bringing to light important issues in the system.

One example of criminal justice reporting is the *Chicago Tribune* series on the death penalty system in Illinois and in Texas. Reporters on this series of articles looked not only at the crimes, but also at the flaws in the death penalty system (Montross & Mulvaney, 2009). The *Tribune's* examination of death penalty policies and practices in the late 1990s led Illinois' governor to impose a moratorium on executions on January 31, 2000. Three years later, Governor George Ryan commuted the sentences of the 167 death row inmates in Illinois, saying he no longer had confidence in the state's administration of the death penalty (Ryan, 2003). The system, he said, when halting executions, had "proven to be so fraught with error and has come so close to the ultimate nightmare, the state's taking of an innocent life" (Armstrong & Mills, 2000). At that time, 13 people on death row had been found to have been wrongfully convicted.

Another example of news coverage that resulted in changes to the criminal justice system is the reporting on the backlog of as many as 400,000 rape kits that went untested in cities and counties across the nation (Associated Press, 2017; Atassi & Dissell, 2013; Ross, 2002; Shamus, 2017). DNA evidence from sexual assault kits sat in storage, often due to the high cost of genetic tests, sometimes until the statute of limitations ran out. The issue had been known since the early 2000s when New York City's medical examiner undertook the largest effort to eliminate the backlog of 16,500 rape kits between 2000 and 2003 (Peterson, Johnson, Herz, Graziano, & Oehler, 2012). The problem persisted until local coverage of the issues brought it to the public attention. In 2008, Los Angeles County reported 10,895 untested evidence samples, and the following year Detroit prosecutors discovered more than 11,000 neglected DNA samples in storage. And in 2011, the Ohio attorney general called for law enforcement to submit old evidence for DNA testing in response to media reports of thousands of untested rape kits across the state (Atassi & Dissell, 2013). When those results came back, the Cleveland Plain Dealer found at least 12 serial rapists responsible for as many as 50 attacks in the early 1990s.

The reporting on the untested DNA evidence, wrongful convictions, flaws in the death penalty system, and other similar examples have one thing in common—these stories all examine systemwide problems, not individual incidences of crime. These types of in-depth analyses take months or years to develop and write, which is an expensive proposition for an industry that is trimming overhead. But these examinations of trends and systemic issues can educate and influence readers and viewers, as well as lawmakers.

In response to the spate of wrongful convictions that have come to light, the district attorney in Dallas, Texas, created a Conviction Integrity Unit in 2007 to examine closed cases where the prosecutors had won a conviction (Barber, 2014). The purpose of the controversial unit was to find and fix the wrongful convictions that the office had won. Under then District Attorney Craig Watkins, who founded the CIU, more than 30 people were exonerated (Pishko, 2018). The Dallas effort has since led 28 other district attorneys to create similar programs (National Registry of Exonerations, 2016).

Similarly, following the reporting on the untested rape kits, Congress designated money to test DNA evidence in federal criminal cases and states have tackled the issue by ordering law enforcement to audit, track, and test sexual assault evidence.

Contrast that type of reporting with crime reporting, which Montross and Mulvaney (2009) characterize as "superficial, sensationalist, and catering to the worst instincts of its readers" (p. 1433). This type of reporting is rarely probing or analytical and sometimes is a mere rewrite of press releases provided by the police or district attorney's office. The news reports based on this information are generally limited to the facts of a single incident and no attention is paid to greater factors often present in the lives of many criminal defendants—poverty, drug addiction, and a failing social safety net (Montross & Mulvaney, 2009).

Though criminal defendants have an advocate in the courtroom, an attorney hired or appointed to represent their interests in front of the judge, they rarely have the ability to respond to press inquiries through a spokesperson. When crime reporting relies on prepackaged information in the form of press releases, that information becomes the easiest to include in an article. The perspective is rarely matched by the defense attorney, who may not have time to respond before a deadline, as public defenders are notoriously overworked. Further, the defense attorney may have a good reason to avoid speaking publicly about a case, to avoid tipping his or her hand to the prosecutor about a defense strategy.

The increase in crime reporting and the decrease of in-depth reporting on criminal justice issues is a function of a corporate priority to place profits over public interest. There are some cases that cost a lot to cover and which the media cannot ignore. The murder trial of O.J. Simpson for the death of two people, his ex-wife Nicole Brown Simpson and her friend Ronald Goldman, was always going to be a high-profile crime story. The case involved celebrity culture and a shockingly violent crime, and it happened in one of the largest media markets in the country. This was always going to be a spectacle. It did, however, raise public awareness of domestic violence and race relations in Los Angeles (Edelman, 2016). Likewise, some crimes are illustrative of larger social issues, such as how the shooting of Trayvon Martin and the subsequent trial and acquittal of George Zimmerman spurred a national conversation about race, guns, and justice (Dukes, & Gather, 2017).

Coverage of individual crimes may differ depending on who the victim is. When it comes to homicide, one study showed that newspapers tended to write longer stories where the victim was female, there was more than one victim, or where the perpetrator was a stranger (Buckler, 2005). Racial and ethnic minorities are also less likely to be depicted as crime victims than Whites in television coverage (Bjornstrom et al., 2010).

This was illustrated in the media coverage of the Laci Peterson case, which was a near daily news story when she was missing and in the aftermath of the discovery of her body. Around the same time, LaToyia Figueroa, a 24-year-old Black woman, disappeared from her Philadelphia home (Moody, Dorries, & Blackwell, 2009). Both women were pregnant. In each case, police were suspicious of the missing woman's romantic partner. But unlike the Laci Peterson coverage, which typically quoted her family and always mentioned her pregnancy, reports on Latoyia Figueroa largely identified her as "the missing Philadelphia woman" and downplayed her pregnancy. This discrepancy in the quality of media attention between White and non-White victims came to be known as the "missing White woman syndrome"—a disproportionate amount of news coverage for White crime victims while failing to adequately cover minority victims.

Research has also demonstrated that racial minorities are overrepresented as criminals or perpetrators, compared to White counterparts (Bjornstrom, et al., 2010; Chiricos, & Eschholz, 2002). This could "promote racial or gender stereotypes or reinforce public hostility" toward those groups shown as perpetrators (Bjornstrom et al., 2010, p. 269). It can also mislead the public about who is "the most vulnerable to crime, or who should fear crime" (Bjornstrom et al., 2010, p. 269)

These misperceptions matter as they can spur a fear of crime, even as statistics show crime rates dropping (Beale, 2006; Heath & Gilbert, 1996). In the 1990s, the United States saw a decline of violent crime rates. By 2000, homicide and robbery rates were at their lowest in 25 years, and other violent crimes continued to show sharp declines. But continual exposure to crime reporting can lead viewers and readers to become more fearful of crime, despite the lessened threat. Their reaction to that fear is to support harsher penalties for crime that focus on punitive instead of preventative methods to address criminal behavior (Beale, 2006).

Front-Row Seat to Justice: Cameras in the Courtroom

Court proceedings are open to the public, with a very few exceptions, and anyone can walk in and watch the proceedings. Unless the judge has closed the court for a specific reason, such as to hear a defendant's attempt to fire his or her attorney or other confidential proceeding, the doors to the courtroom are presumed to be open so citizens can observe what is going on in their name. This, of course, takes time that most people do not have, and traditionally they relied on accounts by reporters who cover courts.

In 1980, the Supreme Court held that the public has a First Amendment right of access to criminal proceedings, which can only be overcome by a finding of specific threats to a fair trial. (*Richmond Newspapers, Inc. v. Virginia*, 1980). The First Amendment, in conjunction with the Fourteenth Amendment, bars governments from "abridging the freedom of speech, or of the press; or the right of the people peaceably to assemble, and to petition the Government for a redress of grievances." In *Richmond*, Chief Justice Warren Burger stated that "[t]hese expressly guaranteed freedoms share a common core purpose of assuring freedom of communication on matters relating to the functioning of government. Plainly it would be difficult to single out any aspect of government of higher concern or importance to the people than the manner in which criminal trials are conducted."

It is one thing to have a reporter observe a criminal trial with a pen and notepad. It is quite different to bring television cameras into the court. Television broadcasts of trials have opened a new window into courtrooms, allowing the public to watch the justice system at work. All 50 states have enacted laws permitting cameras in the courtroom, with judges having the discretion to keep cameras out if the publicity would harm the defendant's right to a fair trial. No camera or recording is permitted in United States' district courts or federal trial courts. Only three circuit courts of appeal permit cameras to record arguments to appellate panels. Those circuits are the Second, Third, and Ninth circuits. The Ninth Circuit not only records appellate arguments, it permits live audio streaming of the arguments and posts the videos so the public can view them later.

The Supreme Court is notoriously camera shy. The justices permit no photography and no video recording, though the court records audio of the argument, which is then made available online. The audio recordings of Supreme Court arguments date back to the 1957–1958 term. In 2012, Congress sought to force the Court to permit live video streaming of the arguments on the Patient Protection and Affordable Care Act. While the Court did not allow the media request for cameras, it did agree to release the audio recording the same day.

Courts have many concerns about permitting cameras to record court proceedings. Judges are tasked with ensuring that everyone who appears in front of them get a fair trial, and while the courtroom is a public proceeding, permitting news media to record and broadcast trials could be prejudicial to the parties, could intimidate witnesses, and could have an effect on how lawyers and others in the courtroom do their jobs. This fear that public observation will make a trial into a media circus is not limited to cameras in the courtroom, as there have been many trials in the past that ran amok when the media consisted of radio and newspaper reporters.

Famously, the trial of Dr. Sheppard, later inspiration for the movie *The Fugitive*, highlighted the dangers of what can happen when a judge loses control of the courtroom.

Dr. Samuel Sheppard was convicted of second-degree murder for the death of his pregnant wife but successfully appealed the verdict, arguing that he did not receive a fair trial due to pervasive and prejudicial publicity surrounding the case during the pretrial period and during the trial (*Sheppard v. Maxwell*, 1966). Among his complaints were that news media aired allegations besides the charges Sheppard faced; he was subjected to a 5-hour televised inquest 3 months before trial; a newspaper published the names and addresses of prospective jurors, causing them to receive letters and phone calls about the case; reporters took over nearly the entire courtroom during trial, sitting so close to Sheppard that he couldn't have a private discussion with his attorney; and the media had unfettered access to the jurors until the jury was sequestered for their deliberations.

The Supreme Court agreed with Sheppard and held that he was denied a fair trial. The trial judge failed to protect his rights by controlling access to the news media. While the trial judge must respect the right of the public to have access to the proceedings, the jury's verdict must be based solely on the evidence introduced in open court, not from outside sources. When the First Amendment and the Sixth Amendment collide, the trial court must protect the defendant's right to a trial free from the influence of outside sources.

The judge does not have to ban cameras—if that were even possible—to protect the defendant's rights. Other remedies are available, such as gag orders on the parties, change of venue, sequestering the jury, or extensive questioning of potential jurors during *voir dire* (Morant, 2001). This can address some risk of prejudice in high-profile cases.

These remedies do not lessen all of television's effect on the people in the courtroom. The knowledge that the audience extends beyond the courtroom can have an effect on the players—the attorneys, judge, witnesses, and defendant. For example, in the highest of high-profile cases, the murder trial of O.J. Simpson, "some of the court participants' actions, i.e., Judge Ito's concern with hair grooming, and the attorneys' grandstanding and flair for the dramatic in arguments, appeared motivated by the presence of a television audience" (Morant, 2001, p. 378). Witnesses, too, may be aware of the presence of a television camera and the resulting publicity from news coverage. "Awareness that one's every action is recorded or broadcast heightens self-consciousness, and can consciously or unconsciously influence cognitive strategies and behavior" (Morant, 2001, p. 375). This type of influence may be subtle and hard to measure, but judges must be mindful of it.

The Future of Crime and Criminal Justice Reporting

Cameras in the courtroom gave the public an inside view of judicial proceedings. A 24-hour news cycle sped up the pace at which the public expects to learn developments. But those two advances in media consumption pale in comparison to how new technology quickens the pace of criminal justice reporting. The public no longer has to wait for a reporter to verify facts before a news story is sent out into the world. Social media and mobile technology allow users to share news faster, increases the media options, and with live-streaming of unfolding events can even make witnesses of us all. This unfiltered coverage isn't vetted by reporters or editors. It is up to each viewer to judge the credibility of the source. The footage is instant, and if it's compelling enough, it can go global in a short time.

Two high-profile examples of that are the shooting deaths of Michael Brown in Ferguson, Missouri, and Philando Castile in the suburb of St. Paul, Minnesota. Brown, an unarmed 18-year-old African American man, was shot and killed by a police officer on August 9, 2014. The shooting sparked outrage, a national wave of protests, and the birth of the Black Lives Matter movement. Thanks to Twitter, the news of Brown's death spread quickly—far faster than traditional news sources could keep up with. Those on the ground shared news, images of the protests, and pushed back against the media portrayal of unrest as a "mob" (Jackson & Welles, 2016).

Less than 2 years later, an African American man, Philando Castile, was fatally shot by a Minnesota police officer during a routine traffic stop as he reached for his driver's license (Wright & Unah, 2017). Castile's girlfriend livestreamed the immediate aftermath of the shooting on Facebook, which was widely shared and sparked outrage and protest actions. Within a day, the video was viewed at least 2.5 million times (Peterson, 2016). The video was briefly taken down by Facebook but returned after an uproar by social media users.

But new technology can also provide a forum for more in-depth criminal justice reporting, such as the 2014 podcast *Serial*. The episodic audio series examined the 1999 murder of Baltimore teenager Hae Min Lee and the subsequent trials and conviction of her boyfriend Adnan Syed. Hosted by Sarah Koenig, the popular series became the fastest podcast to reach 5 million downloads—and that was before the end of its first season (CNN, 2014). By the end of 2014, it had been downloaded an estimated 40 million times.

The detailed reporting in *Serial* raised questions about whether Syed, who is serving a sentence of life imprisonment plus 30 years, should have been convicted. In 2016, Syed was granted a new trial, a decision that the state of Maryland has appealed (Prudente, 2018). The series also spurred an interest in true crime podcasts, such as *74 Seconds*, produced by Minnesota Public Radio, and *In the Dark*, by American Public Media. *74 Seconds*, which won a Peabody Award, examines the shooting of Philando Castile and the trial of the police officer who shot him, as well as the cultural and societal issues Castile's death raised (Mumford & Buetow, 2017). Similarly, the first season of *In the Dark* took one crime—the 1989 sexual assault and murder of Jacob Wetterling—and examined how the police handled the investigation and how Jacob's death changed the public's awareness and drove fears of child abduction (Baran, 2016). While some podcasts do focus on crime reporting and delve into individual incidents of missing persons or unsolved murders, there are multiple examples like *74 Seconds* and *In the Dark* that demonstrate the viability of long-form criminal justice reporting in this new medium.

Further, new media companies have sprung up to showcase longform journalism, some of which covers criminal justice issues. The Marshall Project, a nonprofit news organization, is devoted to coverage of the U.S. criminal justice system. It publishes in-depth reporting on its site and partners with other news organizations to produce stories on systemic issues such as policing, immigration, the death penalty, and juvenile justice. Its efforts have resulted in multiple awards, including an Edward R. Murrow Award for Overall Excellence in 2018.

New technology and forms of media have certainly changed how the public receives its news—and news about criminal justice in particular. It can be a faster source of information, and it has provided a more diverse spectrum of voices and views. The use of social media and digital platforms does come with a caveat—readers and viewers must be better versed in critical thinking and media literacy to know which sources are reliable and trustworthy.

Discussion Questions

1. After reading about how previous changes to the news media landscape have affected criminal justice issues, what are some predictions you have for how new technology in communication and media will affect criminal justice in the future?

2. Think of a high-profile crime story that received national media attention. What makes that story newsworthy for the entire country as opposed to being important on a local level?

3. This chapter named several examples of criminal justice reporting that have affected attitudes or inspired changes in the law, such as DNA exonerations of the wrongfully convicted and the backlog of rape-kit testing. What other examples of criminal justice reporting can you find that have had similar effects? What are some criminal justice issues that are ripe for this type of reporting?

For Further Reading

For in-depth coverage of criminal justice issues, visit the Marshall Project: https://www.themarshallproject.org/

To listen to the *Serial* podcast, visit the website: https://serialpodcast.org/

To listen to archived Supreme Court arguments, visit Oyez: www.oyez.org

References

Armstrong, K., and Mills, S. (2000, Jan. 31). Ryan Suspends Death Penalty. Chicago Tribune. Retrieved from https://www.chicagotribune.com/news/ct-xpm-2000-01-31-0002010058-story.html

Associated Press. (2017, March 26). Second backlog of 555 untested Detroit rape kits found in storage. *Detroit Free Press*. Retrieved from https://www.freep.com/story/news/local/michigan/detroit/2017/03/26/second-backlog-555-untested-detroit-rape-kits-found-storage/99675180/

Atassi L., & Dissell, R. (2013, August 5). Serial rapists terrorized Cleveland's women and children in 1990s, while police set cases aside. *Cleveland Plain Dealer*. Retrieved from: https://www.cleveland.com/rape-kits/index.ssf/2013/08/serial_rapists_terrorized_clev.html

Baran, M. (Reporter/Host). (2016, August). *In the Dark*, season 1 [Audio podcast]. Retrieved from https://www.apmreports.org/in-the-dark/season-one

Barber, E. (2014, May 25). Dallas targets wrongful convictions and revolution starts to spread. *Christian Science Monitor*. Retrieved from https://www.csmonitor.com/USA/Justice/2014/0525/Dallas-targets-wrongful-convictions-and-revolution-starts-to-spread

Beale, S. (2006). The news media's influence on criminal justice policy: How market-driven news promotes punitiveness. *William & Mary Law Review*, 48(2), 397-482.

Bjornstrom, E., Kaufman, R., Peterson, R., & Slater, M. (2010). Race and ethnic representations of lawbreakers and victims in crime news: A national study of television coverage. *Social Problems*, 57(2), 269-293.

Buckler, K. (2015). *Assessing the newsworthiness of homicide events: An analysis of coverage in the Houston Chronicle. Journal of Criminal Justice and Popular Culture*, 12(1), 1–25.

Chiricos, T., & Eschholz, S. (2002). The racial and ethnic typification of crime and the criminal typification of race and ethnicity in local television news. *Journal of Research in Crime and Delinquency*, 39(4), 400–420.

Dukes, K., & Gaither, S. (2017). Black racial stereotypes and victim blaming: Implications for media coverage and criminal proceedings in cases of police violence against racial and ethnic minorities. *Journal of Social Issues*, 73(4), 789–807.

Edelman, E. (Producer/Director). (2016). *O.J.: Made in America* [Television broadcast]. United States: ESPN Films.

Heath, L., & Gilbert, K. (1996). Mass media and fear of crime. *American Behavioral Scientist*, 39(4), 397–386.

Jackson, S. & Welles, B. (2016). #Ferguson is everywhere: initiators in emerging counterpublic networks. *Information, Communication & Society*, 19(3), 397-418.

Light, J. (2017, May 12). What is media consolidation and why should anyone care? *Moyers & Company*. Retrieved from https://billmoyers.com/story/media-consolidation-should-anyone-care/

Miller, A. (1961, December 31). Sayings of the Year: A Further Selection of 1961's More Notable Comments. *The Observer*, p. 9.

Moody, M., Dorries, B., & Blackwell, H. (2009). How national media framed coverage of missing black and white women. *Media Report to Women*, 37(4), 12-18.

Morant, B. (2001). *Resolving the dilemma of the televised fair trial: Social facilitation and the intuitive effects of television*. Virginia Journal of Social Policy and Law, 8(2), 329-396.

Montross, W., & Mulvaney, P. (2009). Virtue and vice: Who will report on the failing of the American criminal justice system? *Stanford Law Review*, 61(6), 1429-1461.

Mumford, T. & Buetow, H. (Producers). (2018, May). *74 seconds* [Audio podcast]. Retrieved from https://www.mprnews.org/topic/philandocastile

National Registry of Exonerations. (2016). Exonerations in 2016. *Newkirk Center for Science and Society*, Irvine, CA: University of California, Irvine.

Policinski, G. (2014). *Setting the docket: News media coverage of our courts—Past, present and an uncertain future. Symposium: The Art, Craft, and Future of Legal Journalism: A Tribute to Anthony Lewis*. Columbia, MO: University of Missouri.

Peterson, A. (2016, July 7). Why the Philando Castile video disappeared from Facebook and then came back. *Washington Post*. Retrieved from https://www.washingtonpost.com/news/the-switch/wp/2016/07/07/why-facebook-took-down-the-philando-castile-shooting-video-then-put-it-back-up

Peterson, J., Johnson, D., Herz, D., Graziano, L., & Oehler, T. (2012, June). Sexual assault kit backlog study. National Institute of Justice. Retrieved from https://www.ncjrs.gov/pdffiles1/nij/grants/238500.pdf

Pishko, J. (2018, May 15). No county for innocent men. *D Magazine*. Retrieved from https://www.dmagazine.com/frontburner/2018/05/dallas-county-exonerations-innocent-conviction-integrity-unit/

Prudente, T. (2018, May 14). Adnan Syed case: Prosecutors ask Maryland's highest court to reverse ruling of new trial for 'Serial' subject. *Baltimore Sun*. Retrieved from http://www.baltimoresun.com/news/maryland/crime/bs-md-ci-adnan-syed-appeal-20180514-story.html#

Reporters Committee for Freedom of the Press. (2018, November 19). *Cameras in courtrooms.* Retrieved from *Richmond Newspapers, Inc. v. Virginia,* 448 U.S. 555 (1980)

Rosenstiel, T., Just, M., Belt, T., Pertilla, A., Dean, W., & Chinni, D. (2007). *We interrupt this newscast: How to improve local news and win ratings, too.* Cambridge, MA: Cambridge University Press.

Ross, B. (2002, August 30). Solving rape cases: 20/20 helps pay for DNA tests police say they can't afford. *ABC.* Retrieved from https://abcnews.go.com/2020/story?id=123852&page=1

Ryan, G. (2003). In Ryan's words: "I must act." *New York Times.* Retrieved from https://www.nytimes.com/2003/01/11/national/in-ryans-words-i-must-act.html

Shamus, K. J. (2017, April 2). What happened to Detroit's untested rape kits?. *Detroit Free Press.* Retrieved from https://www.freep.com/story/news/local/michigan/detroit/2017/04/01/untesteddetroit-rape-kits/99845762/

Sheppard v. Maxwell, 384 U.S. 333 (1966)

Turner, S. D. (2014). *Cease to resist: How the FCC's failure to enforce its rules created a new wave of media consolidation.* Florence, Massachusetts:Free Press

United States Courts. (n.d.). *History of cameras in courts.* http://www.uscourts.gov/about-federalcourts/cameras-courts/history-cameras-courts

Wright, V., & Unah, I. (2017). Media exposure and racialized perceptions of inequities in criminal justice. *Social Sciences, 6*(3), 67.

IV

Special Topics

Chapter 12

Globalizing Criminal Justice Education
Building Cultural Bridges for Career Enhancement[1]

John P. J. Dussich

Introduction

In this paper the terms **global** and **international** are used interchangeably even though they are different: *over the entire planet* vs. *in many countries*. A closely allied concept to these two words and one that is familiar to most criminologists is the term **comparative**: the "apples and oranges" approach. The phrase *comparative criminology* provides a platform in the search for **universal truths.** It begs the question, "Does causality stand the test when it is applied to the unique variables of different countries and cultures?

Are some of the criminal justice practices that work well in such dissimilar countries as Sweden, Germany, Spain, France, Italy, China, Japan, Australia, South Africa, Israel, Indonesia, England, or Australia applicable in the United States? Ultimately, providing our students with a globalized criminal justice education greatly expands the scope of solutions and options for enhancing their career decision making and eventually provides the opportunity for more efficient and effective criminal justice systems. The potential for globalizing criminal justice education significantly multiplies many aspects of preparing CJ professionals for their increasingly complex future challenges. Addressing the importance of developing an international perspective in criminal justice education, a professor from John Jay College of Criminal Justice, Mangai

---

1 *Based on a speech "Globalizing Criminal Justice Education" presented at the First International Education Colloquium on Criminal Justice, California State University, Sacramento, April 21, 2017.

Natarajan (2002) from India, reminds us of the impact of the terrorist attacks of September 11, 2001 by stating, "[W]e can no longer afford to be parochial in our outlook" (Natarajan, 2002, p. 1). The ideal way to maximize the sharing of knowledge and practices within our field is to build new bridges and new paradigms for our faculty and our students, recognizing that these new byways are not just for access to new career destinations of U.S. students, but also for helping multiply the opportunities for those from other countries who come to this country to learn. It is an important reality for us to take stock that most universities host significant numbers of international students, which is also true in our criminal justice programs.

As a researcher in the field of criminology and victimology, I have been personally been intrigued by the very different rates of victimizations among nations, differences that suggest causality from the combination of such variables as types of governments, cultural norms, laws systems, public policies, policing styles, religions, levels of education, poverty levels, etc. Some of my direct experiences, professional and personal, are reflected in this paper: U.S. Army Military Police officer in Bavaria, Germany; multiple international symposia on victimology and criminology in Italy, Israel, Germany, Japan, Croatia, Australia, Netherlands, Canada, Brazil, South Africa, and China; director of a 6-week faculty/student summer course in Scandinavia for 22 U.S. students; a full-time researcher in a criminological research institute, in Hannover, Germany; a director of a victimological research and educational center, which hosted conferences and seminars and published an international journal and special topic books (Tokiwa International Victimology Institute), in Mito, Japan for 10 years; ethnically Italian/Croatian/American; extensive lecturing and consulting in Europe, Latin America and Asia; and publishing articles and books in English, Spanish, Italian, Chinese, Japanese, Croatian, and German, based on conducting criminological research, delivering victim services, and providing criminal justice teaching and training in multiple foreign countries over a career of 58 years.

The Logic Behind Globalization

Embracing and applying the concept of globalization offers a quantum leap to criminal justice educators and a broader range of criminal justice information and options. The current availability of all kinds of valuable information about criminals; victims; criminal justice systems; human rights; criminal, civil and religious laws; and social institutions from around the world is unprecedented. Thus, a university criminal justice teacher today has extensive research and practical resources available to *compare* the American criminal justice system with those of many other countries, thereby greatly enhancing the scope and relevance of his or her academic work and significantly broadening his or her own career as well as those of his or her students. The best example of a vast data base is at the Vienna-based headquarters of the United Nations' Office on Drugs and Crime (UNODC): the primary agency of the UN that deals with criminal justice issues and provides all their key documents in English, Spanish, Russian, French, Arabic, and Chinese. It is important to note that a large percentage of the nongovernment organizations that participate at UN events are staffed by college professors of criminal justice, sociology, psychology, political science, and law.

Methods and Models

Today, there is a great abundance of ways to become globally involved: publish in international publications, conduct annual field trips abroad, collaborate with foreign scholars and institutions, host overseas faculty and student guest exchanges, and become involved with external events hosted by such organizations as the quintennial United Nations Crime Congresses, the triennial World Society of Victimology Symposia, the annual International Association of Chiefs of Police Conferences, and the triennial International Society of Criminology Congresses—to mention only a few. These events are extremely rich events that provide criminal justice scholars and students from around the world with the opportunity to mingle, share, and interact socially, administratively, and educationally, thereby galvanizing relationships among its participants that usually last a lifetime and result in vastly improved careers.

To realize these benefits, travel resources for students and faculty are usually available, especially when linked to formal faculty-student research projects, field trips, or conferences within divisions, departments, colleges, and at the university level. In the last few decades there has been a dramatic rise in the active global recruiting of international students and faculty, which has helped to enhance diversity and higher standards at the receiving institutions that elect to internationalize their curriculum, student body, and faculty make-up. One of the easiest ways to recruit both national and international faculty and students is through "job boards" of the international professional organizations, their websites, and at their conferences. Also, most foreign embassies have "cultural attaches" who are usually more than willing to help locate organizations and top universities within their countries to facilitate promoting university recruitment efforts as well as to help identify resources available to support future research and educational activities in respective countries.

Globalize Curricula, Courses, Texts, and Journals

One of the foundations for globalizing criminal justice education programs is the creation of new courses that reflect the clear will of the faculty to include the internationalization of subjects with upgraded course titles and texts such as "Comparative Criminology and Criminal Justice," "Criminal Justice Systems of the World," "International Law Enforcement," "Comparative Corrections," "Juvenile Delinquency in the World," "Crime in the World," and "Comparative Responses to Violence Behaviors." Most publishers of criminal justice and criminology texts publish textbooks that support these themes with such books titles as *World Criminal Justice Systems* (Terrill, 2012), *Comparative Policing* (Haberfeld & Cerrah, 2008), *Comparative Criminal Justice Systems* (Dammer & Albanese, 2014), *Prisons of the World Over* (Simon & De Waal, 2026), *Juvenile Justice in Global Perspective* (Zimering, Langer, & Tanaenhaus, 2017), and *The World of Crime* (Van Dijk, 2008), to mention a few. Some of the top publishers of transnational and comparative texts are SAGE Publications in Thousand Oaks, California; Oxford University Press in London; Springer Verlag in Berlin, Heidelberg, Dordrecht, Germany, and New York; Macmillan International Higher Education in London, England; McGraw-Hill Education in New York; John Wiley & Sons in Hoboken, New Jersey; Cambridge University Press in Cambridge, the United Kingdom; Wolfe Legal Publishers in the Netherlands; Routledge Press in London, England; Prentice-Hall in Upper Saddle

River, New Jersey; Wadsworth Publishing in Belmont, California; Yale University Press in New Haven, Connecticut; and, Seibundo Publishing in Tokyo, Japan. Also, there are many journals dedicated to the comparative/global perspective: *Comparative Criminology; International Journal of Comparative and Applied Criminal Justice; International Journal of Offender Therapy and Comparative Criminology, International Journal of Prisoner Health, International Annals of Criminology; International Review of Victimology; International Journal of Risk, Security, and Crime Prevention, International Journal of Law, Crime, and Justice;* and *Policing: An International Journal of Police Strategy and Management.* Of course, many other generic journals also publish articles with global and comparative themes, for example some new relatively ones are *Journal of Victimology and Victim Justice; Journal of Law Enforcement and Homeland Security* (student-run and peer reviewed); *Journal of Forensic Psychology Practice; Journal of Criminal Justice Education; Journal of Juvenile Justice;* and *Journal of International Affairs* (which often has criminologically dedicated issues).

It is clear that published English language materials covering the field of global criminology and criminal justice are now in great profusion. It is significant to remind ourselves that books and journals on criminal justice in other languages also exist in great abundance. This is especially true for Chinese, French, and Spanish, and computer-assisted translation is available online. Thus, the challenge for a new criminal justice educational program is not whether scholarly works are available, but rather which are the most accessible to students and faculty, which are the highest quality, and which are the most appropriate to support courses offered.

Funding Sources or Opportunities to Support Faculty and Students

Most overseas education programs are hosted by universities and the education departments of most states, primarily for their own faculty and students. This is especially true when connections are hosted by foreign partner universities, when sister city relationships already exist, or when local ethnic organizations are present in U.S. communities willing to partner with their local universities to foster closer ties with foreign cultural exchange programs. University faculty sabbaticals continue to encourage faculty to challenge themselves to collaborate with foreign research scholars as partners. Also, foreign universities and institutes and are often willing to provide financial and in-kind support. Although they may not be able to afford funds, often they will sometimes provide other resources such as lodging accommodations, administrative support, and even student interns.

In my judgement, a model criminology/criminal justice program would be similar to the one at the California State University, Fresno. Of course, I am biased; however, putting that aside, most of the examples and suggestion in this chapter actually came from Fresno State's Criminology Department. It has a very culturally heterogeneous faculty and staff reflected in very different origins: Germany, Mexico, England, South Africa, Belgium, Japan, and Canada. Our dean is very supportive of international travel and faculty/student field trips every year, and our curriculum (as well as our university's commitment to globalization) are infused with a wide variety of international/global perspectives: study abroad, International Gateway, international students/exchange students/visiting scholars programs, the American English Institute for foreign students from abroad, and partnership opportunities that encourage agreements with foreign institutions. These resources significantly support a global/international criminal justice education and makes Fresno State a model in this area.

Many private educationally focused U.S. foundations (with dedicated websites) will provide funds for U.S. academic activities abroad. Here are five: (a) The Charles Koch Foundation; (b) the Public Library of Science; (c) the 100,000 Strong in the Americas, supported by the U.S. Department of State; (d) Partners of the Americas; and (e) NAFSA: The Association of International Educators—the world's largest non-profit association dedicated to international education and exchange.

Future Directions

Some of the CJ hot topics at the international level now being highlighted and projected into the future by the United Nations, at NGO conferences, and in many journals' "on-board universities" in program development are crimes against humanity, genocide, war crimes (Stromseth, 2017), treatment for human trafficking victims (Polaris, 2017), responding to femicide (Academic Council on the United Nations System, 2018), creating crime-prevention programs (Commission on Crime Prevention and Criminal Justice, 2018), hosting victim services training (National Organization for Victim Assistance, 2018), promoting human rights for indigenous people (United Nations, 2008), understanding trans global organized crime (United Nations on Drug and Crime, 2016), engaging innovations in juvenile justice practices (Decker & Marteache, 2017), developing programs to prevent terrorism (Harris-Hogan, Barrell, & Zammit 2016), conducting refugee and migration studies (Kury, Dussich, & Wertz 2018), identifying and supporting vulnerable groups (Ekblom, 2005), establishing truth and reconciliation efforts (Scharf, 1999), exploring new correctional strategies (Reiter, 2014), and establishing alternative justice models (Saleh-Hanna, 2008). Greatly enhancing the research in these and many other areas is the vast availability of *international digitized secondary data* and the openness of foreign scholars and institutions to collaborate with American scholars and students. Three examples of these types of specialized data bases are (a) ICVS, the International Crime Victims Survey (which also includes crime victim data from the European Union), meant for professionals skilled in research methods and advanced statistics and available from the United Nations Interregional Crime and Justice Research Institute (UNICRI) with headquarters located in Turin, Italy; (b) the International Statistics on Crime and Justice provided by the European Institute for Crime Prevention and Control, affiliated with the United Nations and hosted by HEUNI in Helsinki, Finland (Harrendorf, Heiskanen, & Malby, 2010); and (c) the Bureau of Justice Statistics of the Office of Justice Programs at the U.S. Department of Justice which, in addition to extensive national data sets, maintains extensive international crime data sets from many nations, allowing comparisons with the United States and other countries (Bureau of Justice Statistics, 2018). Also keep in mind that other nations (especially from developed countries) provide crime data sets free of charge, which are relatively easy to access. If one has the skill and the ability to navigate in foreign languages, the resources available are easily doubled. My experience has been that free secondary data is generally underutilized by most faculty and students. In a globalized criminal justice educational program, the research resources mentioned should be the bedrock of scholarly research databases.

My Recommendations

For a typical university, the first order of business would be for the college, school, department, or program in question to jointly and officially decide to embrace the concept of globalization for criminal justice education. Then, I would suggest that at least one faculty member be selected (with release time) to dedicate a minimum of one semester to create a well-researched and well-balanced **five-year criminal justice education globalization plan**, tailored to its unique needs and wishes. Input should then be solicited from each faculty member; then site visits should be made to at least 10 other campuses with existing programs to create a data base of potential options *commensurate* with available resources. Outcomes might include at least three new course titles; job specs for at least three full-time international faculty; at least one annual overseas criminal justice field trip; an exchange program with each sister city partner available; creation of at least five new certificate *training programs* in law enforcement, courts, corrections, juvenile justice, and victim services, with *international* components in such areas as criminal investigation, crime prevention, correctional services, innovations for drug and alcohol treatment, victim treatment, reconciliation and mediation, legal aid studies, applied forensic behavior, criminal justice planning, Latin American criminal justice, organized crime, criminal and juvenile justice, systems' analyses, human trafficking, terrorism, and femicide. All should be tailored to the wishes and skill sets of the local present and future faculty. At the end of this planning semester, a final implementation schedule would be presented for the approval by faculty with specific milestones for annual reviews scheduled over the course of the next five years so that by the end of this period your entity will have the rich variety of international features that *you* want.

Conclusion

One of the champions of globalizing criminal justice education was my friend and colleague Paul C. Friday (1996) who about 20 years ago wrote, "Criminal justice education in general has taken a narrow, pedantic view stressing knowledge of our own system and the dominant American theories of crime. If any comparative material is introduced into the curriculum, it is generally offered as a single special-topics course," which he critically pointed out, "reinforces the notion that the way things are done in the United States is the only way to do things" (p. 231). In some universities, this narrow-biased view has been changed; in many others, the opportunity for change still exists.

The potential for creating a new global criminal justice education program is indeed an exciting prospect! Such a comprehensive program is much more than just an *administrative reset*; success requires embracing *the long view* and an *internal cultural change* **within** a traditional criminal justice program. There is an abundance of resources waiting to be tapped at the federal, state, and local levels, both governmental and private. I predict *that the wealth of benefits of a new international multi-dimensional program could bring in new faculty and students and create a more dynamic environment that could significantly enrich an existing educational platform.*

In my opinion, the most obvious areas of immediate upgrading should be student international internships, faculty exchanges abroad, enhanced curricula content, multiple joint degree programs (intra- and extramural), and special summer practitioner certificate training (tailored to the local needs, which is after all the immediate destination of most of the students), especially for students now preparing for careers in corrections, juvenile justice, law enforcement, and victim assistance. These upgrades would easily facilitate the hosting of international conferences on your campus, increase the participation of your faculty and students at overseas symposia, greatly attract more students into your program, invigorate the "summer lulls," and, most importantly, better prepare your students for the challenges of the future and much more. Good luck, be bold, be creative, and be optimistic.

A Case Scenario: A Foreign Country Field Trip

In a medium-sized university in a small southern town, early in the spring semester, the new announcement posted on the Criminology Department's bulletin board announcing a "Scandinavian Corrections Adventure" had the criminology students intrigued; it was the hottest topic of many discussions in and out of the classrooms. "This summer a very special Corrections tour with prison visits and lectures by local professors will be conducted for 7 weeks involving 22 students in an academic trip to Oslo, Norway; Upsala, Sweden; Helsinki, Finland, and two side sightseeing trips to Copenhagen, Denmark and St. Petersburg, Russia." Of course, the handbill had all the administrative details as well as how students might qualify. With the group airline rates, staying at the dorms at three universities, and a travel stipend from the university, the cost was quite reasonable and within reach for most students. The schedule of events allowed for three prison visits per week, interspersed with two 2-hour seminars per week by the course administrator and two 2-hour lectures per week by professors from the each of the three host universities. Two weeks were to be spent visiting prisons in Norway, 3 weeks in Sweden, and 2 weeks in Finland, with exams on the last day of each country's stay. With satisfactory attendance and a passing grade on the exams, the event could earn each student the equivalent of two full-time, on-campus criminology course credits. The students had to be at least juniors or seniors, with 11 females and 11 males, all registered as criminology majors and having a GPA of at least 2.5. The vetting was done during the fourth week of the semester. Preparations involved getting passports, depositing the full amount of the course fee, taking a cultural orientation course with basic Swedish lessons for the following 3 months of the semester, and reading the then best seller book *The Ugly American* (Lederer & Burdick, 1958), which was made into a film in 1963. The plan was that the book would help make the students sensitive to the blunders many American make when being overseas. Well, by the end of the 7-week trip, students were actually using the book's title to criticize each other's cultural mistakes, or "UAs" as they were dubbed. Academically all the students passed the course; from the standpoint of personal maturity, they all grew a lot. Of course, the experience was harder for some than for others, as over two thirds had never even traveled out of their home state and only two spoke a foreign language

(Spanish). Homesickness emerged as one of the early challenges after about the third week and lingered during the entire trip, but the excitement of many new experiences, the kindness of the Scandinavian hosts, and the extensive sightseeing helped take the edge off the hardships of maintaining the academic regime and the rigors of studying for exams. Also challenging was missing their usual diet and having to eat different foods (luckily in each of these major cities, except in Russia, there were McDonalds available); coping with personality conflicts among the students; self-discipline with drinking, smoking, and, yes, experimenting with pot. Managing their personal spending was a dilemma for some and of course being respectful of their local hosts were issues at times as the Scandinavian professors and student hosts were somewhat much more conservative than the students were accustomed. The second to last weekend in Finland was used for a side trip by boat from Helsinki to St. Petersburg, Russia (strictly monitored by Russian authorities), and the last weekend was used to visit Copenhagen, Denmark. From many different perspectives, these 22 students had a major once-in-a-lifetime experience and not only learned a great deal about Scandinavian corrections (theory and practice), but also a great deal about themselves: how to cope in an alien environment, that personal "truths" held prior to this trip are not valid, and becoming aware that they were able to survive in several foreign cultures. Over the following years, as a result, this university conducted more similar field trips. This helped establish many new collaborations in other countries, enriched the basic criminology department's educational offerings, broadened the scope of faculty research, and, in turn, enhanced students' education and ultimately their careers.

Three Students' Statements

One male junior stated, "This trip was a blast! I thought it was gonna be more of a vacation. Even if I am not much of a nerd, our prof made us study and gave exams at the end of each country visit, and I really learned a lot AND still managed to have a ball. I was blown away with how easy the inmates have it in Scandinavia, yet they have lower recidivism rates—that really surprised me. At our state prisons inmates are treated like crap[;] not in Scandinavia—their dignity as real people is respected a lot. I think I can introduce some of what I saw and learned here in the USA."

One female senior stated, "My parents were not keen on me going. They heard all the negative stories, especially about the super liberal Swedes. Okay, I did experiment with pot, elephant beer (really high alcohol content) and I met some cute guys, but we mostly behaved. We did not want to be "Ugly Americans" like we read in the book our teacher required. I was amazed how homesick I became in the second week. After a while I got used to it. Being so deep in three Scandinavian cultures really opened my eyes about a lot of things besides the correctional stuff, like [] strange foods, how normal people obey the law without all the threat of punishment (like we have in the states)[,] how friendly yet critical the Scandinavian students were towards the US. We all spent a lot of time defending the US—that was a big surprise!"

One older female senior stated, "I was the oldest student—I am a mom and at first felt out of place. About into the second week and luckily, we all became like a family. I am also a Latina and so I was dealing with bias from both the American and my Hispanic upbringing. That made me even more different but in a good way. I especially appreciated that our professor had us take some Swedish language classes and he spent a lot of time explaining the cultures as well as the academic stuff. In spite of my age, I still realize I matured a great deal and it would have never happened if I hadn't taken this plunge way outside my comfort zone. My husband and my two kids were dead-against this trip. But I think I will bring a lot of wisdom back to my family thanks to this great experience. It will definitely influence me in a professional way."

In Reflection

An ideal globalized criminal justice education should prepare students for a career in any of the areas within the criminal justice system. At the heart of success in any of those fields is the ability to solve the intricate problems of an ever-increasing complex world that demands having access to a wide range of solution options. Exposure to the international community makes one aware of the vast variety of ways that other nations cope with their criminal justice problems—usually different and sometimes better than us. The Scandinavian corrections field trip dramatically confronted its participants with a broad range of ideas and practices not used in the

United States and potentially available to this nation. This brief case scenario shows how an innovative doable program can impart a life-altering experience that can last as a significant resource for a lifetime and serve career needs after graduation. This suggests that those with these types of global educational experiences will be among those who will stand out in the future because they will have gathered much more knowledge and resources than others without this exposure. In the final analysis, those who received a globalized criminal justice education were those fortunate students who were given a much broader range and depth of skills and a special awareness thanks to the wisdom of their educators. Thus, as a direct consequence they will likely enjoy their future careers at a much higher level, become significantly more qualified as professionals than would have been the case without this type of unique global educational experience, and in the long-run will be able to contribute much more to their society—clearly a value-added change for all stakeholders.

Discussion Questions

1. Can you imagine why it might be important for your criminal justice education to include courses that would help you understand, be sensitive to, and consider embracing criminal justice practices, policies, and philosophies from other nations and other cultures?

2. What new transnational problems exist, already identified by the United Nations, that have a direct bearing on crime problems in the United States for which we are not adequately prepared due to lack of foresight, myopic planning, or paucity of funds?

3. How might we improve our responses to such international issues as human trafficking, illegal emigration, tourist victimization, victim services for U.S. citizens abroad, controlling terrorism, and investigating international organized crime and femicide?

4. Since other countries' crimes are somewhat different and some nations have lower crime rates, what hypotheses might be crafted from these variables: economic conditions, religions, homogeneity vs. heterogeneity, level of industrialization, forms of government, educational levels, cultural differences, and control/freedom tradeoffs?

5. If you were king for a day, had unlimited resources at your disposal, and were aware of the possibilities enumerated in this chapter, what would you change to create an ideal criminal justice education and why?

Application Exercises: A Focus on Globalization and the "Real World"

1. Based on the content of this chapter, what you know, and your opinions, what ideas from what you have already studied about the criminal justice systems around the globe might work in this country and in your state (real world)?

2. Since the contemporary criminal justice systems in most countries around the world have evolved over many years, some that date back to antiquity, and our system is relatively new and inexperienced by comparison, is it realistic for us to imagine we might adopt some of their positive practices in the short term and how could we justify making them happen in our real world?

3. Outside the educational realm, what are the major social challenges for globalizing our criminal justice policies in the real world of the United States?

4. Why is it that your university does not currently have a well-developed globalized criminal justice educational curriculum, and, in your judgement, what are the local barriers to achieving this goal in the real world?

5. Does the real world pose conflicts between national and state political interests and thus pose a challenge in prioritizing studying topics and financial limitation at your university?

6. How do other advanced countries confront their real-world issues of time related to marginalized groups isolated by race, religion, color language, citizenship, and gender?

7. What attitudes among students and faculty at your university, of which you are aware, are in conflict to the adoption of a more globalized criminal justice educational curriculum based on real-world issues today and in the future?

8. How can college graduates who have received a globalized criminal justice education convince persons without this unique education so as to implement practices that seem to be more effective and more efficient yet less punitive?

References

Academic Council on the United Nations System. (2018). Global knowledge hub on the gender-related killings of women and girls. Retrieved from https://acuns. org/global-knowledge-hub/

Bureau of Justice Statititcs. (n.d.). *All data collections*. Retrieved from https:// www.bjs.gov/index.cfm?ty=dca

Commission on Crime Prevention and Criminal Justice. (2018). *Contribution by the Commission on Crime Prevention and Criminal Justice to the Integration Segment on the theme "Innovative communities: Leveraging technology and innovation to build sustainable and resilient societies."* Retrieved from https://www.un.org/ecosoc/ sites/www.un.org.ecosoc/files/files/en/2018doc/2018-integration-segment-ccpcj.pdf

Dammer, H. R., & Albanese, J. S. (2014). *Comparative criminal justice systems*. Belmont, CA: Wadsworth.

Decker, S. H., & Marteache, N. (Eds.). (2017). *International handbook of juvenile justice*. Cham, Switzerland: Springer.

Ekblom, P. (2005). How to police the future: Scanning for scientific and technological innovations which generate potential threats and opportunities in crime, policing and crime reduction. In M. J. Smith & N. Tilley (Eds.), *Crime science: New approaches to preventing and detecting crimes* (pp. 27–55). Cullompton: Willan.

Friday, P. (1996). The need to integrate comparative and international criminal justice into a traditional curriculum. *Journal of Criminal Justice Education, 7*(2), 227–239.

Haberfeld, M. R., & Cerrah, I. (2008). *Comparative policing: The struggle for democratization*. Thousand Oaks, CA: SAGE.

Harrendorf, S., Heiskanen, M., & Malby, S. (2010) International statistics on crime and justice. *European Institute for Crime Prevention and Control*. Retrieved from https://www.unodc.org/documents/data-and-analysis/Crime-statistics/ International_Statistics_on_Crime_and_Justice.pdf

Harris-Hogan, S., Barrell, K., & Zammitt, A. (2016). What is countering violent extremism? Exploring CVE policy and practice. *Behavioral Sciences of Terrorism and Political Aggression, 8*(1), 2–24.

Kury H., Dussich. J. P. J., & Wertz, M. (2018). Migration in Germany: An international comparison on the psychotraumatic stress among refugees. In H. Kury

& S. Redo (Eds.), *Refugees and migrants in law and policy: Challenges and opportunities for global civic education* (pp. 313–354). Cham, Switzerland, Springer.

Lederer, W., & Burdick, E. (1958). *The ugly American.* New York, NY: Norton.

Natarajan, M. (2002). International criminal justice education: A note on curricular resources. *Journal of Criminal Justice Education, 13*(2), 479–498.

National Organization for Victim Assistance. (2018). *Crisis response team training.* Retrieved from https://www.trynova.org/crtdraft/?gclid=EAIaIQobChMIy4_lwNaQ3AIVAwZpCh2i0weKEAAYAiAAEgLjWvD_BwE

Polaris. (2017). *The facts.* Retrieved from https://polarisproject.org/human-trafficking/facts?gclid=EAIaIQobChMI4oTHgNKQ3AIVBRxp-Ch0mwgAcEAAYBCAAEgKw5PD_BwE

Reiter, K. (2014). Making windows in walls: Strategies for prison research. *Qualitative Inquiry, 20*(4), 417–428.

Saleh-Hanna, V. (2008). Colonial systems of control: Criminal justice in Nigeria. Ottawa, Canada: University of Ottawa Press.

Scharf, M. P. (1999). The amnesty exception to the jurisdiction of the International Criminal Court. *Cornell International Law Journal, 32*(3), 407–427.

Simon, R., & De Waal, C. (2009). *Prisons of the world over.* Lenham, MD: Lexington.

Stromseth. J. (2017). Why the U.S. needs the Office of Global Criminal Justice led by a Senate-confirmed ambassador-at-large. *Just Security.* Retrieved from https://www.justsecurity.org/43554/u-s-office-global-criminal-justice-led-sen-ate-confirmed-ambassador-at-large/

Terrill, R. J. (2016) *World criminal justice systems: A comparative survey* (9th ed.). New York, NY: Anderson.

United Nations. (2008). *United Nations declaration on the rights for indigenous people.* Retrieved from http://www.un.org/esa/socdev/unpfii/documents/DRIPS_en.pdf

United Nations on Drug and Crime. (2016). Organized crime has globalized and turned into a security threat. Retrieved from https://www.unodc.org/unodc/index.html

United Nations Interregional Crime and Justice Research Institute. (2018). Retrieved from http://www.unicri.it/

Van Dijk, J. (2008). *The world of crime.* Thousand Oaks, CA: SAGE.

Zimering, F. E., Langer, M., & Tanenhaus, D. S. (Eds.) (2017). *Juvenile justice in global perspective.* New York, NY: New York University Press.

Chapter 13

From Past to Present

Understanding the Influence of Immigration Status on the Criminal Justice System

Mercedes Valadez

Introduction

The United States maintains a complex identity as a country that was founded by immigrants. The conversation surrounding early U.S. immigration focuses on nostalgic feelings of pride and history. Even though most European immigrant groups were met with prejudice and negative immigrant stereotypes, it was easier for them to assimilate based on race. However, the racial and ethnic makeup of the immigrant community began to change during the 1960s. The 1965 Immigration and Nationality Act (enacted in 1968) reshaped immigration in the United States. (Chishti, Hipsman, & Ball, 2015). The act removed national quotas, which were typically reserved for European immigrants. This change allowed Asian and Latin American immigrants to qualify for entry based on family ties, education, and/or skills. Figure 13.1 provides an illustration of immigrant population trends based on census data between 1960–2010. Since 1965, the migration flow has been primarily Latin American (over half) and Asian (over a quarter) (Chishti, Hipsman, & Ball, 2015; Gibson & Lennon, 1999; U.S. Census Bureau, 2011). The foreign-born population has grown from approximately 9.6 million in 1965 to approximately 45 million in 2015, with the majority being Latino (Chishti, Hipsman, & Ball, 2015; Gibson & Lennon, 1999; U.S. Census Bureau, 2011).

Latinos are now the largest ethnic or racial minority in the United States, making up 17% of the total U.S. population (Stepler & Brown, 2016). The majority are of Mexican descent. Furthermore, foreign-born Latinos comprise roughly 35% of the Latino population (Stepler &

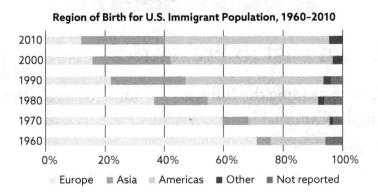

Region of Birth for U.S. Immigrant Population, 1960–2010

Europe Asia Americas Other Not reported

FIGURE 13.1   Region of birth for U.S. immigrant population, 1960–2010.

Brown, 2016). The growth of the Latino immigrant population has generated a need to better understand this segment of the population and how they fare in criminal justice system outcomes (Light, 2014; Light, Massoglia, & King, 2014; Wang, 2012). The increase in migration from Latin American countries has been followed by the demonization of Latino immigrants (Massey, 2009). Recent research suggests that Latinos are now the most disadvantaged group in the criminal court system (Light, 2014).

Growth of non-White immigrant population can result in alarmist, group threat, and nativist attitudes. When Americans overestimate the number of racial and ethnic minorities, relative to the number of Whites, they tend to be more supportive of anti-immigrant policies (Alba, Rumbaut, & Marotz, 2005). Since 1965, attitudes about immigrants have primarily been reflective of alarmist themes (Chavez, 2001). Immigrants are often described as a threat to culture, national security, jobs, etc. Alba and colleagues' (2005), negative immigrant perceptions and restrictive policies focus on Latino immigrants. Within the last decade, several state and federal legislative policies have been enacted with the purpose of deterring unauthorized migration and criminalizing immigrants (see Beason-Hammon Alabama Taxpayer and Citizenship Protection Act; Illegal Immigration Relief Act Ordinance, 2006; Support Our Law Enforcement and Safe Neighborhoods Act, 2010; and the Trump Administration's Family Separation or "zero-tolerance" policy).

Politicians have a history of making distinctions between desirable immigrant groups and unwanted immigrants. Congress enacted legislation to set national origin quotas and exclude immigrants by race, among other discriminatory restrictions. These policies help reinforce the perception that some immigrants (Whites) are worthy of inclusion, whereas others (non-White) are disposable. Latino immigrants are often discussed in disparaging terms in the immigration debate. For example, during a Congressional hearing, a representative from Mississippi voiced his concern that "a bunch of Mexicans" take away American jobs (Newton, 2008, p. 143). During his presidential bid, Trump stated, "When Mexico sends its people, they are not sending their best. They are not sending you. They're not sending you. They're sending people that have lots of problems, and they're bringing those problems with us. They're bringing drugs. They're bringing crime. They're rapists. And some, I assume, are good people" (*Newsday*, 2016). Not only do politicians run on a "get-tough-on-crime" campaign, but they are also known to run on a "tough-on-immigration" campaign.

Once in office, the anti-immigrant rhetoric turns to anti-immigrant legislation. Several significant legislative pieces have led to a current broken immigration system that focuses on criminalizing immigrants. The 1986 passage of the Immigration Reform and Control Act (IRCA) marked the last time the United States government focused on creating a legal pathway for undocumented immigrants. IRCA allowed undocumented immigrants (approximately 2.7 million), living in the United States prior to 1982, to obtain temporary legal status (Chrishti, Meissner, & Bergeron, 2011). However, IRCA was coupled with increased border enforcement and security. It also created employer sanctions for knowingly hiring undocumented workers, which in turn led to an increase in use of fraudulent identification documents. Criminal provisions focused on use of fraudulent documents and knowingly harboring, bringing in, or transporting unauthorized immigrants. These are still aggressively enforced and are in the top five most common immigration-related charges (Chrishti, Meissner, & Bergeron, 2011).

A decade after IRCA, President Clinton signed the Illegal Immigration Reform and Immigrant Responsibility Act (IIRIRA) into law. IIRIRA broadened the definition of an "aggravated felony" and increased the types of crimes that could lead to deportation. The law was also applied retroactively (Kanstroom, 2005), allowing the deportation of those who were convicted of crimes prior to 1996. This allowed legal permanent residents to be deported for minor crimes. The act also increased funding for border patrol agents and created an expedited removal process to deport immigrants without holding a formal hearing. IIRIRA also included Section 287(g) of the Immigration and Nationality Act (INA) (American Immigration Council, 2017). It now plays a prominent role in immigration enforcement at the state and local level. That same year, Clinton also signed the Anti-Terrorism and Effective Death Penalty Act (AEDPA), which authorized fast-track immigrant deportation procedures. IIRIRA and AEDPA created drastic changes to immigration laws in the name of safety and enforcement, which still haunt both undocumented and legal status immigrants. For example, IIRIRA decreased the monetary amount that served as a threshold for deportation based on an offense such as theft (Warner, 2005). One of the other changes was that after 1996, crimes of "moral turpitude" were punishable by deportation. After 1996, a non-U.S. citizen convicted of a first-time misdemeanor shoplifting offense became eligible for deportation (Warner, 2005). IIRIRA coupled with AEDPA helped usher in a system of criminalizing immigrants, which has had a detrimental effect on criminal justice related outcomes for the last 20 years.

More recently, Congress passed the 2002 Homeland Security Act (HSA), which transferred all functions of the U.S. Immigration and Naturalization Service (INS) to the newly created Department of Homeland Security (DHS). DHS includes U.S. Customs and Border Protection (CBP), U.S. Immigration and Customs Enforcement (ICE), and the U.S. Citizenship and Immigration Services (USCIS). Spending on immigration enforcement more than quadrupled between 1985 and 2002 (Dixon & Gelatt, 2005). The annual budget for ICE and CBP has continued to increase since the creation of DHS (American Immigration Council, 2017; U.S. Department of Homeland Security, 2018a). The policies and practices outlined are in part influenced by the myth of the criminal immigrant (Mears, 2001; Rumbaut & Ewing, 2007).

Immigration and Crime

One of the arguments often used to justify anti-immigrant policies is that immigrants are more dangerous and criminally prone relative to native born U.S. citizens. However, the data on crime rates and the literature on the relationship between immigration and crime dispute those misconceptions (Hagan & Palloni, 1999; Ousey & Kubrin, 2014; Sampson, 2008; Stowell, Messner, McGeever, & Raffalovich, 2009). Immigrant stereotypes have always been part of American's history. The only difference is that the race and ethnicity of the dominant migrant group changes overtime. Since the mid to late 1960s, Latino immigrants bear the brunt of the anti-immigrant rhetoric.

Today, immigrant-related fears and prejudice revolve around the stereotypes that immigrants are a threat to employment availability, wages, language, culture, crime, and national security (Chávez, 2001; Chávez, 2008; Massey, 2009). In his article, Roman (2000) argues that Americans are often exposed to the dangerous Latino criminal stereotype. Latinos, especially Latino males, are regularly portrayed in television and films as gangsters, drug dealers, violent, and undocumented. These caricatures generate prejudice and stereotypes that help push the narrative that Latinos are dangerous "outsiders" who aim to cause harm and disrupt the American way of life.

Not all immigrants are viewed with fear and skepticism; some are welcomed to the United States. In a White House meeting with several members of Congress, Trump is cited as having said that the United States welcomes too many immigrants from "shithole countries" and too few from countries like Norway (Gjelten, 2018). In other words, the country would do better to allow more European immigrants rather than those from more impoverished countries. This also signals that there is a level of superiority among some immigrants compared to others.

One of the groups often seen as inferior or criminal is Latino. More specifically, Central Americans and Mexicans are viewed as dangerous drug lords or MS-13 gang members. Now, Latino immigrants are being described as less than human. In one of his speeches, Trump stated, "We have people coming into the country, or trying to come in and we're stopping a lot of them, but we're taking people out of the country. You wouldn't believe how bad these people are. These aren't people. These are animals" (as cited by Oliphant & Esposito, 2018). When asked about the comments he made, he doubled down stating that "MS-13—these are animals.... We need strong immigrant laws.... We have laws that are laughed at on immigration. So when the MS-13 comes in, when the other gang members come into our country, I refer to them as animals and guess what, I always will" (as cited by Oliphant & Esposito, 2018). However, Mexican nationals find themselves at the forefront of the anti-Latino immigrant rhetoric. This trend emerged before Trump, but he helps to foster it. According to Massey (2009), Mexicans are "increasingly subject to processes of racialization that have rendered them more exploitable and excludable than ever before" (p. 12). The inflammatory comments made against immigrants serve to activate voters' beliefs and stereotypes, which in turn influence voters on immigration policies (Newman, Shah, & Collingwood, 2018). Painting immigrants as dangerous and instituting anti-immigrant policies provides the narrative that Trump is addressing the immigrant problem.

The Trump administration has put forth an appeal for additional restrictive immigration policies, building a border wall across the U.S.-Mexico border, expanding use of detention centers, and increasing deportations as a means of public safety. Trump has regularly used erroneous links between immigration and crime to justify anti-immigrant rhetoric and policies. In response to the myth of the criminal immigrant, the attorney general created a taskforce aimed at reducing crime in the following areas: "illegal immigration, drug trafficking, and violent crime" (White House, 2017). Trump also directed the Department of Homeland Security to create the Victims of Immigration Crime Engagement (VOICE) office with assisting and publicizing "crimes committed by individuals with a nexus to immigration" (Department of Homeland Security, 2018, pg. 1). The Trump administration is focused on fostering the myths and misconceptions surrounding immigration and crime despite overwhelming evidence that immigrants are not more dangerous nor criminal.

There is a long body of work showing that immigrants have lower crime rates compared to native-born U.S. citizens (Bersani & Piquero, 2016; Ewing, Martinez, & Rumbaut, 2015; Ousey & Kubrin, 2014; Vaughn, Salas-Wright, DLisi, & Maynard, 2014). Studies dating back to over a century ago consistently found that immigrants had lower rates of criminality compared to their native U.S. born peers (Ghandnoosh

& Rovner, 2017). This includes both violent and nonviolent criminal offenses and arrest rates (Vaughn, Salas-Wright, DLisi, & Maynard, 2014). These findings also apply to juveniles. For example, in a study using data from 1994–2002, researchers found that immigrant middle and high school youth had lower delinquency rates for nonviolent offenses (e.g., drug-related crimes, drugs, property damage, and theft) relative to their native-born peers (Powell, Perreira, & Mullan Harris, 2010). Immigrant status can serve as a protective rather than a risk factor. There are also benefits to living in a neighborhood with a high concentration of immigrants. Sampson, Morenoff, and Raudenbush (2005) found lower rates of violence among Mexican Americans compared with Whites. This was "explained by a combination of married parents, living in a neighborhood with a high concentration of immigrants, and individual immigrant status" (Sampson et al., 2005, p. 231). The current undocumented population is primarily composed of Latino, young, poor males, with little formal education (Ewing, Martinez, & Rumbaut, 2015). Even though they face so much disadvantage, they are more likely to be law abiding compared to their native-born peers. Additionally, an increase in the immigrant population, including undocumented immigrants, coincide with historic crime drops (Brown & Stepler, 2016; Ghandnoosh & Rovner, 2017). Yet, immigrants remain under a cloud of suspicion and are overly policed.

Immigration and Policing

The federal government is responsible for immigration enforcement. However, Immigration and Customs Enforcement (ICE) works alongside state and local law enforcement agencies to fulfill its mission of enforcement. The 287(g) program allows state and local law enforcement agencies to enter a partnership with ICE. They do so under a joint memorandum of agreement (MOA), which grants state and local agencies authority in their jurisdictions over immigration enforcement matters. The first MOA was signed by Florida in 2002 per the request to train officers in combating terrorist threats. The Obama administration was instrumental in expanding the 287(g) program. Participation in the program allows DHS to deputize state and local law enforcement agents to perform the duties of federal immigration agents. According to the

U.S. Department of Homeland Security (2018b), ICE currently holds agreements with 78 law enforcement agencies in 20 states. The type of support they provide is primarily jail enforcement. Criticism often cited against using state and local law enforcement agencies for immigration enforcement includes eroding public trust between police and immigrant communities.

In recent years, state and local law enforcement agencies have taken on a larger role within the context of immigration enforcement. To that end, it has resulted in some unintended consequences including undermining public safety and creating distrust between police and immigrant communities (Ghandnoosh & Rovner, 2017). Theodore (2013) assessed the effect of Latino and immigrant perceptions of police involvement in immigration enforcement. He found that when state and local law enforcement agencies are perceived as taking on more of an immigration enforcement role, as many as 70% of undocumented immigrants say that they are less likely to contact law enforcement if they are the victims of a crime. In addition, 58% of undocumented immigrants reported feeling under more suspicion now that local law enforcement agencies became more involved in immigration enforcement. Furthermore, 78% of undocumented respondents said that police officers stop Latinos without good reason or cause very or somewhat often. These findings point to the costs to public trust in law enforcement as state and local police agents take on federal enforcement responsibilities. It sets up an already vulnerable population to be victimized at greater numbers because they will be too fearful to report victimization. Immigrants who feel distrust for police will not be as willing to come forward as witnesses of crime because of fear of deportation. Theodore (2013) found that 67% of undocumented respondents were less likely to voluntarily offer information about crimes committed because of fear that police will ask them or other people they know about their immigrant status. State and local police agencies are aware of the risk that participation in immigration enforcement can have on the communities they serve, and some have spoken out against the practice.

Police officers are often referred to as the gatekeepers of the criminal justice system. When asked about working with immigrant communities, some police groups have expressed a need to build trust within immigrant communities rather than instill fear. For example, Boston Police

Commissioner William Evans stated the following when asked about building trust in immigrant communities: "The last thing we want is for people to be afraid of us. And I think that's what's going on in a little bit now. People are afraid that, all of a sudden, we are going to be rounding them up and sending them out.... They won't report crimes or help us in their communities if they afraid of us" (Ellement, 2017, pg 2). Detective Brent Hopkins of Los Angeles echoed the same sentiment when it came to the ramifications of police distrust in immigrant communities. He stated, "I'm losing my witnesses or my victims because they're afraid that talking to me is going to lead to them getting deported" (Cave & Heisler, 2014, p. 1). Once arrested or detained, immigrants often move through the next stage of the criminal justice system.

Immigration and the Courts

Aggressive immigration enforcement, coupled with legislation aimed at criminalizing immigrants, has led to increased immigrant-related court cases. Given the increase of immigrant defendants in the criminal court system, there is a growing interest in studying this segment of the population. Researchers seek to understand how non-U.S. citizen defendants fare in courtroom outcomes. To this end, a growing body of literature focuses on the role of citizenship status on sentencing outcomes (Albonetti 2002; Demuth, 2002; Hartley & Armendariz, 2011; Logue, 2009; Mustard 2001). Research suggests that non-U.S. citizens are sentenced more punitively compared to U.S. citizen offenders (Steffensmeier & Demuth, 2000). Light (2014) found that noncitizens were three times more likely to be incarcerated compared to similarly situated U.S. citizens. Other studies find that non-U.S. citizen defendants receive longer prison sentences and obtain fewer benefits based on guideline departures (Albonetti, 2002; Mustard, 2001). Other studies, though, find no association between citizenship status and courtroom outcomes (Everett & Wojtkiewickz, 2002; Kautt & Spohn, 2002). Moreover, other studies show mixed findings with respect to the association between citizenship status and sentencing outcomes (Wolfe, Pyrooz & Spohn, 2010; Wu & DeLone, 2012). Wolfe and colleagues (2010) found that while noncitizens are more likely to be incarcerated, they received shorter prison sentences compared to U.S. citizens. Another area of study that has emerged is looking at the effect of legal status or nationality on sentencing outcomes.

Research suggests that immigrants, especially those who are undocumented, are punished more severely than similarly situated U.S. citizens (Demuth, 2002; Light, 2014; Valadez, 2013; Valadez & Wang, 2017). In one study, Demuth (2002) found that among federal drug offenders, legal residents were 30% more likely to be incarcerated relative to U.S. citizens. He also found that undocumented immigrants were 44% more likely to be imprisoned relative to U.S. citizens. However, he did not find a significant difference in sentence length outcomes. Valadez (2013) found that among Latino immigrants, Mexican nationals were more likely to be incarcerated and serve longer prison terms compared to other Latino subgroups. Valadez and Wang (2017) examined the moderating effects of race/ethnicity, age, and gender on sentencing outcomes for federal drug offenders between 2006–2008. They found that young Hispanic, male, noncitizen and undocumented immigrants have the greatest odds of imprisonment compared to similarly situated defendants. These findings support the influence of the dangerous, young, Latino male on courtroom outcomes. The stereotypes discussed earlier may seep into the courtroom and influence the judge, who is supposed to be impartial.

Judges are not immune or protected from the influences of what takes place outside a courtroom. While judges are supposed to remain free of bias, that is not always the case. In fact, judges have used negative immigrant stereotypes in their rational during the sentencing phase of a case (*U.S. v. Borrero-Isaza*, 1989; *U.S. v. Gomez*, 1986). In the case of *U.S. v. Gomez* (1986) a judge used stereotypes of Latino drug offenders as he made his sentencing decision. The case was appealed, but the appellate court sided with the judge and upheld the 15-year prison sentence on the basis that the judge didn't use the defendant's nationality to target him specifically. Instead, the judge used the defendant's nationality to send a message to other South Americans against committing drug offenses. However, other judges have been much more open about their bias against immigrant defendants. In *U.S. v. Onwuemene* (1991) the trial judge stated the following:

You are not a citizen of this country. This country was good enough to allow you to come in here to confer upon you ... a number of the benefits of this society, form of government, and its opportunities and you repay that kindness by committing a crime like this. We have got enough criminals in the United States without importing any (as cited in Logue, 2009, p. 427).

In another case, Judge Edith Jones' impartiality was questioned after she was accused of claiming that Hispanics are criminally prone, as well as expressing bias against Mexican nationals (Committee on judicial conduct and disability of the judicial conference of the United States, 2015). These cases show that judicial bias against immigrants is brought into the courtroom and used as part of the rationale during sentencing. Defendants are punished for both being non-U.S. citizens or undocumented in addition to the crimes they allegedly commit. As more and more immigrants are processed and sentenced to prison, it's created a booming business for private prisons and private detention centers.

Immigrants and Imprisonment

The Justice Department through the Bureau of Justice Statistics (BJS) provides an overview of inmate demographics under the jurisdiction of the state and federal correctional facilities (Carson, 2018). Approximately 21% (39,956 of 189,192) of federal prisoners imprisoned in 2016 were non-U.S. citizens. This number excludes individuals detained by the U.S. Department of Homeland Security. With respect to state-level incarceration, an additional 43,600 noncitizens were imprisoned at the end of 2016. According to Carson (2018), these data exclude those housed in private prisons, local jails, or other jurisdictions. However, the Bureau of Prisons (BOP) counts inmates housed in contract facilities and those detained who are awaiting deportation. As of May 2018, the Federal Bureau of Prisons estimates that 20.1% of the prison population is made up of non-U.S. citizens. Of these, 12.8% (23,532) are Mexican nationals, and 7.1% (12,115) of inmates are incarcerated for immigration offenses (Federal Bureau of Prisons, 2018). In 1992, non-U.S. citizen Latinos made up 16% of sentenced offenders, whereas 20 years later, non-U.S. citizen Latinos made up 76% of sentenced offenders (Light, Lopez, &

Gonzalez-Barrera, 2014). The increase of immigrant imprisonment or confinement has created a demand for housing, resulting in the rise of private immigrant jails and detention centers.

The business of imprisoning immigrants is booming. The Trump administration's zero-tolerance policy and increased enforcement efforts have also contributed to the demand of additional detention centers. In fiscal year (FY) 2001, ICE identified approximately 209,000 immigrants for detention or removal. However, by 2016 that number increased to approximately 353,000 immigrants processed through one of the over 200 immigration detention centers in the United States (Luan, 2018). Figure 13.2 provides an illustration of immigrant removals, returns, and apprehensions between FY 1968 and 2016 (U.S. Department of Homeland Security, 2017). Removal refers to the deportation of those with an order of removal, whereas return refers to immigrants deported without an order of removal. Apprehension refers to border patrol and ICE administrative arrests. Removals increased each decade, with the lowest number (9,590) in 1968. Returns do not reflect a steady increase overtime, instead reaching a peak of 1,570,127 in 1998. That same year, apprehensions were also high at 1,679,439. By August of 2016, approximately 75% of detained immigrants were held in private prisons, whereas a decade prior they were primarily held in ICE-contracted state prisons or local jails. Privately run immigration detention centers house immigrants being processed or awaiting removal, asylum seekers, and those waiting for a hearing in immigration court. CoreCivic and GEO

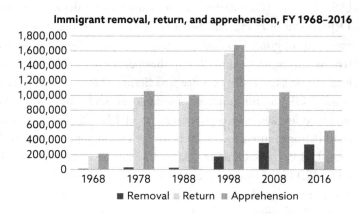

FIGURE 13.2   Immigrant removal, return, and apprehension, FY 1968–2016.

Group manage about half of the private prison contracts for both immigrant and non-immigrant detention centers (Luan, 2018). Both made sizable contributions to Trump's presidential campaign and donated $250,000 for inaugural activities (Luan, 2018). Several human rights groups and even the U.S. Justice Department have found that privately run immigrant detention centers do not meet safety and security standards (Burnett, 2017; Luan, 2018). Immigration detention facilities are plagued with claims of sexual assault, abuse, inadequate medical care, and other forms of mistreatment (Speri, 2018). Despite these findings, in 2018, ICE requested proposals by private companies to house additional immigrant detainees (Geller, 2018). Given the issues of abuse in private detention facilities, there are calls to address enforcement practices and detention facility conditions.

Immigration Issues, Present and Future

The United States has come under criticism for violations of due process and abuse of immigrants. The United Nations' Human Rights Office has denounced Trump's family separation policy, noting that "the use of immigration detention and family separation as a deterrent runs counter to human rights standards and principles" and that the "practice of separating children from their parents is being applied to both asylum-seekers and other migrants in vulnerable situations" (United Nations Human Rights Office of the High Commission, 2018, p. 2). Due to forced family separation, more toddlers and children are being ordered into court for their own deportation proceedings (Jewett & Luthra, 2018). These children cannot be expected to articulate the reasons they fled their home country. Possibly due to some of the public outcry and backlash, the administration altered the family separation policy through an executive order (Gonzales, 2018). However, the order makes it possible to house children with parents in detention facilities indefinitely, essentially creating immigrant family prisons.

Conclusion

The focus on immigration remains on enforcement, prosecution, detention, and deportation. In fact, Trump's fiscal year 2019 proposed budget requested $47.5 billion toward the Department of Homeland Security (DHS), which is a 7.8% in increase from the year prior (Department of Homeland Security, 2018). The influence of immigrant status crosses all areas of the criminal justice system. Increased enforcement leads to more prosecutions, a backlog of immigrant-related cases, and overflowing immigrant detention centers, fostering an environment ripe for human rights abuses.

Discussion Questions

1. Despite all evidence to the contrary, why do politicians continue to claim that immigrants commit crime at greater rates than native born citizens?
2. What are the ethical and moral dilemmas with family separation and indefinite family detention of immigrants and asylum seekers?

References

Alba, R., Rumbaut, R. G., & Marotz, K. (2005). A distorted nation: Perceptions of racial/ethnic group sizes and attitudes toward immigrants and other minorities. *Social Forces*, 84(2), 901–919.

Albonetti, C. A. (2002). The joint conditioning effect of defendant's gender and ethnicity on length of imprisonment under the federal sentencing guidelines for drug trafficking/manufacturing offenders. *Journal of Gender, Race, and Justice*, 6, 39–60.

American Immigration Council. (2017). Fact sheet: The cost of immigration enforcement and border security. Retrieved from https://www.americanimmigrationcouncil.org/sites/default/files/research/the_cost_of_immigration_enforcement_and_border_security.pdf

American Immigration Council. (2017). *The 287(g) program: An overview.* Retrieved from https://www.americanimmigrationcouncil.org/sites/default/files/research/the_287g_program_an_overview_0.pdf

Beason-Hammon Alabama Taxpayer and Citizenship Protection Act, 2011, Alabama House Bill 56.

Bersani, B. E. & Piquero, A. R. (2016). Examining systematic crime reporting bias across three immigrant generations: Prevalence, trends, and divergence in self-reported and official reported arrests. *Journal of Quantitative Criminology*, 33(4) 835–857.

Brown, A., & Stepler, R. (2016). Statistical portrait of the foreign-born population in the United States. Pew Research Center. Retrieved from http://www.pewhispanic.org/2016/04/19/statistical-portrait-of-the-foreignborn-population-in-the-united-states-key-charts/#2013-fbpopulation

Burnett, J. (2017). Big money as private immigrant jails boom. NPR. Retrieved from https://www.npr.org/2017/11/21/565318778/big-money-as-private-immigrant-jails-boom.

Cave, D., & Heisler, T. (2014, June). Day 20: The politics of crime and immigration. *New York Times*. Retrieved from https://www.nytimes.com/interactive/2014/us/the-way-north.html?_r=3#p/20

Carson, A. (2018). Prisoners in 2016. U.S. Department of Justice. Retrieved from https://www.bjs.gov/content/pub/pdf/p16.pdf/.

Chávez, L. R. (2001). Covering immigration: Population images and the politics of the nation. Berkeley: University of California Press.

Chávez, L.R. (2008). The Latino threat: Constructing immigrants, citizens, and the nation. Stanford, CA: Stanford University Press.

Chishti, M., Hipsman, F., & Ball, I. (2015). Fifty years on, the 1965 Immigration and Nationality Act continues to reshape the United States. *Migration Policy Institute*. Retrieved from https://www.migrationpolicy.org/article/fifty-years-1965-immigration-and-nationality-act-continues-reshape-united-states

Chishti, M., Meissner, D., & Bergeron, C. (2011). At its 25th anniversary, IRCA's legacy lives on. *Migration Policy Institute*. Retrieved from https://www.migrationpolicy.org/article/its-25thanniversary-ircas-legacy-lives.

Committee on judicial conduct and disability of the judicial conference of the United States (2015). In RE: Complaint of Judicial Misconduct. Retrieved from https://www.uscourts.gov/sites/default/files/ccd-14-01order-final-02-19-15.pdf

Demuth, S. (2002). The effect of citizenship status on sentencing outcomes in drug cases. *Federal Sentencing Reporter*, 14(5), 271–275.

Dixon, D. & Gelatt, J. (2005). Immigration enforcement spending since IRCA. The Migration Policy Institute. Retrieved from https://www.migration policy.org/pubs/FactSheet_Spending.pdf.

Ellement, J. R. (2017). Police "need to build trust" with immigrant community, Evans says. *Boston Globe*. Retrieved from https://www.boston.com/news/local-news/2017/01/31/police-need-tobuild-trust-with-immigrant-community-evans-says.

Everett, R.S., &Wojtkiewicz, R.A. (2002). Difference, disparity, and racial/ethnic bias in federal sentencing. *Journal of Quantitative Criminology, 18*, 189-211.

Ewing, W. A., Martinez, D. E., & Rumbaut, R. G. (2015). The criminalization of immigration in the United States. American Immigration Council (AIC). Retrieved from https://www.americanimmigrationcouncil.org/research/criminalization-immigration-unitedstates.

Geller, A. (2018). Companies propose immigrant detention centers for Midwest. U.S. News. Retrieved from https://www.usnews.com/news/us/articles/2018-05-11/companies-proposeimmigration-detention-centers-for-midwest.

Ghandnoosh, N., & Rovner, J. (2017). Immigration and public safety. *Sentencing Project*. Retrieved from https://www.sentencingproject.org/publications/immigration-public-safety/

Gibson. C. J., & Lennon. E. (1999). Historical census statistics on the foreign-born population of the United States: 1850–1990. *U.S. Census Bureau*. Retrieved from https://www.census.gov/population/www/documentation/twps0029/twps0029.html

Gjelten, T. (2018). President Trump's idea of good and bad immigrant countries has a historical precedent. *NPR*. Retrieved from https://www.npr.org/2018/01/13/577808792/president-trumps-idea-of-good-and-bad-immigrant-countries-has-a-historical-prece

Gonzales, R. (2018). Trump's executive order on family separation: What it does and doesn't do. NPR. Retrieved from https://www.npr.org/2018/06/20/622095441/trump-executive-order-onfamily-separation-what-it-does-and-doesnt-do.

Hagan, J. & Palloni, A. (1999). Sociological criminology and mythology of Hispanic immigrants and crime. *Social Problems, 46*(4), 617–632.

Hartley, R. D., & Armendariz, L. F. (2011). Border justice? Sentencing federal narcotics offenders in southwest border districts: A focus on citizenship status. *Journal of Contemporary Criminal Justice, 27*(1), 43–62.

Illegal Immigration Reform and Enforcement Act, 2011, Georgia House Bill 87

Jewett, C., & Luthra, S. (2018). More toddlers appear alone in court for deportation under family separation. PBS. Retrieved from https://www.pbs.org/newshour/health/more-toddlers-appearalone-in-court-for-deportation-under-family-separation.

Kanstroom, D. (2007). *Deportation nation: Outsiders in American history*. Cambridge, MA: Harvard University Press.

Kautt, P., & Spohn, C. (2002). Race/ethnicity and sentencing outcomes among drug offenders in North Carolina. *Journal of Contemporary Criminal Justice, 24,* 371-398.

Light, M. T. (2014). The new face of legal inequality: Noncitizens and the long-term trends in sentencing disparities across U.S. district courts, 1992–2009. *Law & Society Review, 48*(2), 447–478.

Light, M. T., Lopez, M. H., & Gonzalez-Barrera, A. (2014). Changing demographics of sentenced offenders. *Pew Research Center.* Retrieved from http://www.pewhispanic.org/2014/03/18/3-changing-demographics-of-sentenced-offenders/.

Light, M.T., Massoglia, M., & King, R.D. (2014). Citizenship and punishment: The salience of national membership in U.S. criminal courts. *American Sociological Review, 79,* 825-847.

Logue, M. A. (2009). The price of being Mexican: Sentencing disparities between noncitizen Mexican and non-Mexican Latinos in the federal courts. *Hispanic Journal of Behavioral Sciences, 31*(4), 423–445.

Luan. L. (2018). Profiting from enforcement: The role of private prisons in U.S. immigration detention. Migration Policy Institute. Retrieved from https://www.migrationpolicy.org/article/profiting-enforcement-role-private-prisons-usimmigration-detention.

Massey, D. (2009). Racial formation in theory and practice: The Case of Mexicans in the United States. *Race and Social Problems, 1*(1), 12–26.

Mears, D. P. (2001). The immigration–crime nexus: Toward an analytic framework for assessing and guiding theory, research and policy. *Sociological Perspectives, 44*(1), 1–19.

Mustard, D. (2001). Racial, ethnic, and gender disparities in sentencing: Evidence from the U.S. federal courts. *Journal of Law and Economics, 44*(1), 285–314.

Newton, L. (2008). *Illegal, alien, or immigrant: The politics of immigration reform.* New York, NY: New York Press.

Newman, B. J., Shah, S., & Collingwood, L. (2018). Race, place, and building a base: Latino population growth and the nascent Trump campaign for president. *Public Opinion Quarterly, 82*(1), 122–134.

Oliphant, J., & Esposito, A. (2018). Trump says 'animals' comment refers to criminals, Mexico protests. *Rueters.* Retrieved from https://www.reuters.com/article/us-usa-immigration-mexico/trump-says-animals-comment-refers-to-criminals-mexico-protests-idUSKCN1II2AT

Ousey, G. C., & Kubrin, C. E. (2014). Immigration and the changing nature of homicide in US cities, 1980–2010. *Journal of Quantitative Criminology, 30*(3), 453–483.

Powell, D., Perreira, K. M., & Mullan Harris, K. (2010, June). Trajectories of delinquency from adolescence to adulthood. *Youth & Society, 41*(4), 475–502.

Rumbaut, R.G., & Ewing, W. (2007). The myth of immigrant criminality and the paradox of assimilation. Retrieved from https://www.americanimmigrationcouncil.org/research/mythimmigrant-criminality-and-paradox-assimilation.

Sampson, R. J. (2008). Rethinking crime and immigration. *Contexts, 7*(1), 28–33.

Sampson R. J., Morenoff J., & Raudenbush S. W. (2005). Social anatomy of racial and ethnic disparities in violence. *American Journal of Public Health, 95*(2), 224–232.

Speri, A. (2018). Detained, then violated. *The Intercept.* Retrieved from https://theintercept.com/2018/04/11/immigration-detention-sexual-abuse-ice-dhs/.

Steffensmeier, D., & Demuth, S. (2000). Ethnicity and sentencing outcomes in U.S. federal courts: who is punished more harshly? *American Sociological Review, 65,* 705–729.

Stepler, R., & Brown, A. (2016). 2014, Hispanics in the United States statistical portrait, Hispanic trends. *Pew Research Center.* Retrieved from http://www.pewhispanic.org/2016/04/19/2014-statistical-information-on-hispanics-in-united-states/

Stowell, J. I., Messner, S. F., McGeever, K. F., & Raffalovich, L. E. (2009). Immigration and the recent violent crime drop in the United States: A pooled, cross-sectional time-series analysis of metropolitan areas. *Criminology, 47*(3), 889–928.

Support Our Law Enforcement and Safe Neighborhoods Act, 2010, Arizona Senate Bill, 1070

Theodore, N. (2013). Insecure communities: Latino perception of police involvement in immigration enforcement. *University of Illinois at Chicago: Department of Urban Planning and Policy.* Retrieved from https://www.policylink.org/sites/default/files/INSECURE_COMMUNITIES_REPORT_FINAL.PDF

White House. (2017). *Presidential executive order on a task force on crime reduction and public safety.* Retrieved from https://www.whitehouse.gov/presidential-actions/presidential-executive-ordertask-force-crime-reduction-public-safety/

Wolfe, S.E., Pyrooz, D.C., & Spohn, C. (2011). Unraveling the effect of offender citizenship status on federal sentencing outcomes. *Social Science Research, 40,* 349-362.

Wu, J, & DeLone, M.A (2012). Revisiting the normal crime and liberation hypotheses: citizenship status and unwarranted disparity. *Criminal Justice Review, 37,* 214–38.

Valadez. M. (2013). *"We have got enough criminals in the United States without importing any"*: *An examination of the influence of citizenship status legal status and national origin among Latino subgroups in federal sentencing outcomes* (Doctoral dissertation). Retrieved from https://search.proquest.com/openview/ec0bc-0d38ebed675c18308f51c41dd70/1?pq-origsite=gscholar&cbl=18750&diss=y

Valadez, M., & Wang, X. (2017). Citizenship, legal status, and federal sentencing outcomes: Examining the moderating effects of age, gender and race/ethnicity. *Sociological Quarterly, 58*(4), 670–700.

Vaughn, M. G., Salas-Wright, C. P., DeLisi, M., & Maynard, B. R. (2014). The immigrant paradox: Immigrants are less antisocial than native-born Americans. *Social Psychiatry and Psychiatric Epidemiology, 49*(7), 1129–1137.

Wang, X. (2012). Undocumented immigrants as perceived criminal threat: A test of the minority threat perspective. *Criminology, 50*(3), 743–776.

Warner, J.A. (2005). The social construction of the criminal alien in immigration law, enforcement practice and statistical enumeration: Consequences for immigrant stereotyping. *Journal of Social and Ecological Boundaries, 1*, 56–80.

United Nations Human Rights Office of the High Commission (2018). Press briefing on Egypt, United States and Ethiopia. Retrieved from https://www.ohchr.org/EN/NewsEvents/Pages/DisplayNews.aspx?NewsID=23174&LangID=E.

U.S. Census Bureau. (2011). *The foreign-born population in the United States.* Retrieved from https://www.census.gov/newsroom/pdf/cspan_fb_slides.pdf

U.S. Department of Homeland Security. (2017). Table 39. Aliens removed or returned: Fiscal years 1892–2016. Retrieved from https://www.dhs.gov/immigration-statistics/yearbook/2016/table39.

U.S. Department of Homeland Security. (2018a). DHS Budget. Retrieved from https://www.dhs.gov/dhs-budget.

U.S. Department of Homeland Security. (2018b). Delegation of immigration authority section 287(g) immigration and nationality act. Retrieved from https://www.ice.gov/287g

U.S. v. Borrero-Isaza, 887 F.2d 1349, 1352, 9th Cir. (1989)

U.S. v. Gomez, 933 F.2d 650, 651, 8th Cir. (1991)

U.S. v. Onwuemene, 933 F.2d 650, 651, 8th Cir. (1991)

Chapter 14

Trauma-Informed Justice

An Introduction

Lynette C. Lee

Introduction

Many who work in the field of criminal justice, particularly first responders and those who investigate, supervise, or counsel violent crime victims and perpetrators, are disproportionately exposed to events and conditions known to produce trauma. After nearly 50 years of systematic study into psychological trauma, researchers and treatment specialists have a fairly clear understanding for the range of harmful effects that can result from extreme stress and trauma. Brunello and colleagues (2001) provide a thorough overview of negative effects of stress and trauma on individual well-being. Others have reported how traumatic stress is associated with impaired job performance among justice system professionals (Denhof & Spinaris, 2013). Evidence also exists to support the efficacy of certain approaches designed to assist those who experience severe physiological and psychological symptoms resulting from trauma.

The main U.S.-based research on trauma began in the late 1960s with veterans returning from the Vietnam War. Much of the early research focused on the symptoms of trauma and how to classify the condition for treatment purposes. Early treatment tended to rely heavily on medications intended to alleviate the symptoms; later treatments were developed to address root psychological processes thought to be the source of persistent fear-based responses.

The most current understanding is that there are both psychological and physiological causes and consequences of trauma and responses to threatening events and conditions. Some are also exploring the contours of "generational" trauma from both cultural and genetic perspectives. While most psychological theory has focused primarily on processes involved in the formation of belief structures, other theories are drawn from to help understand physiological, cultural, and genetic correlates of trauma.

While trauma-informed practices have been evolving for the past 50 years among treatment specialists, the recognized importance of teaching justice professionals about trauma is quite recent. It's only been within the past decade that justice agency leaders have started to develop more systematic responses to the causes and harmful consequences of trauma on individuals, organizations, and communities. At this point, there are still only a few pioneers within criminal justice system leadership (i.e., administrators within police, courts and correctional agencies) who are beginning to respond with the development of "trauma-informed" practices, including education of personnel.

The purpose of this chapter is to introduce the concept of fear- and stress-based psychological trauma and outline major risk and protective factors associated with a condition called posttraumatic stress disorder (PTSD). A general overview of prevalence of PTSD for those working within criminal justice is presented, as well as evidence-informed approaches on the horizon designed to build resilience within justice-centered populations. A case is made for the importance of those working in the field of criminal justice to take a more pro-active approach to combating trauma as part of their overall wellness regime.

Definitional Issues

Trauma can be studied and understood from a number of different disciplinary and theoretical perspectives. Since different research traditions tend to focus on different aspects of trauma (e.g., psychological, physiological, cultural/historical, biological/genetic) and use different theories and research methods to conduct their studies, it's difficult to provide a universally accepted definition.

For the purpose of this chapter "trauma" is defined as "experiences that can cause intense physical and psychological stress reactions" (Substance Abuse and Mental Health Services Administration (SAMHSA), 2014). This definition is taken from mental-health practitioners who work in clinical settings with traumatized others versus those researching trauma from a specific disciplinary perspective. For the intense stress reaction to be considered problematic from a long-term health perspective, it also needs to produce *lasting adverse effects* on any aspect of the individual's well-being (i.e., physical, social, emotional, or spiritual) (SAMSHA 2014).

A few additional definitional points to consider are that trauma can be caused by a single event (e.g., experiencing a natural disaster), multiple events (e.g., experiencing a natural disaster and losing a loved one) or a set of short- or long-term conditions (e.g., growing up in an abusive household, periodic or regular work with traumatized others). Another major key to understanding trauma is that it's a *subjective* experience—unique to the individual. Different individuals can react differently to the same event or condition. These reactions can be *acute* (short lived), *chronic* (experienced over a long period of time), *accumulative* (built up from multiple events over time), or *delayed* (buried internally for a period of time, resurfacing later in life). We can also respond differently based on the seriousness of an event or condition.

Primary and Secondary Trauma

Experiencing trauma from direct exposure to an event or condition is referred to as *primary trauma*. It's also possible, however, to experience trauma-related stress reactions from exposure to another individual's traumatic experiences. This condition has been referred to as "secondary trauma," "vicarious trauma," or "compassion fatigue." Figley (1995) defines secondary traumatic stress as problematic emotional and behavioral reactions that manifest from indirect exposures to traumatic experiences. Osofsky, Putman, and Lederman (2008) explain that secondary trauma can result from the cumulative effect of working with survivors of traumatic life events, or perpetrators, as part of everyday work.

Researchers have found relatively high rates of secondary trauma in healthcare providers, attorneys, first responders, those who work with crime victims and perpetrators, military personnel, disaster volunteers, and more (Figley, 1995, 2002; Pearlman & Saakvitne, 1995). One of the major findings from a number of different studies on secondary trauma is that although each of these groups can have unique stressors and types of traumatic experiences, the effects are generally the same as those experienced by exposure to primary trauma (Osofsky et al., 2008).

General Effects of Trauma

Although individual differences exist as to whether, how, or when someone experiences trauma, it's also known that almost everyone exposed to a serious "critical incident" (e.g., a serious car accident, an officer-involved shooting, sexual assault) will experience some type of acute stress reaction (Bryant, 2016). This type of reaction includes a predictable set of symptoms. In other words, the human psyche and physiology, or *mind–body complex* is similar enough that in most cases we experience certain automatic reactions when exposed to a serious event. Those employed in the field of criminal justice can significantly benefit from an understanding of how these reactions may be present when working with crime victims, suspects, and perpetrators.

Given the significance of how the mind–body complex responds to a serious shock or critical incident, it's helpful to get a general idea of what happens when someone is exposed to an event or situation where he or she fears violent injury or death. When first faced with a seriously threatening event or condition, the person's mind–body complex automatically moves energetic resources away from the neocortex, the brain center responsible for more deliberative, rational thought, and begins to operate from the "lower" or "survival" part of the brain (sometimes called "reptilian" brain). This part of the brain specializes in instinctual survival, so when faced with a perceived threat, it sends out the message for the organism to either fight, flee, or freeze. While "freeze" is normally the initial reaction for most, some systems then move into either fight or flight mode.

If the signal for "freeze" persists, the system shuts down blood to the brain. If enough blood is cut off, the person faints. If the signal for fight or flight is sent out from this brain center, the mind–body complex immediately performs the necessary functions to go into survival mode. Hormones such as adrenaline and cortisol are instantly released into the bloodstream. These hormones, combined with electric impulses sent to targeted nerve centers, direct energy away from systems needed for long-term survival (e.g., digestion and immune systems) and toward muscles and organs perceived as essential for immediate survival (e.g., the lungs for increased oxygen, major motor muscles in legs and arms necessary to fight or flee). This survival response to a perceived extreme threat can be observed in physical signs such as an increased heart rate, sweating, tunnel vision, shaking, and nausea.

After the perception of an immediate threat subsides, most systems still demonstrate predictable reactionary effects for the next several days to a month. These include psychological, physiological, and behavioral symptoms such as an inability to sleep or self-regulate thoughts and emotions, hyper-vigilance, trouble concentrating, disassociation ("zoning out"), being quick to anger, and withdrawal from others. And even when the body is able to regain balance, it can take the mind much longer to adjust to the traumatic event or condition.

From a physiological perspective, Jeffreys (2018) states that a long-term traumatic response can be understood as "a dysregulation of the *hypothalamic–pituitary–adrenal* (HPA) axis and the balance between excitatory and inhibitory brain neurocircuitry" (para. 8). In other words, mechanisms designed to tell the body–mind complex that it needs to be on high alert won't shut off. Extended periods of this type of stress to the system can produce long-term impairment to brain circuitry and functioning.

From one modern psychological perspective (i.e., cognitive-behavioral based on social learning theory) it's believed that an inability to rebalance thoughts and feelings after a traumatic event or condition—assuming no major inherent physiological dysfunction—is due to an inability to cognitively and/or emotionally adjust to that event or condition. In other words, people can have trouble integrating extreme events or conditions into their existing view of themself, others, or how the world works (or should work). The experience is perceived as either too painful to think about or feel (cognitive or affective avoidance) and/or doesn't fit with existing core beliefs (cognitive dissonance). If the person's mind–body complex isn't able to regain balance within a few days to weeks, it's possible he or she may be suffering from a condition called *posttraumatic stress disorder* (PTSD).

Posttraumatic Stress Disorder

PTSD can be thought of as a persistent imbalance of the human mind–body complex. This condition was first studied closely in U.S. veterans returning from the Vietnam War. In 1980, the American Psychiatric Association (APA) included PTSD as a condition in its diagnostic manual (DSM-III). Since that time, a vast body of literature has been produced that addresses the causes, consequences, and best practices to effectively respond to what's identified as the fifth most common psychiatric disorder in the United States (Keane, Marx, & Sloane, 2009). In addition to recognized attention by the medical and treatment communities, several domestic and international conferences and professional journals are dedicated to the presentation and publication of research focused on trauma, loss, and PTSD.

According to the most recent edition of the Diagnostic and Statistical Manual (DSM-5) (American Psychiatric Association, 2013) a person must display one or more of the symptoms from the following categories to be diagnosed with PTSD after a traumatic event or condition:

+ *Intrusive thoughts* such as repeated, involuntary memories; distressing dreams; or flashbacks of the traumatic event.
+ *Avoiding reminders* of the traumatic event, which may include avoiding people, places, activities, objects, and situations that bring on distressing memories.
+ *Negative thoughts and feelings*, which may include ongoing and distorted beliefs about oneself or others (e.g., "I am bad," "I don't feel like living"); ongoing fear, horror, anger, guilt, or shame; much less interest in activities previously enjoyed; or feeling detached or estranged from others.
+ *Arousal and reactive symptoms*, which may include being irritable and having angry outbursts; behaving recklessly or in a self-destructive way; being easily startled; or having problems concentrating or sleeping.

It is essential to note that the majority of individuals exposed to a perceived threat are likely to temporarily experience an *acute stress response*. This response will include some of these symptoms. If the symptoms persist beyond a month, however, the person may be diagnosed with PTSD. It's also possible for full PTSD symptoms not to appear until months or years after the event or condition (*delayed*). These symptoms can also be triggered by later life events such as a child rape victim who is sexually harassed as adult. In addition, chronic PTSD sufferers often display other disorders such as depression, substance and alcohol abuse and have trouble managing daily activities (Brunello et al., 2001; Gillespie, Phifer, Bradley, & Ressler, 2009).

Knowing the short- and long-term harmful effects of serious psychological trauma on the body and mind, for both those who experience the trauma as well as those who attempt to assist, is why there's such a need for trauma-informed justice professionals. In addition to understanding major causes and consequences of trauma, in general, and for PTSD specifically, it's also helpful to consider what factors increase or decrease the likelihood of experiencing harmful impacts of trauma.

PTSD Risk Factors

Risk factors for PTSD are conditions that increase the likelihood that someone will experience a prolonged stress reaction when confronted with an event or condition perceived to cause serious injury or death. To provide some idea for the prevalence with which members of the general public are at risk for PTSD, it has been estimated that approximately 4–10% of the U.S. adult population will experience PTSD at some point in their life (Kilpatrick et al., 2013).

There are a number of *individual, group,* and *environmental* factors that can increase the chances that someone will experience PTSD. For example, Kessler, Chiu, Demler, Merikangas, and Walters (2005) have reported that women are more than twice as likely to experience PTSD as men, but also found a 16% prevalence rate for both men and women in post-conflict settings (i.e., war veterans). Rates can be even higher for populations exposed to conflict zones (e.g., war refugees), major disasters (natural or human-made), severe child abuse, or those who lack support from friends or family (Gillespie et al., 2009). Relationships between PTSD and a host of other individual, group, and environmental factors such as personality or temperament, race, culture, neurobiology or genetic make-up, and poverty have also been studied.

For example, studies examining the effects of environment on genetic expression (epigenetics) have demonstrated that a predisposition for trauma can be passed down through generations (Almli, 2014). Similarly, Maria Yellow Horse Brave Heart (2003) has defined the condition of historical trauma as "cumulative emotional and psychological wounding over the lifespan and across generations, emanating from massive group trauma experiences" (p. 7). Historical or multi-generational trauma can be experienced by specific cultural groups such as Native Americans/

First Nation People, African Americans, families living in intergenerational poverty, immigrants, genocide survivors, and refugees. Criminal justice professionals can benefit from understanding these and other types of trauma since they can impact a person's perception of a situation, trust in authority figures, ideas about what's appropriate conduct in a given situation, etc.

While a great deal is known about how certain individual and group characteristics and dynamics can put someone at risk for experiencing PTSD, there are also major environmental factors that should be considered by those operating within the criminal justice system. The two major environmental factors known to increase the likelihood of experiencing PTSD include *where the person lives* (i.e., those exposed to abusive family settings or violent neighborhoods are at greater risk) and *where they work* (i.e., some occupations and professions are at higher risk than others).

Risk Based on Living Environment

From a social learning perspective, it is evident that *where* we are raised and *how* we are raised shapes our beliefs, values, and assumptions about the world, and hence how we think and feel about, and act toward others and ourselves. One landmark study that helped highlight the incredible strength of the relationship between environment and behavior is called the Adverse Childhood Experiences (ACE) study. This was a large-scale study conducted in the mid 1990s that examined the relationship between exposure to *adverse childhood experiences* and later life conditions (i.e., health, lifestyle, likelihood to come in contact with the justice system).

The three main categories of adverse childhood experiences examined, via self-reported survey data, were as follows:

+ Abuse (psychological, physical, or sexual)
+ Neglect (emotional and physical)
+ Household dysfunction (i.e., mother abused; living with members who were substance abusers, mentally ill, suicidal or spent time in prison; living with non-biological parent)

Findings from this study revealed that the greater the mistreatment or adversity during childhood, the greater the likelihood for poor health and lifestyle conditions during adulthood (Felitti et al., 1998). One of the most striking findings, however, was the prevalence of mistreatment in the population studied (Kaiser Permanente medical patients). Approximately 67% of respondents reported having at least one adverse childhood experience, and more than 20% reported three or more ACEs (Felitti et al., 1997).

This study helps illustrate what's now considered a fact that childhood experiences, positive or negative, can impact future involvement in violence—both victimization and perpetration—as well as lifelong health and social opportunity, including coming in contact with the criminal justice system. Given these results, as well as multiple replications that have produced similar findings, it's possible to state that one of the main risk factors for PTSD (as well as violence and victimization) is exposure to adverse childhood experiences.

Justice professionals who are aware of both the prevalence of trauma in the general population—which is even higher in victim and offender populations—as well as harmful effects of trauma, can be better prepared to perform their duties more safely and effectively. For example, knowing that common PTSD symptoms include conduct such as avoidance, angry outbursts, and self-destructive behavior may help a police officer understand why a person might be reacting negatively to his or her presence or sincere attempt to initiate a positive contact. Or, when a judge is hearing a case or a probation officer is working with a youth, knowing the individual's trauma background could be relevant to how the case is processed or how the youth is supervised.

Risk Based on Work Environment/Criminal Justice Settings

In addition to where someone lives, certain types of jobs, such as those performed by many justice workers, are also considered major risk factors for PTSD. High rates of moderate to severe traumatic stress symptoms have been reported in samples of correctional staff, probation officers, law enforcement, and attorneys (Denhof & Spinaris, 2013; Levin et al., 2011; Skogstad et al., 2013). Specifically, those working with violent crime victims or perpetrators, as well as frequent exposure to child abuse, injury, and death, are the conditions that put officers at greatest risk for experiencing both primary and secondary PTSD than general populations.

While it may seem reasonable to assume that rates of PTSD for police officers have increased over the years, the evidence does not support this view. For example, more than 3 decades ago Gerson (1989) reported a prevalence rate of PTSD for those working in local U.S. law enforcement departments between 7 and 19% (nearly twice the rate of the general population at 4 to 10%). More recently, Hartley (2013) reported a very similar finding of 15% in male officers and 18% in female officers. Higher rates were found in the same study for female officers with frequent exposure to abused children and homicide victims.

While those working in law enforcement are at risk for both primary and secondary trauma, those working in the courts are often more susceptible to secondary trauma. This tends to come from repeated exposure to detailed case histories and personal backgrounds of victims and perpetrators of violent crimes. Some studies have examined secondary trauma experienced by jurors (Lonergan, Leclerc, Descamps, Pigeon, & Brunet, 2016). Although fewer studies have been conducted on the courts than police or corrections, progressive judicial leaders in both Canada and the United States are taking steps to adopt trauma-informed educational and training programs for court personnel, as well as special court practices and conditions for those suffering from severe stress and trauma.

Those working in correctional settings can be particularly at risk for both primary and secondary trauma given the characteristics of work environments including violent inmate populations. Kilpatrick (2013) estimates that approximately 30% of male and 60% of female inmates are experiencing PTSD at any one time. And Gillece (2009) estimated that as many as 85% of women in correctional settings have an early experience of physical or sexual abuse—a condition that makes them more susceptible to PTSD.

These insights may help explain recent findings by James and Todak (2018) that 19% of prison workers were found to meet the criteria for PTSD (the same rates as Iraq and Afghanistan war veterans). In the same study the authors reported the following:

- Women, Blacks, and those with more than 10 years on the job were found to have the highest rates within the sample of correctional workers
- The security level of the institution didn't make any difference in detected rates of PTSD symptoms

James and Todak (2018) also noted that although severe stress and trauma is a major problem in correctional settings, limited evidence exists on specific risk and protective factors to inform targeted interventions. In other words, the state of knowledge in this field of study—trauma in justice-related settings—is still in its infancy. A more complete understanding for PTSD risk factors within these settings can assist leadership design and operate more safe, effective, and healthy work environments.

PTSD Protective Factors and Evidence-Informed Practices

Protective factors for PTSD can be methods used to reduce or eliminate the harmful negative effects of extreme stress and trauma (i.e., treatment) or conditions that diminish the likelihood of experiencing or not quickly recovering from extreme stress and trauma (i.e., prevention). Over the past 50 years a number of different approaches have been developed to treat symptoms of PTSD.

Treatment

Treatment for PTSD can be thought of as a method to protect the individual from further harm due to prolonged trauma symptoms. Although PTSD treatment for children is typically different from that for adults, current PTSD treatment for criminal justice personnel does not differ from that used with other adults. The most common therapeutic interventions employed today for PTSD include some form of trauma-focused psychotherapy and the use of pharmaceuticals. The most common pharmacological therapies for PTSD treatment include the use of anti-depressants and anti-anxiety medications. Evidence-based psychotherapies include trauma-informed cognitive-behavioral or cognitive-processing therapy, exposure therapy, and eye movement desensitization and reprocessing (Torchalla and Strehlau, 2018; Watkins, Sprang & Rothbaum, 2018).

+ Cognitive-behavioral or cognitive-processing therapy: Teaches victims to reframe negative thoughts about the trauma. It involves talking with providers about negative thoughts and doing short writing assignments.
+ Prolonged exposure (PE): Teaches victims how to gain control by facing your negative feelings. It involves talking about trauma with a provider and doing some of the things a victim may have avoided since the trauma.
+ Eye-movement desensitization and reprocessing: Helps victims process and make sense of their trauma. It involves calling the trauma to mind while paying attention to a back-and-forth movement or sound (like a finger waving side to side, a light, or a tone).

The essential goal of PTSD treatment is to help the person suffering regain some degree of psychological and physiological balance. The first or "front-line" approach is generally psychotherapy. If this type of treatment isn't successful, or if the trauma is particularly extreme, pharmaceuticals may be used to help stabilize physiological and psychological symptoms. This rebalancing allows the person, as appropriate and available, to engage in psychotherapeutic techniques designed to work directly with the negative thoughts and feelings (which are believed, according to some theories, to drive the majority of the other symptoms including *arousal and reactivity*).

One of the limitations of most traditional "talk therapies," such as the cognitive-behavioral family of interventions, is that they attempt to directly address less functional thoughts and feelings. While working directly with psychological aspects of PTSD has demonstrated effectiveness for many, evidence is pointing toward the importance of incorporating more integrated mind–body practices. For example, in a recent study on the efficacy of emerging PTSD treatments, Metcalf and colleagues (2016) pointed out that the four most promising non-traditional practices (meditation, yoga, acupuncture, and emotional freedom technique/"tapping") are all based on a theoretical model that assumes a direct connection between the mind and body.

Trauma Education in Justice Agencies

Trauma-informed practices within criminal justice generally include providing police, court, and correctional personnel with information on causes and consequences of trauma, as well as how to most appropriately work with those believed to be suffering from PTSD. Early agency-based educational initiatives started within a few local agencies approximately 10 years ago. A few police and sheriffs' departments, courts, and correctional agencies (field and institutional services), for example, have developed in-house training programs for personnel on how to identify and work with those suffering from PTSD. Some states now include information on PTSD under mental health sections of mandated training for justice personnel. For example, as of 2010, the State of California passed legislation requiring training on PTSD and traumatic brain injuries for all police personnel (California Senate Bill 1296).

In an effort to expand the reach of this type of training, federal agencies such as the U.S. National Institute of Justice have sponsored seminars to prepare trauma-informed probation officers in federal, state, and local agencies. One extremely progressive approach to providing PTSD education and support to public safety personnel, as well as a wide range of other health and wellness challenges, is presently being established in Canada. The Canadian Institute for Public Safety Research and Treatment is a collaborative effort between Canadian government and university entities. The purpose of the institute is to identify best practices and provide robust, quality mental health support and services to public safety workers and their families. Another example of cutting edge trauma-informed training is that recently provided to all California state juvenile courts judges. The purpose of the training is to help judges minimize secondary trauma. It was delivered by a nonprofit organization that focuses on mind–body practices, the Niroga Institute.

Although beyond the scope of this chapter, the use of more mind–body practices is now being explored more systematically in criminal justice settings. Readers may want to explore research conducted by Chopko and Schwartz (2013) that summarizes the effectiveness of mindfulness, a meditation practice, for police suffering from PTSD.

Prevention

Unlike the existence of evidence-informed treatment approaches, much less is known about how to prevent extreme stress and trauma. Authors of a recent meta-analysis of trauma-informed practices within the U.S. juvenile justice system noted, for example, that only half of the studies examined included any information on PTSD prevention practices for youth, staff, or the broader agency environment (Branson, Baetz, Horwitz, & Hoagwood, 2017). The most common approach employed to date to help those living or working in stressful environments is to provide information or educational materials on the causes and consequences of trauma and training on how to build and apply trauma-informed skills.

More generally, evidence-based programs and practices designed to protect employees from high rates of stress and trauma include the following:

- Good physical (including nutritional), mental and emotional health
- Strong social support networks (including faith communities and spiritual practices, for some)
- Positive relationships with supervisors and coworkers

Research also exists on the value of a treatment protocol called post-traumatic growth (PTG), as well as practices specifically designed to build individual (and organizational) resilience (Chopko et al., 2018). PTG treatment approaches are designed to help individuals consider how the traumatic event or situation can help them continue to develop more of their own potential (e.g., for forgiveness, acceptance of "what is," capacity to take the perspective of others). Since this practice isn't typically adopted until after the person has sought help for PTSD, it's only considered "preventative" in terms of relapse. Having mental and emotional skills that allow for greater psychological flexibility can strengthen a person's ability to quickly process the trauma if/when faced with another extreme event or situation.

Another approach to prevention is to focus on building resilience. Resilience practices are based on the assumption that taking care of our physical, mental, emotional, and, for some, spiritual health is the best way to prevent long-term harmful effects of stress and trauma. A considerable body of research has examined the relationship between resilience and employee effectiveness, with some studies even focusing on those within criminal justice (Christopher et al., 2018; McCraty & Atkinson, 2012). Those interested in these types of strengths-based, pro-active approaches to trauma prevention are encouraged to explore the literature on the benefits of developing physical, mental, emotional, and spiritual resilience. The vast potential of resilience-oriented approaches to promote optimal health and well-being for criminal justice personnel remains highly untapped.

It's likely that additional understanding for how to best prevent and respond effectively to extreme stress and trauma will require the development of new theoretical models of the human condition (Lee & Stohr, 2011). For example, a tremendous body of theory and evidence already exists on the effectiveness of ancient Eastern cultural practices on human health and development. In addition to the mind–body practices, many also report tremendous value from the use of faith-based and spiritual models of therapy and wellness (Pearce, Haynes, Rivera, & Koenig, 2018). The logical next step is to design and test theories of human wellness and development based on more integrated models of mind, body, and spirit.

Conclusion

There's a tremendous need for those within criminal justice to understand the causes, consequences, and most effective responses to extreme stress, trauma, and PTSD. For many service professionals, becoming "trauma-informed" requires a shift in mind-set and the development of a specific set of skills. In summary, a trauma-informed justice professional should be able to do the following:

+ Define key concepts such as primary trauma, secondary trauma, and PTSD
+ Recognize the prevalence of trauma within communities, agencies, and dominant service populations
+ Summarize the major risk and protective factors for PTSD
+ Put this knowledge into practice

+ Avoid engaging in practices known to traumatize or retraumatize others

Many leaders within the field of criminal justice have begun to seriously consider how this body of knowledge on stress, trauma, and PTSD can be used to guide the design, implementation, and evaluation of trauma-informed justice policy, programs, and practices. For example, the extremely harmful effects of extreme stress and trauma on human development are now evident. And since trauma experienced in early childhood produces the most severe negative consequences, support for children and families should be a central focus from a long-term public health and safety perspective.

Applications of this knowledge within the field of criminal justice are slowly beginning to appear. The progress already made within the past 5 to 10 years is a good example of how empirical evidence can be used to guide organizational decision making. Continuous improvement of justice-centered policies and practices will require leadership that understands and values the less apparent aspects of organizational effectiveness and the well-being and development of agency personnel. From a human growth and development perspective, a necessary aspect of effective leadership requires not only a commitment to provide treatment to those in need, but also to work proactively to prevent injuries such as PTSD. One way this can be done is by developing creative ways to encourage and assist employees build their own resilience and further their own growth potential.

Leaders can begin by developing a personal practice designed to promote their own healing, resilience, and ongoing growth of physical, mental, and emotional capacities. Some will also choose to incorporate practices that explicitly strengthen their personal faith and/or sense of deeper connectedness to all living beings. As a cautionary note, as we develop our capacity for higher-order thinking and analysis, it becomes easier to see what and how *others* need to change. Making sure that we're actively, consciously working on our own growth potential ("be the change ...") allows us to become better prepared to help others do the same.

In conclusion, there are an unlimited number of things that can be done to help build more healthy mind-sets, behaviors, relationships, and systems. With the necessary attention to individual and organizational health and development, everyone can help minimize the harm, and expand the potential of justice-related personnel and agencies to make positive impacts on our communities and societies.

Discussion Questions

1. Assume you're in a leadership role in a criminal justice agency (i.e., police, courts or corrections). Now, write down three things you could do to help your employees build their:

   a) physical resilience to extreme stress and trauma,

   b) emotional resilience,

   c) mental resilience, and

   d) spiritual resilience.

2. What would you include (or are you currently doing) in your own personal practice to build each of these four types of resilience?

(Write down your responses, and try to be as specific as possible. Then share and discuss your responses with others in your group.)

References

Almli, L., Fani, N., Smith, A., & Ressler, K. (2014). Genetic approaches to understanding post-traumatic stress disorder. *International Journal of Neuropsychopharmacology, 17*(2), 355–370. doi:10.1017/S1461145713001090

American Psychiatric Association. (2013). *Diagnostic and statistical manual of mental disorders (DSM-5)* (5th ed.). Washington, DC: Author.

American Psychiatric Association. (2018). *What is posttraumatic stress disorder?*. Retrieved from https://www.psychiatry.org/patients-families/ptsd/what-is-ptsd

Branson, C., Baetz, C., Horwitz, S., & Hoagwood, K. (2017). Trauma-informed juvenile justice systems: A systematic review of definitions and core components. *Psychological Trauma: Theory, Research, Practice, and Policy, 9*(6), 635–646. doi:10.1037/tra0000255

Brunello, N., Davidson, J. R., Deahl, M., Kessler, R. C., Mendlewicz, J., Racagni, G., ... & Zohar, J. (2001). Post-traumatic stress disorder: Diagnosis and epidemiology, comorbidity and social consequences, biology and treatment. *Neuropsychobiology, 43*(3), 150–162.

Bryant, R. A. (2016). Acute stress disorder. In P. R. Casey & J. J. Strain (Eds.) *Trauma- and stressor-related disorders: A handbook for clinicians* (pp. 81–98). Arlington, VA: American Psychiatric Publishing, Inc.

Chopko, B., Palmieri, P., & Adams, R. (2018). Relationships among traumatic experiences, PTSD, and posttraumatic growth for police officers: A path analysis. *Psychological Trauma: Theory, Research, Practice, and Policy, 10*(2), 183–189. doi:10.1037/tra0000261

Chopko, B., & Schwartz, R. (2013). The relation between mindfulness and posttraumatic stress symptoms among police officers. *Journal of Trauma and Loss, 18*(1), 1–9. doi:10.1080/15325024.2012.674442

Christopher, M., Hunsingera, M., Goerlinga, R., Bowena, S., Rogersa, B. Grossd, R., ... & Pruessnere, J., (2018). Mindfulness-based resilience training to reduce health risk, stress reactivity, and aggression among law enforcement officers: A feasibility and preliminary efficacy trial. *Psychiatric Research, 264*, 104–113. doi:10.1016/j.psychres.2018.03.059

Denhof, M. D., & Spinaris, C. G. (2013). *Depression, PTSD, and comorbidity in United States corrections professionals: Prevalence and impact on health.* Florence, CO: Desert Waters Correctional Outreach.

Figley, C. R. (1995). Compassion fatigue as secondary traumatic stress disorder: An overview. In C.R. Figley (Ed.), *Compassion fatigue: Coping with secondary traumatic stress disorder in those who treat the traumatized* (pp. 1–20). New York, NY: Brunner/Mazel.

Figley, C. R. (2002). *Treating compassion fatigue. Psychosocial stress book series.* New York, NY: Routledge.

Filitti, V., Anda, R., Nordenberg, D., Williamson, D., Spitz, A., Edwards, V., & Marks, J. (1998). Relationship of childhood abuse and household dysfunction to many of the leading causes of death in adults. *American Journal of Preventative Medicine, 14*(4), 245–258. doi:10.1016/S0749-3797(98)00017-8

Gersons, B. (1989). Patterns of PTSD among police officers following shooting incidents: A two-dimensional model and treatment implications. *Journal of Traumatic Stress, 2*(3), 247–257. doi:10.1002/(ISSN)1573-6598

Gersons, B. P., Carlier, I. V., Lamberts, R. D., & van der Kolk, B. A. (2000). Randomized clinical trial of brief eclectic psychotherapy for police officers with posttraumatic stress disorder. *Journal of Traumatic Stress, 13*(2), 333–347. doi:10.1023/A:1007793803627

Gillece, J.B. (2009). Understanding the effects of trauma on lives of offenders. *Corrections Today, 71*(1), 48–51.

Gillespie C. F., Phifer, J., Bradley, B., & Ressler, K. J. (2009). Risk and resilience: Genetic and environmental influences on development of the stress response. *Depress Anxiety, 26*(11), 984–992.

Hartley, T., Sharkisian, K., Violanti, J., Andrew, M., & Burchfiel, C. (2013). PTSD symptoms among police officers: Associations With frequency, recency, and types of traumatic events. *International Journal of Mental Health, 15*(4), 241–253.

Heart, M. (2003). The historical trauma response among natives and its relationship with substance abuse: A Lakota illustration. *Journal of Psychoactive Drugs, 35*(1), 7–13. doi:10.1080/02791072.2003.10399988

James, L., & Todak, N. (2018). Prison employment and post-traumatic stress disorder: Risk and protective factors. *American Journal of Industrial Medicine, 61*(9), 725–732. doi:10.1002/ajim.22869

Jeffreys, M. (2018). *Clinicians guide to PTSD medications.* Retrieved from https://www.ptsd.va.gov/professional/treat/txessentials/clinician_guide_meds.asp

Keane, T. M., Marx, B. P., & Sloan, D. M., (Eds.). (2009). *Post-traumatic stress disorder: Definition, prevalence, and risk factors.* New York, NY: Humana Press.

Kessler, R. C., Chiu, W. T., Demler, O., Merikangas, K. R., & Walters, E. E. (2005). Prevalence, severity, and comorbidity of 12-month DSM-IV disorders in the National Comorbidity Survey Replication. *Archives of General Psychiatry, 62*(6), 617–627. doi:10.1001/archpsyc.62.6.617

Kilpatrick, D. G., Resnick, H. S., Milanak, M. E., Miller, M. W., Keyes, K. M., & Friedman, M. J. (2013). National estimates of exposure to traumatic events and PTSD prevalence using DSM-IV and DSM-5 criteria. *Journal of Traumatic Stress, 26*(5), 537–547. doi:10.1002/jts.21848

Lee, L., & Stohr, M. (2011). A qualified critique of "correctional quackery." *Journal of Contemporary Criminal Justice, 28*(1), 96–112. doi:10.1177/1043986211432203

Levin, A. P., Albert, L., Besser, A., Smith, D., Zelenski, A., Rosenkranz, S., & Neria, Y. (2011). Secondary traumatic stress in attorneys and their administrative support staff working with trauma-exposed clients. *Journal of Nervous and Mental Disease, 199*(12), 946–955. doi:10.1097/NMD.0b013e3182392c26

Lonergan, M., Leclerc, M. E., Descamps, M., Pigeon, S., & Brunet, A. (2016). Prevalence and severity of trauma- and stressor-related symptoms among jurors: A review. *Journal of Criminal Justice, 47,* 51–61. doi:10.1016/j.jcrimjus.2016.07.003

McCraty, R., & Atkinson, M. (2012). Resilience training program reduces physiological and psychological stress in police officers. *Global Advances in Health and Medicine, 1*(5), 42–64.

Metcalf, O., Varker, T., Forbes, D., Phelps, A., Dell, L., DiBattista, A., ... & O'Donnell, M. (2016). Efficacy of fifteen emerging interventions for the treatment of posttraumatic stress disorder: A systematic review. *Journal of Traumatic Stress, 29*(1), 88–92. doi:10.1002/jts.22070

Osofsky, J., Putman, F., Lederman, C. (2008). How to maintain emotional health when working with trauma. *Juvenile and Family Court Journal, 59*(4), 91–102.

Pearce, M., Haynes, K., Rivera, N., & Koenig, H. (2018). Spiritually integrated cognitive processing therapy: A new treatment. *Global Advances in Health and Medicine, 7*, 1–7. doi:10.1177/2164956118759939

Pearlman, L. A., & Saakvitne, K. W. (1995). Treating therapists with vicarious traumatization and secondary traumatic stress disorders. In C. R. Figley (Ed.), *Compassion fatigue: Coping with secondary traumatic stress disorder in those who treat the traumatized* (pp. 150–177). New York, NY: Brunner/Mazel.

Skogstad, M., Skorstad, M., Lie, A., Conradi, H. S., Heir, T., & Weisæth, L. (2013). Work-related post-traumatic stress disorder. *Occupational Medicine, 63*(3), 175–182. doi:10.1093/occmed/kqt003

Substance Abuse and Mental Health Services Administration. (2014). *Key terms: Definitions*. Retrieved from https://www.samhsa.gov/samhsaNewsLetter/Volume_22_Number_2/trauma_tip/key_terms.html

Torchalla, I., & Strehlau, V. (2018). The evidence base for interventions targeting individuals with work-related PTSD: A systematic review and recommendations. *Behavior Modification, 42*(2), 273–303. doi:10.1177/0145445517725048

Watkins, L. E., Sprang, K. R., & Rothbaum, B. O. (2018). Treating PTSD: A Review of Evidence-Based Psychotherapy Interventions. *Frontiers in behavioral neuroscience, 12*, 258. doi:10.3389/fnbeh.2018.00258

Chapter 15

Approaches to Transitional Justice

Two Cases from Africa

Ernest Uwazie and Nicole Fox

Introduction

In the past 30 years or so, transitional justice mechanisms have emerged on the global stage as tools for achieving reconciliation after human rights abuses and loss of government legitimacy, or regime change. The range and adaptability of transitional justice mechanisms are praised as providing a flexible pathway for addressing the chaos and popular distrust of the state in the aftermath of mass atrocity and gross human rights abuses. Such mechanisms, through interim laws, governments, and institutions, strive to transition societies out of destruction and toward democracy and development as well as restoration of trust. Judicial processes during transitions can create promising opportunities for countries who hope to face past injustices, confront impunity, and prevent future violence but are not without challenges and limitations.

This chapter provides a succinct overview of emerging transitional justice processes and their variance, followed by a description of two African cases: Rwanda and South Africa. These two cases illuminate how transitional justice approaches can best be used in combination with one another and explores the ways in which demands for redress and justice by different stakeholders take distinctive shape and form. The lessons from these case studies have implications for establishing a credible justice system, with the applicable institutions for enforcement of rule of law and the prevention of future atrocity crimes.

Transitional Justice

Transitional justice (TJ) refers to both the judicial pursuits utilized to facilitate democracy after human rights abuses and the heuristic that such processes are a necessary and appropriate response to state-sponsored crimes. The belief that countries must address past wrongs to have a more functioning society is not a new idea but has become more widely adopted in the past 30 years, coinciding with the "justice cascade" (Sikkink, 2012). One aspect that makes transitional justice pursuits differ from normative law is the context in which justice occurs, with the former being a site of pervasive human rights violations and the decimation of a nation. Because TJ often occurs with little institutional support and resources, and when complete justice is close to impossible, there is no perfect solution. Such circumstances prevent transitional justice mechanisms from emulating "the ideal rule of law" (Teitel, 2003, p. 76), and rather function as an adjustable model for the best possible model of justice and reconciliation for that moment in time and place.

TJ efforts can be mobilized from grassroots campaigns, new regimes, and international bodies such as the United Nations. Judicial pursuits have materialized in the implementation of diverse TJ approaches ranging from amnesties, to truth commissions, to local courts and reconciliation programs (Barsalou & Baxter, 2007; De Brito, Gonzaléz-Enríquez, & Aguilar, 2001). The variance in approaches is qualitatively important, as such flexibility makes TJ mechanisms able to adjust to a country's stability, resources, and specific history of violence (Barsalou & Baxter, 2007).

Trials are an example of a retributive form of transitional justice, focusing on proportional punishment for crimes committed. They take place in courtrooms requiring trained judges, attorneys, and jurors and can have various levels of impact, such as advancing legal jurisdiction, bringing perpetrators to justice, and shaping public policy (Dieng, 2011; International Criminal Tribunal for Rwanda, 2007; Sadat, 2012). However, trials can often be expensive and slow or alien to the average citizen, which was the case of the International Court Tribunal of Rwanda (Jones, 2009; Reydams, 2005).

In contrast to the retributive nature of trials, restorative justice approaches focus on the needs of the victim rather than legal discourse and can produce outcomes such as social or financial reparations or restitution. An example of restorative justice in Rwanda is how some perpetrators paid for the property they damaged or stole during the genocide, to the victim or their family. In restorative justice practices, victims are active in the process and offenders are believed to make right by repairing the harm they caused to the victim and their community through service, apologies, or payment (Dandurand & Griffith, 2006; Hamber & Wilson, 2002). Another way of healing the country is through active participation of truth commissions.

Advocates of truth commissions assert that to achieve unity and peace after human rights violations, establishing an official truth is essential (Crocker, 2000; Hayner, 2011; Phelps, 2004). Establishing a truth is a process that frequently involves an official investigation that produces easily accessible, public, historical knowledge and details about crimes committed (and who the perpetrators were). Research finds that when victims can tell their stories of violence and atrocity for truth commissions while others bear witness, victims can begin a process of healing, knowing their story and that loved ones will not be forgotten (Gibson, 2004; Hayner, 2011; Rotberg & Thompson, 2000). Truth programs can support forgiveness, for when victims know who committed the crime, they can begin to forgive that individual (Hayner, 2001). Finally, truth and reconciliation programs can have broad effects on a country's democratic processes. For example, South African therapists reported that after the TRC torture, survivors felt that the public was more respectful and empathetic for their experiences and needs, making them feel less isolated and ashamed (Hayner, 2001). However, such positive ramifications do not always hold true for survivors of gender-based violence, and women more generally (Brounéus 2008; Crosby & Lykes 2011; Goldblatt & Meintjes 1998). Amnesty, an official pardon for one's crime, in exchange for truth telling has found to have both positive and negative effects on reconciliation (Aguilar 1997; Mamdani 2005).

National-level truth commissions and amnesty policies, however, are only a few of the mechanisms associated with the reconciliation process and sometimes have goals of social harmony that are too broad and ambitious to materialize (Barkan & Karn, 2006; Gibson, 2004, 2006). Localized reconciliation programs also work to find practical solutions to post-conflict tensions (Arzt, 2006; Barkan & Karn, 2006; Clark &

Kaufman, 2009; Engel & Munger, 1996). In Rwanda, these programs range from free legal assistance to those accused of genocidal acts (such as looting and property disputes), soccer teams (with children of both victims and perpetrators), church groups (to discuss coping and church involvement in the genocide), and orphan educational programs (for those whose parents are in jail or deceased).

Macro-level government-sponsored transitional justice mechanisms can include forced regime change or compensation to victims. Lustration processes meet a public need to punish the perpetrators of past injustices without violating individuals' rights. Compensation from state entities is another form of transitional justice focused more squarely on the victims. Compensation awards victims of atrocity crimes or human right abuses some form of reparation to acknowledge and atone for their suffering. National and local efforts may also include addressing a difficult past through reimagining the physical landscape. Because national monuments and memorials demonstrate the values, historical relevance, and collective memory of a nation in the built environment, during periods of transition they may need recontextualization or removal. Such efforts could mean recontextualizing or removing statues, monuments, or street names associated with the previous regime or creating memorials or museums that commemorate and educate about past human rights abuses.

The Case of Rwanda

On April 7, 1994, after years of civil war and political instability, a 100-day genocide erupted in the small, densely populated, East African country of Rwanda. The violence was organized and included elements such as hate speech radio broadcasts, road blockages that prevented victims from leaving the country, and false "safety zones" that in actuality were sites of mass killings, ultimately claiming the lives of more than 800,000 people (Mamdani, 2001; Straus, 2006). The culmination of ethnic tension[1], orchestrated by colonial powers for several decades, was mass atrocity, property crimes, and wide-spread violence.

The aftermath of the genocide in 1994 included not only the loss of a generation, but also a demolished infrastructure, decimated country, refugee disaster, and a traumatized citizenry. Children were orphaned; those who survived often endured horrific conditions including but not limited to rape, torture, being forced to kill others to survive, sexual slavery, hiding under corpses, witnessing the murder of family members, and extreme living conditions such as starvation and dehydration. When the new regime began organizing society post-genocide and pursing justice, jails overflowed with suspected perpetrators. To move forward, the international community, along with the new Rwandan government, worked to instill multiple transitional justice mechanisms. These included an international tribunal, courts and memorials honoring those who were killed in the genocide, among others such as local reconciliation, poverty reduction, and/or education programs.

A year after the genocide, in 1995, the United Nations Security Council created a specific tribunal for Rwanda, called International Court Tribunal for Rwanda (ICTR). The ICTR was intended to be a special court to try the highest criminal acts of genocide, including genocidal rape, organization of genocidal killings, and executing plans of mass killing. This international court was the first to hand down international criminal punishments since the 1945 Nuremberg trials.

The ICTR made legal history in 1998 when it handed down the world's first convictions of genocide and genocidal rape, which impacted legal precedent in international courts for years to come. At the end of

---

1 Prior to colonialization Rwanda had three main groups centered on class-based differences (amount of cows one owned, occupation, etc.): the Hutu, Tutsi, and Twa. These groups intermarried and shared the same language and culture. However, during colonialization, Germany and Belgium constructed these groups as fixed ethnic categories, requiring identity cards in 1933. They believed the Tutsi were most similar to Europeans, so they placed them in positions of power, marginalizing the majority Hutu. Such unequal relations set the stage for the uprisings of the 1960s and the resentment that fueled anti-Tutsi violence culminating in the 1994 genocidal violence (Hintjens, 2001; Mamdani, 2001).

the ICTR's tenure in 2012, 93 individuals had been indicted, resulting in 62 sentences (United Nations, n.d.). While the ICTR made legal history, it also had it shortcomings. Because of its location outside of Rwanda in Arusha, Tanzania, what transpired in court was seldom reported or shared to local Rwandans, with the exception of highly educated Rwandans living in urban areas. When cases were in process, the majority of Rwandans did not know the status of them or even how they were managed. It was also often impossible for witnesses to travel to Tanzania if they wanted to testify or attend a trial of a suspected killer because of cost. In the early years, the ICTR experienced resource and logistical problems, as well as lacking proper training on both Rwandan culture and trauma (Des Forges & Longman, 2004; Mullins, 2009). Proper training on trauma, especially sexual assault, is key to making tribunals and truth commissions meaningful and safe for those participating. For some, the ICTR was inefficient in the amount of time it required to prosecute a handful of suspects.

To try more than a handful of perpetrators like the ICTR, the new Rwandan government developed a court system that could try hundreds of thousands of cases in a more localized and efficient manner. In 2000 Rwanda implemented an innovative court system called Gacaca, which was primarily based on an assumption that civic involvement in restorative judicial processes are vital for reconciliation in Rwanda. Gacaca was not invented in 2000, but rather was a judicial system in place before colonial rule to solve disputes over land, marriage, and village conflicts (Brehm, Uggen, & Gasanabo, 2014). Traditional Gacaca was informal, as it would litigate problems mainly between family members and neighbors based on the assumption that such disagreements are pertinent to the community and not simply an individual's problem (Karekezi, 2004).

Adjusted for post-genocide Rwanda, Gacaca tried all suspected criminals, including those of property crimes (such as looting) except those who were the more serious criminals, who were tried in the ICTR. Within Gacaca's tenure, 10,000 lay judges tried almost two million cases on hills, community centers, or soccer fields. Nearly every week perpetrators offered confessions in exchange for freedom, reduced sentences, or community work, and survivors declared accusations and provided testimony. Gacaca challenged traditional notions of justice by insisting on a local and participatory process. Hearings also served in some cases as a form of truth telling where survivors gained information on when, how, and where their loved ones were murdered or buried (De Ycaza, 2010).

Like all transitional justice mechanisms, Gacaca faced several challenges. While cathartic for some victims who participated as witnesses, it was traumatizing for some, especially for women who survived rape and/or were infected with HIV/AIDS, as truth telling became more traumatizing than healing (Brounéus, 2008). Within the international community, debates arose about Gacaca's lack of due process and legal representation (Meyerstein, 2007). Finally, false accusations and fabricated testimony occurred as a form of revenge, compromising the integrity of some of the cases.

The creation of memorials and museums dedicated to remembering those who died in the genocide is also a vehicle for transitional justice and can illuminate aspects of truth and reconciliation after atrocity (Barsalou & Baxter, 2007). Rwandan citizens, along with the help of international non-governmental organizations (NGOs) and donors, have created over 500 memorials of various sizes and shapes throughout the country. Among these memorials are seven national sites supported by the Rwandan government, several of which house both the bodily remains of victims and evidence of genocidal violence, such as bloodied walls, weapons, and genocidal propaganda. Some survivors find these spaces essential for reconciliation and healing, as they acknowledge the violence they endured and commemorate their loved ones and all lost in the genocide (Fox, in press). Some memorials have become educational sites in which the next generation learns about the precursors of mass violence and how to promote social harmony and peaceful coexistence.

Memorials, like all other mechanisms, come with challenges. Debates have arisen over the validity and purpose of showing exposed bones in memorials, as well as the lack of discussion of war crimes in such memorial narratives (Longman, 2017; Thomson, 2013). Memorial narratives have varied in their approaches to discussing gender-based violence, with some discussing and acknowledging gender-based violence and others remaining silent due to the difficulty of the topic or fear of traumatizing the public (Fox, in press). Survivors have found the silence around gender-based violence problematic. Finally, not unique to Rwanda, contention is felt over contested or forgotten narratives that are not included in the national memorials (Fox & de Ycaza, 2014). Taken together, these mechanisms have assisted in transitioning Rwanda from destruction to its current state of stability.

TABLE 15.1   Timeline of Key Political-Legal Events

1962	Independence from Belgium, after episodes of violence between Tutsi and Hutu. President Kayibanda (a Hutu) is elected as the first independent president.
1973	President Kayibanda (a Hutu) is removed in a military coup and replaced by the newly elected Preseident Habyarimna (also a Hutu).
1978	New constitution is established making the National Revolutionary Movement for Development the only legal political party and eradicating presidential term limits.
1990	The Rwandan Patriotic Front (RPF), a rebel group of mostly exiled Tutsis, invade Rwanda from neighboring Uganda, marking the start of a 3-year civil war.
1991	New multiparty constitution adopted.
1993	President Habyarimana signs power-sharing agreement with the RPF, agreeing to a UN peace-monitoring mission, marking the official end of the civil war.
1994 (April)	Unknown assailants shot down the plane carrying the presidents of Rwanda and Burundi (neighboring country) as it attempted to land in Kigali, Rwanda, effectively ending the Peace 1993 agreement and signaling the start of a well-planned and organized genocide led by extremist Hutus against Tutsis and moderate Hutus.

1994 (August)	New Rwandan government agrees to the UN ICTR trials.
1995	ICTR for Rwanda announces first indictments against eight suspects for genocide and crimes against humanity.
1996	Mass repatriation from Zaire begins; the Rwandan government orders a moratorium on arrests of suspected genocide perpetrators. Trials begin for Hutu genocide suspects.
1996	Trials begin for Hutus involved in 1994 genocide.
1997 (January)	First case trial in the ICTR in Arusha, Tanzania, against Jean Paul Akayesu, a local government official accused of ordering mass killings in his area.
1997 (February)	In Gikongoro, Rwanda, Venuste Niyonzima is the first man tried locally for crimes against humanity in his own village. Frodouald Karamina, leader of a Hutu extremist political movement, is sentenced to death for his involvement in the genocide.
1997 (July)	Creation of a ICTR unit for gender issues and assistance to victims of genocide.
1998 (May)	Former Interim Government Prime Minister Jean Kambanda pleads guilty to genocide. This marks the first time that an accused person admits responsibility for genocide, conspiracy to commit genocide, and crimes against humanity. By accepting his plea, the ICTR becomes the first international tribunal since Nuremberg to issue a judgement against a former head of state.
1999 (March)	Creation of the National Unity and Reconciliation Commission.
1999 (December)	A leader of a Hutu militia, Georges Rutaganda, is found guilty of genocide and crimes against humanity and is sentenced to life in prison.
2000	The trials of Jean Bosco Barayagwiza, Ferdinand Nahimana, and Hassan Ngeze result in the first verdicts by an international tribunal holding members of the media responsible for broadcasts intended to inflame the public to commit acts of genocide.

2001	Gacaca is implemented in local communities.
2011	Pauline Nyiramasuhuko is the first woman to be indicted and arrested by an international criminal tribunal.
2003	New constitution implemented, proscribing ethnic hatred or "divisionism" of any form, as well as any public categorization or pronouncements of ethnicity.
2004	Re-education camps (Ingando) introduced for rehabilitation of ex-prisoners/soldiers who participated in the genocide. Ingando is later applied to returning refugees and other Rwandan citizens.
2005	Mass prisoner release by the government due to overcrowded prisons and the implementation of Gacaca.
2008	Prohibition against genocide ideology. Rwanda's famous singer Simon Bikindi sentenced to 15 years for inciting violence during the genocide.
2012	Gacaca courts close and deliver final judgements.
2013	ICTR overturns the genocide convictions of two former government ministers.
2015	ICTR holds last hearings, with 93 total convictions.
2017	President Kagame is re-elected president, after a constitutional referendum passed allowing for him to serve a third term.
2018	President Kagame pardons over 2,000 prisoners, including leading opposition leader Victoire Ingabire, who was jailed in 2012.

Modified from BBC, 2018a; Frontline, n.d.; and United Nations International Residual Mechanism for Criminal Tribunals, 1994.

The Case of South Africa

Following the legal abolition of the racist and violent Apartheid regime of South Africa under the 1993 Interim Constitution, the Truth and

Reconciliation Commission (TRC) was created under the Promotion of National Unity and Reconciliation Act, No. 34 of 1995, and its related amendments through 2003. Among other provisions, the act was "[t]o provide for the investigation and the establishment of as complete a picture as possible of the nature, causes and extent of gross violations of human rights committed during the period from 1 March 1960" to 1994 (p. 1). Chapter 2 of the act established the Truth and Reconciliation Commission with the "objectives to promote national unity and reconciliation in a spirit of understanding which transcends the conflicts and divisions of the past" (p. 4). The TRC was empowered to document the extent and circumstances of the gross human rights violations of the apartheid era (by both the state government forces and rebel or opposition groups as well as the perspectives of the victims) grant amnesty to qualified confessors, disclose the whereabouts and fate of victims as well as provide them the opportunity to be heard publicly, recommend reparations to the victims, and compile the relevant facts and findings of the gross human rights violations and recommendations for their prevention. Pursuant to the TRC charge and goal of Act No. 34 of 1995, several other organs were established to facilitate the mandate of the TRC, with specific jurisdictions and functions, including committees on human rights violations, amnesty, and reparation and rehabilitation. Members of the commission were appointed by the president of South Africa, with the power of removal with justification and under specified guidelines. The 17-member commission of nine men and eight women was chaired by the Nobel Peace Laureate Archbishop Desmond Tutu.

By the time the TRC concluded its work in 2002, presented its report to President Nelson Mandela in 1998, and received an extension to 2002, it achieved the following (U.S. Institute of Peace, 1995):

+ Heard the testimonies of over 21,000 victims, with 2,000 of them at public hearings
+ Received 7,112 amnesty applications, granted 849 and denied 5,392; others were withdrawn
+ Recommended compensation of $3,500/each year for 6 years to each victim

- Selected prosecution in certain cases of denial or no request for amnesty with the applicable evidence under the country's laws and constitution
- President Mandela accepted the report and issued national apology to all victims on behalf of the state/government
- In 2006 the government set up a group to monitor implementation of the recommendations on reparations and exhumations. A missing person's taskforce was established to exhume and rebury victims and continue investigations of missing persons or disappearances

With fewer trials than expected or confessed crimes, there were limited convictions in small numbers of cases, long payment delays, and lower than the recommended amounts for reparations to the 21,000 victims and presidential special pardons. Additionally, the nation's intelligence apparatus deliberately destroyed relevant documents of human rights violations and abuses. Taken together, there were mixed reviews on the effectiveness of the TRC in achieving its stated objectives and mission and was seen as more of an "objectification" and "commodification" of survivor memories (Ehrenreich, 2011). However, the TRC is widely viewed as an international model for healing, peace, and reconciliation after mass atrocities, through "truth"-telling, and/or public confession by the perpetrator and active voice of the victim. The TRC is heralded as acknowledging the past to facilitate a reconciled future. The TRC prioritized truth discovery as fundamental to national reconciliation and personal healing, with the hope of promoting restorative versus punitive justice in the new democratic South Africa. The TRC experience was intended to illustrate the strong African tradition of forgiveness and "ubuntu" spirit of community and collective interests (Ehrenreich, 2011).

The South African TRC is a clear example of a transitional justice mechanism, purposefully created by legislation after large-scale government-sponsored or sanctioned human rights violations against its citizens. It is designed to re-establish new political-legal order, create legitimacy of the new social order, and promote public confidence in the new justice system. After decades of the Apartheid political regime and separation laws (1913–1990), it was evident that an enabling political mechanism was needed to repair the harm done to individuals and institutions and to create a more balanced formal system of social control, in contrast to the previous system of total racial subjugation of the majority Black population by the White minority government, including punitive racial segregation and restrictive pass laws (Nicholson, 1986). It is also to be noted that many South African Whites also opposed the Apartheid regime and participated in the struggle for its abolition. Further, the Black resistance groups also committed human rights violations against civilian populations, including the current ruling and then banned African National Congress party.

An example of the government's brutal rule was revealed during the TRC hearings on the government's response to the 1961 Sharpeville Massacre (Svicevic, 2016). In 1960, Black anti-apartheid parties organized a massive protest, with Black citizens walking around without restrictive passes and freely submitted to arrest. The protest was exercised as an act of peaceful civil disobedience. However, when the youth protesters encountered the police, one of the police officers, alleging that the crowd was getting violent, panicked, and ultimately over 69 people were killed by the police (South African History Online, 2017). In response to the civil or monetary claims by the victims of the Sharpeville massacre against the government leaders and the state agents, the government passed the Indemnity Act 61 of 1961. This act prohibited the courts from hearing both criminal and civil claims against the government or agents for any events that occurred between March 1960 and July 1961 (Svicevic, 2016), thereby nullifying the legal claims. This act was one of the many abuses of abuse of power that sanctioned the government to exploit its Black citizens and avoid responsibility for its role in the Sharpeville Massacre. In essence, the formal legal system was used to create, promote, and consolidate a culture of impunity that also raised the resolve of the oppressed groups.

The TRC experience and process were not without critics. Some criticized the TRC for focusing on the more serious crimes of political motivations committed against South Africans by the government and opposition forces and relying on the lower standard of proof in regular criminal cases. This focus on more heinous crimes may have ignored the lesser but more pervasive human rights violations, or the "day-to-day injustices" (Glaser, 20001, p. 227). However, it is to be noted that the commission's mandate was specifically to "find the truth" and not necessarily determine "guilty" as in the regular justice process. The TRC was thought to have achieved a balance between seeking pure retributive justice and overusing their ability to pardon (Glaser, 20001).

The case of "Black Sunday" is often criticized as illustrative of the selective search for the truth, even in serious politically motivated crimes, but ignored by the TRC. In 1952, the towns of Port Elizabeth and East London experienced violent clashes between militant anti-apartheid and government forces. The ANC had condoned "organized civil disobedience," but these protesters were considered to be operating outside of ANC policy. These protesters had violently engaged government armed forces, resulting in the killing of between 9–200 of the primarily Black protesters by the police. Although nine people were officially reported killed, it is believed the number was nearer to 200. It is widely believed that family members secretly buried the dead in their familial cemeteries to avoid having to report their family member's involvement in anti-government protests (Bank & Carton, 2016). Given the notoriety and the ambiguity of the event, it would seem the TRC had more than enough incentive to discover the truth of this event, among other serious incidents.

Despite the criticisms, there is enough evidence to argue that the TRC was very effective in exposing South Africa's apartheid system to the world. South Africans tend to believe that TRC was successful in revealing a vast amount of truth about the brutality of the Apartheid era, but fell short of full reconciliation. For example, the Afrikaners had a lower perceived value of effectiveness of reconciliation than English and Xhosa (Vora & Vora, 2004). Surprisingly, the Xhosa had the highest perception of the TRC's reconciliation impact (Vora & Vora, 2004). Overall, South Africans believed that the TRC brought about truth but did not bring about reconciliation. The creation of the Apartheid museum in 2001 documents the rise and fall of the apartheid, including the impact and memories of the apartheid system and the struggles to end it, leading up to TRC.

TABLE 15.2   Key Developments in South Africa Politics of Justice (see also BBC News, 2018b)

1964	ANC leader Nelson Mandela sentenced to life imprisonment.

1970s	More than three million people forcibly resettled in Black "homelands."
1976	More than 600 killed in clashes between Black protesters and security forces during uprising, which started in Soweto.
1984–1989	Township revolt; state of emergency imposed.
1989	FW de Klerk replaces PW Botha as president; meets Mandela. Public facilities desegregated. Many ANC activists freed.
1990	ANC unbanned; Mandela released after 27 years in prison, effectively dismantling apartheid.
1991	Start of multi-party talks. De Klerk repeals remaining apartheid laws; international sanctions lifted.
1993	Agreement on interim Constitution.
1994	April: ANC wins first non-racial elections; Mandela becomes president; Government of National Unity formed; South Africa takes seat in UN General Assembly after 20-year absence.
1995	Promotional National Unity and Reconciliation Act No. 34.
1996	Truth and Reconciliation Commission chaired by Archbishop Desmond Tutu begins hearings on human rights crimes committed by former government and liberation movements during apartheid era.
1998	Truth and Reconciliation Commission report brands apartheid a crime against humanity and finds the ANC accountable for human rights abuses.
2001	Apartheid Museum created.
2002 (April)	Court acquits Dr. Wouter Basson, dubbed "Dr. Death," who ran apartheid-era germ warfare program. Basson had faced charges of murder and conspiracy.

2002 (October)	Bomb explosions in Soweto and a blast near Pretoria are thought to be the work of right-wing extremists. Separately, police charge 17 right-wingers with plotting against the state.
2004 (April)	Ruling ANC wins landslide election victory, gaining nearly 70% of votes. Thabo Mbeki begins a second term as president.
2005 (March)	Investigators exhume the first bodies in a Truth and Reconciliation Commission investigation into the fates of hundreds of people who disappeared in the apartheid era.
2005 (May)	Geographical names committee that recommends that the culture minister should approve a name change for the capital from Pretoria to Tshwane.
2005 (August)	Around 100,000 gold miners strike over pay, bringing the industry to a standstill.
2006 (December)	South Africa becomes the first African country, and the fifth in the world, to allow same-sex unions.
2007 (June)	Hundreds of thousands of public-sector workers take part in the biggest strike since the end of apartheid. The strike lasts for 4 weeks and causes widespread disruption to schools, hospitals, and public transport.
2008 (May)	Wave of violence directed at foreigners hits townships across the country.
2009 (July)	Township residents complaining about poor living conditions mount violent protests.
2010 (June)	South Africa hosts the World Cup football tournament.
2010 (August)	Civil servants stage nation-wide strike.
2012 (August)	Marikana massacre. The killing of 34 striking miners at the Marikana platinum mine shocked South Africa. The government sets up judicial commission of inquiry.

2012 (July)	Member of White extremist group found guilty of plotting to kill Mandela and trying to overthrow government.
2012 (October)	Platinum mine owner Amplats fires 12,000 striking miners as wave of wildcat strikes shows little sign of abating.
2013 (December)	Nelson Mandela dies at age 95. Tributes to "the father of the nation" flood in from throughout the world.
2015 (February)	President Zuma announces plans to limit farm sizes and ban foreign farmland ownership in an attempt to redistribute land to Black farmers
2015 (March–April)	A spate of anti-immigrant attacks leaves several people dead.
2016 (March)	Supreme Court rules President Zuma violated the Constitution for not repaying public money used to improve his private residence.
2018 (February)	President Zuma resigns under pressure from the governing ANC over corruption charges, which chooses veteran trade unionist and businessman Cyril Ramaphosa as his successor.

Conclusion

This chapter provided an overview of the most common transitional justice mechanisms and analyzed two African case studies who utilized transitional justice after atrocity. In summary, this chapter did the following:

+ Described a range of transitional justice mechanisms, some restorative and some retributive
+ Demonstrated how transitional justice mechanisms often work best in combination with one another
+ Provided two case studies as examples of transitional justice. The first, Rwanda, implemented several mechanisms, all having their own particular strengths and challenges (tribunals, local courts, and memorialization). The second, South Africa, emphasized

truth telling by both victims and perpetrators of violence as key to personal healing and national reconciliation

+ Illustrated some pathways for rebuilding a formal justice system after state moral or political collapse, thereby re-establishing a new system of peace and order that commands public confidence and attracts international legitimacy

Discussion Questions

1. How might practices of transitional justice be applied to historical or contemporary cases in the United States?
2. What U.S. experience of injustice(s) could benefit from any of the mechanisms discussed? Specify the injustice and justify your proposed mechanism.
3. What challenges might the United States face when trying to implement transitional justice?
4. Compare the South African TRC and Rwanda Gacaca, indicating their strengths and weaknesses.
5. Can you imagine or create a system of justice and governance that will preempt the need for transitional justice? Explain.

Research Project

Research a case of transitional justice not described in this chapter (such as Sierra Leone; Greensboro, North Carolina; Poland; Germany; Bosnia/former Yugoslavia; Argentina; or Guatemala) and present to the class the following:

1. The context in which transitional justice occurred
2. The mechanism(s) the country used
3. The benefits and challenges of that mechanism(s)
4. The overall impact on the current formal justice system

References

Aguilar, P. (1997). Collective memory of the Spanish Civil War: The case of the political amnesty in the Spanish transition to democracy. *Democratization, 4*(4), 88–109.

Arzt, D. E. (2006). Views on the ground: The local perception of international criminal tribunals in the former Yugoslavia and Sierra Leone. *Annals of the American Academy of Political and Social Science, 603*(1), 226–239.

Bank, L. J., & Carton, B. (2016). Forgetting apartheid: History, culture and the body of a nun. *Africa: The Journal of the International African Institute, 86*(3), 472–503.

Barkan, E., & Karn, A. (Eds.). (2006). *Taking wrongs seriously: Apologies and reconciliation*. Stanford, CA: Stanford University Press.

Barsalou, J., & Baxter, V. (2007). The urge to remember: The role of memorials in social reconstruction and transitional justice. In [AU: Add editor(s) name(s)] *Stabilization and Reconstruction* (pp. 1–24). Washington DC: United States Institute for Peace.

BBC. (2018a). *Rwanda profile–Timeline*. Retrieved from https://www.bbc.com/news/world-africa-14093322

BBC. (2018b). *South Africa profile–Timeline*. Retrieved from https://www.bbc.com/news/world-africa-14094918

Brehm, H. N., Uggen, C., & Gasanabo, J. (2014). Genocide, justice, and Rwanda's Gacaca courts. *Journal of Contemporary Criminal Justice, 30*(3), 333–352.

Brounéus, K. (2008). Truth-telling as talking cure? Insecurity and retraumatization in the Rwandan Gacaca courts. *Security Dialogue, 39*(1), 55–76.

Clark, P., & Kaufman, Z. (Eds.). (2009). *After genocide: Transitional justice, post-conflict reconstruction and reconciliation in Rwanda and beyond*. New York, NY: Columbia University Press.

Crocker, D. (2000). Truth commissions and transitional justice. In School of Public Affairs (Ed.), [AU: Add title of book] (pp. 23–31). College Park, MD: University of Maryland: Institute for Philosophy and Public Policy.

Crosby, A., & Lykes, B. M. (2011). Mayan women survivors speak: The gendered relations of truth telling in postwar Guatemala. *International Journal of Transitional Justice, 5*(3), 456–476.

Dandurand, Y., & Griffith, C. T. (2006). United Nations handbook on restorative justice programmes. In United Nations Office on Drugs and Crime (Ed.), *Criminal justice handbook series, IV* (pp. 105). Vienna, Austria: United Nations Publications.

De Brito, A., Gonzaléz-Enríquez, C., & Aguilar, P (Eds.). (2001). *The politics of memory: Transitional justice in democratizing societies.* Oxford, UK: Oxford University Press.

De Ycaza, C. (2010). Performative unctions of genocide trials in Rwanda: Reconciliation through restorative justice? *African Journal on Conflict Resolution, 10*(3), 9–28.

Des Forges, A., & Longman, T. (2004). Legal responses to genocide in Rwanda. In E. Stover & H. Weinstein (Eds.), *My neighbor, my Enemy: Justice and community in the aftermath of mass atrocity* (pp. 49–68). Cambridge, UK: Cambridge University Press.

Dieng, A. (2011). Capacity-building efforts of the ICTR: A different kind of legacy. *Northwestern Journal of International Human Rights, 9*(3), 401–422.

Ehrenreich, V. (2011). Commodification of traumatic stories: Memory, performance and the TRC in South Africa's post independence stage. In E. Uwazie & C. Ridley (Eds.), *Contemporary issues in African studies: A reader* (pp. 44–59). Dubuque, IA: Kendall Hunt Publishing.

Engel, D. M., & Munger, F. W. (1996). Rights, remembrance, and the reconciliation of difference. *Law & Society Review, 30*(1), 7–53.

Fox, N. (2014). *"It Is Here That I Remember My Beloved": Memorials and Commemorations in Post-Genocide Rwanda.* PhD Dissertation. Waltham, MA: Brandeis.

Fox, N. (in press). Memory in interactions: The remembering and forgetting of gender-based violence during atrocity. *Signs.*

Fox, N. & De Ycaza, C. (2013). Narratives of mass violence: The role of memory and memorialization in addressing human rights violations in post-conflict Rwanda and Uganda. *Societies Without Borders, 8*(5), 344–372.

Frontline. (n.d.). Rwanda chronology. *PBS.* Retrieved from https://www.pbs.org/wgbh/pages/frontline/shows/rwanda/etc/cron.html

Jones, N. (2009). *The courts of genocide: Politics and the rule of law in Rwanda and Arusha.* New York, NY: Routledge.

Gibson, J. L. (2004). *Overcoming apartheid: Can truth reconcile a divided nation?* New York, NY: Russell Sage Foundation.

Glaser, D. J. (20001). *Politics and society in South Africa: A Critical Introduction.* [London: Sage Publications].

Goldblatt, B., & Meintjes, S. (1998). Dealing with the aftermath: Sexual violence and the Truth and Reconciliation Commission. *Agenda: Empowering Women for Gender Equity, 13*(36), 7–18.

Hamber, B., & Wilson, R. A. (2002). Symbolic closure through memory, reparation and revenge in post-conflict societies. *Journal of Human Rights, 1*(1), 35–53.

Hayner, P. B. (2011). *Unspeakable truths: Transitional justice and the challenge of truth commissions.* New York, NY: Routledge.

Hintjens, H. M. (2001). When identity becomes a knife: Reflecting on the genocide in Rwanda. *Ethnicities, 1*(1), 25–55.

International Criminal Tribunal for Rwanda. (2007). Symposium on the Legacy of International Criminal Courts and Tribunals in Africa.": International Center for Ethics, Justice, and Public Life, Brandeis University, Waltham, MA.

Karekezi, U., Nshimiyimana, A., & Mutamba, B. (2004). Localizing justice: Gacaca courts in post-genocide Rwanda. In E. Stover & H. Weinstein (Eds.), *My neighbor, my enemy: Justice and community in the aftermath of mass atrocity* (pp. 69–84). Cambridge, UK: Cambridge University Press.

Longman, T. (2017). *Memory and justice in post-genocide Rwanda.* New York, NY: Cambridge University Press.

Mamdani, M. (2001). *When victims become killers: Colonialism, nativism and the genocide in Rwanda.* Princeton, NJ: Princeton University Press.

Mamdani, M. (2005). Amnesty or impunity? A preliminary critique of the report of the Truth and Reconciliation Commission of South Africa (TRC). *Diacritics, 32*(3), 33–59.

Meyerstein, A. (2007). Between law and culture: Rwanda's Gacaca and postcolonial legacy. *Law and Society Inquiry, 32*(2), 467–508.

Minow, M. (1998). *Between Vengeance and Forgiveness: Facing History After Genocide and Mass Violence.* Boston: Beacon Press.

Mullins, C. W. (2009). He would kill me with his penis: Genocidal rape in Rwanda as a state crime. *Critical Criminology, 17*(1), 15–33.

Nicholson, C. (1986). Nothing really gets better: Reflections on the twenty-five years between Sharpeville and Uitenhage. *Human Rights Quarterly, 8*(3), 511–516. doi:10.2307/762274

Phelps, T. (2004). *Shattered voices: Language, violence and the work of truth commissions.* Philadelphia, PA: University of Pennsylvania Press.

Promotion of National Unity & Reconciliation Act, No. 34 (1995). Retrieved from http://www.justice.gov.za/legislation/acts/1995-034.pdf

Reydams, L. (2005). The ICTR ten years on: Back to the Nuremberg paradigm? *Journal of International Criminal Justice, 3*(4), 977–988.

Rotberg, R., & Thompson, D. (Eds.). (2000). *Truth commissions and the provision of truth, justice, and reconciliation.* Princeton, NJ: Princeton University Press.

Sadat, L. N. ed. (2012). *The legacy of the International Criminal Tribunal for Rwanda.* Whitney R. Harris World Law Institute (pp. 1-20). Washington University: St. Louis, MO.

Sikkink, K. (2012). *The justice cascade: How human rights prosecutions Are changing world politics.* New York, NY: Norton.

South African History Online. (2017, March 21). *Sharpeville Massacre, 21 March 1960.* Retrieved from https://www.sahistory.org.za/topic/sharpeville-massacre-21-march-1960

Straus, S. (2006). *The order of genocide: Race, power, and war in Rwanda.* Ithaca, NY: Cornell University Press.

Svicevic, M. (2016). Law and justice: Reviewing positive law in post-apartheid South Africa. *Africa Policy Journal, 11,* 20–30.

Teitel, R. G. (2003). Transitional justice genealogy. *Harvard Human Rights Journal, 16,* 69–94.

Thomson, Susan. (2013). *Whispering Truth to Power: Everyday Resistance to Reconciliation in Postgenocide Rwanda.* Madison: University of Wisconsin Press.

United Nations. (n.d.). International residual mechanism for criminal tribunals: ICTR in brief. Retrieved from http://unictr.irmct.org/en/tribunal

United Nations International Residual Mechanism for Criminal Tribunals. (1994). *The United Nations establishes the ITCR.* Retrieved from http://unictr.irmct.org/en/ictr-milestones

U.S. Institute of Peace (1995). *Truth Commission: South Africa.* Retrieved from https://www.usip.org/publications/1995/12/truth-commission-south-africa

Vora, J., & Vora, E. (2004). The effectiveness of South Africa's Truth and Reconciliation Commission: Perceptions of Xhosa, Afrikaner, and English South Africans. *Journal of Black Studies, 34*(3), 301–322.

V

Additional Perspectives

Highlight A

Principled Policing

An Evolution

Eric Jones

Recently, there have been a number of 21st-century and other policing initiatives that illustrate an evolution of policing. These initiatives have in common three primary shifts for local law enforcement in the areas of relationships and trust building, the use of new metrics, and more focused data-driven enforcement. These contemporary policing shifts in today's challenging world have an overarching philosophy of certain principles and values for which the industry of law enforcement must stand.

The term "smarter policing" relates to the use of intelligence-led and evidence-based strategies and is about being data driven and strategic in the delivery of public safety services to the community. Smarter policing includes innovation and technology to improve service delivery. But if smarter policing is the manner of how the job is done, then "principled policing" is really what the agency stands for and is the reason the men and women in law enforcement do what they do. Smarter policing, therefore, must be driven by principled policing to ensure the profession of law enforcement is procedurally just and legitimate. Law enforcement agencies must use effective crime-fighting strategies that also continue to build trust within the community. This link between trust and crime reduction is clear.

Principled policing contains all the components used to increase the community's trust of their police department and officers. Principled policing stands on the premise that law enforcement should be based on its founding principles. Back in 1829, the Peelian principles were developed on the tenets of police transparency, integrity, fairness, and accountability—all critical to legitimizing policing in the eyes of the public and securing bonds of trust with the community. Arguably, these principles apply even more now than they did in 1829. Community tensions with police are high, but with today's best research and data, experts can validate that low community trust exists, but can also determine in which specific communities and why. This provides opportunities to better address distrust, which is through focused deterrence crime strategies, procedural justice and implicit bias training for police officers, and racial reconciliation listening sessions.

Based on these principles, the evolution of policing has brought to law enforcement three shifts in enforcement, relationships, and metrics. Regarding enforcement, police have moved away from "blanket enforcement" and toward strategic and data-driven enforcement. Instead of simply responding to high crime areas and saturating them with zero-tolerance enforcement, police departments are being much more strategic to focus on the very small percentage of community members committing the vast majority of crime.

For relationship building, there is a shift toward recognizing how best to reach out to the most disenfranchised communities. An understanding of the levels and sources of mistrust, especially in our communities of color, and how historical acknowledgments and reconciliation can assist in meaningful dialogue, are building blocks for trust building. Law enforcement agencies are also beginning to recognize the importance of being trauma informed.

Regarding outcomes and measurements, there is less an emphasis on arrests and citations as a police report card for success and a stronger focus on trust-building metrics. Community sentiment and feedback on the policing of our communities is important for a police department's gauge of success. Promising strategies seem to be comprehensive community surveys externally and are a shift from traditional Compstat numbers to collective overviews looking at both crime-fighting and trust-building efforts in departmental meetings internally. Much of the content of these three areas of shift is contained in the California Attorney General's Principled Policing Subcommittee and Statewide Training, the National Initiative on Building Community Trust and Justice, and the President's Task Force on 21st Century Policing, all of which involved Stockton, California.

The success of principled policing relies on leadership at all levels, top to bottom, and on a culture embracing change. It must be ingrained into the policing culture, which is the shared set of values and beliefs. The culture should be one where ideas are evaluated on merits rather than rank or politics, openness is promoted, people are held accountable, and best practices are sought. The principles must be the overarching philosophy that permeates all aspects of policy and culture, but that can also be tangibly infused at the operational level.

Implicit Bias and Law Enforcement

Cecil E. Canton

In 2014, the deaths of Michael Brown in Ferguson, Missouri, Eric Garner in New York City, Tamir Rice in Cleveland, Ohio, the 2016 shooting of Philando Castile in St. Paul, Minnesota, and the 2018 police shooting of Stephon Clark in Sacramento, California, among others, put a spotlight on the killings of African Americans at the hands of law enforcement. Unfortunately, these slayings represent the consequence of implicit bias.

Implicit bias has been identified as the reason for so many deaths of unarmed African American men and women at the hands of law enforcement personnel.

Based on the number of justifiable homicides reported to the FBI, during a 7-year period ending in 2012, a White police officer killed a Black person nearly two times a week in the United States. In fact, according to comprehensive research and data collected by Vice News, an estimated 1,083 Americans have been killed by cop since August 9, 2014, an average of nearly three people a day (Fields, 2015). Of course not all of those killed were African American, but Black people were killed 3.49 times more often than White people (Ross, 2015). However, it is particularly dangerous to assume that everyone who is stopped by the police is actually guilty of a crime.

Implicit bias, oftentimes referred to as unconscious bias, implicit stereotype, or implicit social cognition, refers to the attitudes or stereotypes that affect our understanding, actions, and decisions in an unconscious manner. These biases, which encompass both favorable and unfavorable assessments, are activated involuntarily and without an individual's awareness or intentional control.

Under certain conditions, those automatic associations can influence behavior—making people respond in biased ways even when they are not explicitly prejudiced (Kirwan Institute for Study of Race and Ethnicity, n.d.).

Advances in neuroscience and other social sciences have helped us to understand that people can consciously believe in equality while simultaneously acting on subconscious prejudices they are not aware they harbor. The mind sciences have found that most of our actions occur without our conscious thoughts, allowing us to function in our extraordinarily complex world.

By looking at the complexity of how our brains work, this research has given us a way to understand better how decision making happens in our minds. This means, however, that our implicit biases often predict how we'll behave more accurately than our conscious values. Everyone has implicit biases and preferences that operate on a subconscious level. They could be related to race, gender, disability, religion, etc. (Canton, 2013). This psychological explanation arose as a way to explain why discrimination persists, even though research clearly shows that people oppose it.

And this is especially helpful in our understanding of how that process works in the minds of law enforcement personnel, who, when interacting with Black Americans, often perceive themselves in a threatening life-or-death situation. Current research paints a picture of a nation where a citizen's race or ethnicity may well affect their experience with police—whether an encounter ends with a traffic stop, the use of police force, or a fatal shooting. However, researchers continue to show that Whites persist in maintaining a negative implicit bias against non-Whites (Beer, 2015).

Research also suggests that implicit bias is not always negatively applied. There is evidence that the more one looks like a White person, the more this "protective coloration" serves as a safeguard from police harm and danger. In a study focusing on group bias in the criminal justice system, researchers examined intragroup bias by looking at perceived suspect phenotypic racial stereotypicality (e.g., how strongly members possess physical features typical of their racial group) on severity of police use of force. Regression analyses confirmed that police used less force with highly stereotypical Whites and that this protective effect was stronger than the effect for non-Whites. Study results suggest that intragroup bias is a protective factor for Whites but not for non-Whites, providing an additional route through which racial disparities in law enforcement operate (Kahn, Goff, Lee, & Motamed, 2016; Eberhardt, Davies, Purdie-Vaughns, & Johnson, 2006).

The Kirwan Institute for the Study of Race and Ethnicity (n.d.) at Ohio State University have observed that these associations develop over the course of a lifetime, beginning at a very early age through exposure to direct and indirect messages. In addition to early life experiences, the media and news programming are often cited as origins of implicit associations leading to support for punitive policies (Ghandnoosh, 2014). The lethal cocktail of institutional racism, police and societal expectations of crime as "Black," anti-Blackness ideologies rooted in policing institutions' ties to slavery and slave patrols, and media portrayals of Blacks as thugs and monsters to be feared have reinforced these beliefs in the minds of Whites (Sewell, 2016). In the words of one researcher, "The only thing that was significant in predicting whether someone shot and killed by police was unarmed was whether or not they were black. Crime variables did not matter in terms of predicting whether the person killed was unarmed" (Lowery, 2016).

If we are to improve and strengthen the relationships between police and minority communities, we must reduce the influence of implicit bias on their interactions. Recent studies have suggested that implicit bias contributes to "shooter bias"—the tendency for police to shoot unarmed Black suspects more often than White ones—as well as the frequency of police stops for members of ethnic and racial minority groups (Sadler, Correll, Park, & Judd, 2012; Corell, Park, Judd, & Wittenbrink, 2007). Studies have also found that those with higher implicit bias levels (as measured by instruments such as the Implicit Association Test (IAT)) (Project Implicit, n.d.) against Black people are more likely to categorize non-weapons as weapons (such as a phone for a gun, or a comb for a knife) (Payne, Neimi, & Doris, 2018) and in computer simulations are more likely to shoot an unarmed person (Perception Institute, n.d.). When these biases influence the behavior of law enforcement officers in real time "shoot/don't-shoot" situations, they can do more than hurt feelings; they can lead to a tragic ending.

In conclusion, although mind scientists are in the early stages of determining how to "de-bias" attitudes and behavior, media and makers of popular culture can play a role by ceasing to perpetuate stereotypes in news and pop culture. Despite the challenges, it is possible to address and reduce implicit bias through training and policy interventions with law enforcement agencies. Research suggests that biased associations can be gradually unlearned and replaced with nonbiased ones (Perception Institute, n.d.). Additionally, institutions and individuals can identify risk areas where implicit biases may affect behaviors and judgments. By instituting specific procedures for decision making that encourage mindfulness and understanding of the risks of implicit bias, law enforcement organizations can help their members avoid acting according to biases that are contrary to their conscious values and beliefs. By doing so, there may be an opportunity to mend the harm that racial stereotyping does in the minds of law enforcers and to our public safety.

References

Beer, T. (2015, July 25). Implicit racial bias: Where do we learn whom we should perceive negatively?. *Sociology Toolbox, The Society Pages*. Retrieved from https://thesocietypages.org/toolbox/implicit-bias/

Canton, C. (2013, Spring). A journey into change. *California Faculty: The Magazine of the California Faculty Association*, 17–18.

Correll J., Park, B., Judd, C. M., & Wittenbrink, B. (2007); The influence of stereotypes on decisions to shoot. *European Journal of Social Psychology*, 37, 1102–1117.

Eberhardt, J. L., Davies, P. G., Purdie-Vaughns, V. J., & Johnson, S. L. (2006). Looking deathworthy: Perceived stereotypicality of Black defendants predicts capital-sentencing outcomes. *Psychological Science, 17*(5), 383–386.

Fields, L. (2015, August 9). Police have killed at least 1,083 Americans since Michael Brown's death. *Vice News*. Retrieved from https://news.vice.com/en_us/article/kz9wea/police-have-killed-at-least-1083-americans-since-michael-browns-death/

Ghandnoosh, N. (2014, September 3). Race and punishment: Racial perceptions of crime and support for punitive policies. *The Sentencing Project*. Retrieved from http://www.sentencingproject.org/publications/

race-and-punishment-racial-perceptions-of-crime-and-support-for-punitive-policies/

Kahn, K. B., Goff, P. A., Lee, J. K., & Motamed, D. (2016). Protecting Whiteness: White phenotypic racial stereotypicality reduces police use of force. *Social Psychological and Personality Science, 7*(5), 403–411.

Kirwan Institute for the Study of Race and Ethnicity. (n.d). Implict bias. *Ohio State University.* Retrieved from http://kirwaninstitute.osu.edu/research/understanding-implicit-bias/

Lowery, W. (2016, July 11). Aren't more White people than Black people killed by police? Yes, but no!. *Washington Post.* Retrieved from https://www.washingtonpost.com/news/post-nation/wp/2016/07/11/arent-more-white-people-than-black-people-killed-by-police-yes-but-no/

Payne, K., Niemi, L., & Doris, J. M. (2018, March 27). How to think about "implicit bias." *Scientific American.* Retrieved from https://www.scientificamerican.com/article/how-to-think-about-implicit-bias/

Perception Institute. (n.d.). *Implicit bias.* Retrieved from https://perception.org/research/implicit-bias/

Project Implicit. (n.d.). *Overview.* Retrieved from https://implicit.harvard.edu/implicit/education.html

Ross, C. T. (2015, November 5). A multi-level Bayesian analysis of racial bias in police shootings at the county level in the United States, 2011–2014. *PLoS One, 10*(11), e1041852.

Sadler, M. S., Correll, J., Park, B., & Judd, C. M. (2012). The world is not Black and White: Racial bias in the decision to shoot in a multiethnic context. *Journal of Social Issues, 68*(2), 286–313.

Sewell, A. A. (2016, July 22). Racial bias in lethal police shootings: The need for interdisciplinary research. *The Society Pages.* Retrieved from https://thesocietypages.org/toolbox/racial_bias_police_shootings/

Juvenile Justice Realignment in California

One Decade Later

Lee Seale

O ver the last decade, California has reemerged as a nationwide leader in criminal justice reform, ushering in historic changes to its prison population, the parole process, its approach to drug offenses, the Three Strikes Law, and probation supervision. The impacts of these cataclysmic changes have been the focus of research, media attention, and debate. Nearly overlooked, however, is perhaps the biggest change of all: California's reform and realignment of its juvenile justice system, a milestone legislative act that just marked its 10-year anniversary.

Before this reform, in the 1990s and early 2000s juvenile crime rates soared in California, stoked by nationwide fears of juvenile "super-predators" and a "get-tough" mentality toward crime. Both responding to and reflecting these concerns, California voters passed Proposition 21 in 2000, making it easier for youth to be charged as adults and funneling more young adults into an already badly overcrowded adult prison system. Meanwhile, incarceration in the state's Division of Juvenile Justice surged to a population nearing 10,000 young people. Many jurisdictions, both state and local, faced overcrowded conditions and lawsuits related to their treatment of juveniles. Research-based rehabilitative programs for juveniles were scarce.

Though other more modest juvenile justice reforms were underway, lawmakers, impatient with the pace of change, passed Senate Bill 81 on August 24, 2007, creating a significant realignment and reform of California's juvenile justice system. This seismic shift accomplished three key things. First, it prospectively restricted incarceration in the state juvenile system to only those youth convicted of serious, violent, or sex offenses. Going forward, all other youth whose crimes were not serious, violent, or sex offenses would remain in county custody under the jurisdiction of local probation departments, serving any time in local juvenile detention centers, camps, or ranches. Second, and similarly, it restricted state juvenile parole to only those who have committed serious, violent, or sex offenses. All other youth or young adults released to the community would be supervised by local probation departments. Third, under juvenile realignment, California would provide funding and support to encourage best practices among the counties to implement their expanded responsibilities, particularly in the area of community supervision. Senate Bill 81 specifically incentivized the use of risk and needs assessments, data collection, and evidence-based practices, and created a Youth Offender Block grant to support these new county practices and responsibilities.

The impact of juvenile realignment was immediate and enormous. California's juvenile crime rates, both felony and misdemeanor, plummeted to their lowest rates in decades. Today, they are less than one-third of what they were in 2007 when juvenile realignment was first implemented. During that same 10-year period, the state's youth population in the Division of Juvenile Justice dropped from 2,516 to less than 700.

One would expect that the shift from state to local custody and supervision would have driven local populations higher; however, the opposite occurred. Evidence-based practices and the increased use of risk and needs assessments led to better decisions about which youths belonged in custody and which did not, resulting in reduced custodial populations, greater savings to taxpayers, and better public safety outcomes. Between 2007 and 2017, local populations in youth detention centers, camps, and group homes all were cut by more than half throughout California. Here in Sacramento county, juvenile crime rates have matched statewide reductions, while the number of locally incarcerated youth stands at one quarter of what it was in 2007. Throughout California, juvenile system leaders have reduced young people's unnecessary penetration into the justice system and are doing much more to make community-based treatment and services available that are tailored to the individualized needs of the youth we serve.

Looking ahead, there are several reasons why we must remain committed to the advances achieved under juvenile realignment. First, the premises of realignment—that youth are best served close to home and that local communities are best-suited to serve them—are now recognized as axiomatic among researchers. Those premises, which recognize the protective functions of local families, schools, and faith communities, are the foundation of any successful youth-serving system and must be securely anchored into California's future. Second, the widespread adoption of evidence-based practices among state and local justice systems that began with juvenile realignment is still in its infancy and must continue to expand and mature. The entire juvenile justice system should be outcome driven and predicated on research into what works. Third and finally, juvenile justice practitioners must continue their work in family engagement. Too often it is not just the youth who need treatment and services; it is the whole family unit. Supporting families keeps kids out of the justice system. Continued adherence to these lessons from juvenile realignment will produce another decade of progress in California for youth and families.

About the Authors

Canton, Cecil:

Cecil E. Canton earned his B.A. from the State University of New York at Stony Brook and M.A., M.Ed. & Ed.D., from Teachers College, Columbia University. Canton is a tenured full professor of criminal justice at California State University, Sacramento. He co-authored *The Politics of Survival in Academia: Narratives of Inequity, Resilience, and Success* (Rowman & Littlefield, 2002) and articles on unconscious bias, cultural taxation and anti-racism, and social justice transformations in academia and labor unions.

Dussich, John:

John Dussich received his Ph.D. in criminology/sociology from Florida State University. He is the National Organization for Victim Assistance creator/founder, launched in Fresno, California (1976). He served as secretary-general and president of the World Society of Victimology. He served in the U.S. Army's Military Police Corps, retiring as full colonel. He taught victimology/victim services and was creator/director of the Tokiwa International Victimology Institute and editor in chief of its journal, *International Perspectives in Victimology*. He is a criminology professor emeritus from California State University, Fresno. He has published 16 books, 106 articles, and 203 presentations. He received the 2016 U.S. Attorney-General's Ronald Reagan Public Policy award.

Fox, Nicole:

Nicole Fox, Ph.D., received her doctorate in sociology from Brandeis University and researches how racial and ethnic contention impacts communities, including how remembrances of adversity shape social change, collective memory, and present-day social movements. She is an assistant professor of criminal justice at California State University, Sacramento, and teaches on comparative criminal justice and global criminology. Her scholarship has been published in *Signs, Social Forces, Sociological Forum,* and *Societies Without Borders,* among others. Her work has generously been supported by several organizations including the National Science Foundation and the Andrew Mellon Foundation.

Getty, Ryan:

Ryan Getty is assistant professor of criminal justice at California State University, Sacramento, and coordinator of the division's crime scene lab. He received his Ph.D. in Criminology from the University of Texas at Dallas. He has over 30 years of police-practitioner experience as a full-time licensed officer, investigator, and chief of police in Georgia, Texas, and California. He enjoys teaching undergraduate and graduate research methods/design, statistics, ethics, management, and policing classes. His main scholarly interests include police training and behavior, advanced research designs and statistics, as well as criminological theory as it applies to police (mis)behavior.

Gutierrez, Ricky:

Dr. Ricky S. Gutierrez is a tenured full professor of criminal justice at California State University, Sacramento. He worked as a corrections counselor with the criminally insane for 10 years after completing his B.A. in psychology from Eastern Washington University. He earned his graduate degrees (M.A. and Ph.D.) from Washington State University in criminal justice. He is published in peer-reviewed journals, has published a book on community policing, and continues to publish articles on jails, prisoner reentry, and social justice issues.

Huang, Shihlung:

Shihlung Huang received his Ph.D. in criminology and criminal justice from Sam Houston State University. He currently teaches as an associate professor of criminal justice at California State University, Sacramento. Prior to that he also taught in universities in North Dakota and North Carolina. Dr. Huang had several years of law enforcement experience in immigration and police management in Taiwan. His teaching and research areas have focused on law enforcement, drug policy, and criminal justice administration and management.

Jones, Eric:

Eric Jones is police chief of the Stockton Police Department. He developed and led principled policing with the California State Department of Justice for state-wide training. He led Stockton to be one of only six sites for the National Initiative for Building Community Trust and Justice. His work was profiled in the *New York Times* in July 2016, and in *USA Today* in June 2017.

Kubicek, Laurie:

Laurie Kubicek is a full professor of criminal justice at California State University, Sacramento. Her research interests and legal experience include California criminal law and procedure, criminal justice policy, academic program development, and evaluation of California correctional institutions and multi-jurisdictional drug task forces. She established and serves as director of the Sacramento State Pre-Law Advising program and is the director of Sacramento State's Justice Epstein Judicial Internship program.

Lee, Lynette:

Lynette Lee, Ph.D., is a full professor of criminal justice at California State University, Sacramento. Her teaching and research pursuits have focused on the application of integrally informed models of human development to the design, delivery, and assessment of justice education and training. She is currently working with a small consortium of justice educators to pioneer a concentration of study referred to as "integral justice."

Michaud, Andrew C.:

Andrew C. Michaud received his master's degree in criminal justice from California State University, Sacramento. He has researched and written about various topics, including police legitimacy, Ontario (Canada) police's perception of hate crime, perceptions of criminal sanctions' severity, and post-incarcerated individuals' perceptions of the criminal-legal apparatus. Currently, Andrew is an adult high school instructor for students who have newly immigrated to the United States or who have experienced marginalization, including incarceration. He also volunteers as an instructor at a Sacramento-based reentry program.

Moffatt, Shelby:

Dr. Shelby Moffatt is a retired law enforcement officer with the Sacramento Police Department, adjunct professor of criminal justice at California State University, Sacramento, and director of the Law Enforcement Candidate Scholars' (LECS) career/leadership development program. His research focuses on diversity and recruitment in policing. Dr. Moffatt received his doctorate in educational leadership from California State University, Sacramento, his master's degree in public administration from the University of Southern California, and his bachelor's degree in pre-law/history from the University of the Pacific.

Noble, Jennifer:

Jennifer C. Noble is an assistant professor of criminal justice at California State University, Sacramento. She is a former criminal defense attorney and journalist and directs the Student Hearing Officer grant project on parking violations appeals at California State University, Sacramento. She received a bachelor's degree in journalism from California State University, Sacramento, and a juris doctor at University of the Pacific, McGeorge School of Law, where she graduated with honors. Her first textbook, *White Collar and Financial Crimes: A Casebook of Fraudsters, Scam Artists, and Corporate Thieves,* will be published by University of California Press in 2020.

Repa, Melissa:

Dr. Melissa Repa is the director of the Career Center, previously served as director of Services to Students with Disabilities, Project Rebound, and was first-year seminar instructor at Sacramento State. She graduated with distinction with a Doctorate of Education in Educational Leadership from Sacramento State and received a Wayne K. Miyamoto Public Policy Dissertation Fellowship, a Master of Arts in psychological studies in education from UCLA, and a Bachelor of Science in psychology and a teaching certificate from the University of Michigan.

Sardina, Alexa:

Alexa D. Sardina, Ph.D., is an assistant professor of criminal justice at California State University, Sacramento. Her scholarship focuses on the motivations and justifications of sex offenders, with special attention given to the situational contexts within which child sexual abuse occurs. Her research also combines her experiences as a sex crimes researcher and rape survivor to share the perspective of "survivor scholars" and supports restorative justice as a means to heal victims, offenders, and communities after sexually violent offenses.

Sasere, Davies:

Davies Sasere, M.P.A., Ph.D. is an adjunct professor of criminal justice at California State University, Sacramento. He is also a part-time instructor at Argosy University and Merritt College, Oakland. Davies also works as a parole administrator with the California Department of Corrections and Rehabilitation. His professional experience includes consultant on terrorism and counterterrorism and curriculum development for correctional peace officers' academies. Davies has a bachelor's degree in sociology, a master's degree in public administration, and a Ph.D. in homeland security administration. His academic research explores domestic terrorism and perceptions of law enforcement.

Seale, Lee:

Lee Seale began his career as a criminal prosecutor with the California Department of Justice. He later served as a director in the California Department of Corrections and Rehabilitation. He is currently the chief of probation for Sacramento County and serves as an appointee of California Supreme Court Chief Justice Cantil-Sakauye on her Criminal Law Advisory Committee. Chief Seale holds a J.D. from UC Davis School of Law and recently co-taught a course at UC Davis on California's correctional reforms.

Sowards, Timothy:

Timothy Sowards is a Sacramento County senior deputy probation officer and adjunct professor of criminal justice at California State University, Sacramento, as well as an alumnus of the criminal justice program. He co-founded the Randy Yamada Foundation and Northern California Fraternal Order of Police Lodge. He has a Doctor of Philosophy degree in public policy and administration. Timothy has instructed academy-level students throughout California on the use of force. He is the creator of the Juvenile Force Perceptions Survey.

Uwazie, Ernest:

Ernest E. Uwazie holds a Ph.D. in justice studies from Arizona State University, Tempe. He is a professor and chair of criminal justice and director/founder of the Center for African Peace & Conflict Resolution at California State University, Sacramento. He teaches courses on comparative justice, dispute resolution and restorative justice, minorities and justice, and the justice system and community. He is a renowned ADR (alternative dispute resolution)/mediation trainer, practitioner, scholar, and system designer, with extensive training workshops and seminars in Africa and United States. He has many presentations and publications on peace and conflict resolution, peace education, restorative justice, alternative dispute resolution, and legal pluralism in Africa, including *Peace & Conflict Resolution in Africa* (Ed.) (2018).

Valadez, Mercedes:

Dr. Mercedes Valadez is an assistant professor of criminal justice at California State University, Sacramento. She earned a B.A. in criminal justice from California State University, Bakersfield, an M.S. in criminology from California State University, Fresno, and a Ph.D. in criminology and criminal justice from Arizona State University. Her work largely focuses on underrepresented groups in crime and justice research. More specifically, she investigates disparities and discrimination in criminal justice outcomes based on race, ethnicity, and immigration status. Her work has been featured in the *Sociological Quarterly*. She has presented her research in state, national, and international conferences.

CPSIA information can be obtained
at www.ICGtesting.com
Printed in the USA
LVHW080746120722
723223LV00004B/18